PET REVOLUTION

Animals and the Making of Modern British Life

JANE HAMLETT AND
JULIE-MARIE STRANGE

REAKTION BOOKS

For
Kim and Kelley
and
Pep, Maude, Ronnie and Bernard

Published by
Reaktion Books Ltd
Unit 32, Waterside
44–48 Wharf Road
London N1 7UX, UK

www.reaktionbooks.co.uk

First published 2023
Copyright © Jane Hamlett and Julie-Marie Strange 2023

Printed and bound in Great Britain by
TJ Books Ltd, Padstow, Cornwall

A catalogue record for this book is available from the British Library

ISBN 978 1 78914 686 8

Contents

Introduction

The year 2020 was an extraordinary one for humans and companion animals as a new pandemic caused monumental change in everyday life across the globe. Millions of people brought new animals into their homes to help them cope with lives that were suddenly more restricted and more isolated. In the Western world, countries closed borders and told people to stay home to limit the spread of the COVID-19 virus. In Britain alone that year, 3.2 million households acquired a new pet. By 2021, 17 million homes (59 per cent) in the UK had at least one pet, an increase from just under half of all UK homes between 2011 and 2019 and the first time since such records began that homes *without* pets were in the minority.[1] Cats and dogs were equally the most popular pets (around 24 million in total), and after them came 3.2 million small animals (guinea pigs, hamsters, rabbits and so on), 3 million birds and 1.5 million reptiles. Another 5 million households reported keeping fish in aquaria. The rise in pet numbers during the pandemic meant retailers struggled to meet unprecedented demand for pet food, and trading prices – especially for dogs – rose. But some of these commitments were short-lived. Animal welfare charities prepared for an increase in surrendered animals as the economic effects of the pandemic took its toll on people's income, and humans living with pets for the first time struggled to adapt to animal needs. By March 2021, twelve months after the UK's national lockdown, 5 per cent of new pet keepers were thought to have surrendered their animals.[2] Yet the 'pandemic pets' phenomenon was driven by human belief in the benefits of animal companionship. For some, this was strategic: walking the dog provided a legitimate reason for leaving home during the first

UK national lockdown. But for most new owners, animal companionship went beyond finding reasons to be outdoors. Fifty-nine per cent of new pet owners in 2020 were under 35 years old and acquired their pet to help them cope with the social isolation of lockdown. This strategy worked for 74 per cent of all new owners, who said that pet companionship actively helped their mental health during the pandemic.[3] As the chief executive of Britain's biggest pet product retailer noted in November 2020, pets had been 'a lifesaver for many through this incredibly challenging period'.[4]

This book explains the exceptional role companion animals played in 2020 by charting two hundred years of pet keeping to understand how pets became so integral to the British and their homes. Modernity in the Western world was forged through a series of revolutions, from the industrial and agricultural to the political and commercial. We contend that, in Britain at least, there was another revolution – the pet revolution – whereby households across the social spectrum welcomed animals into their domestic lives on an unprecedented scale. Using a wide range of historical material, our book is the first to explore the changing role of pets, mainly through the lives and words of people who kept them: we consider why people chose pets, how they acquired them and how they became an important part of daily life. Changing ideas about the natural world and the growth of conservation had a powerful impact on how pets were defined. Between the nineteenth and twentieth centuries the boundaries between the home and the natural world and between wild and domestic animals were slowly solidified. From the Victorian period, consumer capitalism, new forms of consumption and a changing retail landscape helped transform the way in which pet animals were acquired and viewed as commodities.[5] Most important of all were the twin engines of home and family life, in which humans co-opted animals into new visions of domesticity and home-making. Pets had a unique role to play in family life – sometimes peripheral, sometimes transformative – befriending the lonely, chumming with children and even intervening between husband and wife. As we will show, however, human–animal homes were not always a vision of domestic bliss and pet keeping has always involved challenges.

FROM CLEOPATRA'S CATS to the black terrier that accompanied Mary Queen of Scots to her execution, from dogs in the Domesday Book and Chaucer's cats to the marmoset accompanying a boy in a painting by Hans Holbein the Younger, humans and animals have lived in companionship for millennia. Studies of dog and wolf DNA suggest that the first dogs were domesticated between 15,000 and 25,000 years ago (although the nature of the relationship between early humans and these 'friendly wolves' is open to speculation).[6] The different social, religious, economic and household infrastructures of specific historical cultures mean that these relationships could look very different from those we identify today. Until at least the Industrial Revolution, many households in the West included accommodation for livestock: sharing living space with animals brought humans warmth in winter and made livestock easier to manage in a context of scant resources.[7] Animals with utility functions, such as hunting, shepherding or killing vermin, might cross into human living space depending on a household's structure while some animals were kept indoors as status symbols. But from the early medieval period onward, we know that elite households kept animals simply for the pleasure of their companionship while members of other social groups, notably religious orders and scholars, might readily forge emotional attachments to animals kept indoors primarily for utility purposes.[8] By the eighteenth century pet keeping – especially of small dogs that could be easily accommodated in boudoirs and drawing rooms – had become sufficiently common in affluent households to encourage satirical comment on those who cared more for animal than human friends and dogs that grew pompous from their own self-importance.[9]

But it was the nineteenth century that witnessed the expansion of pet keeping across different social classes and its widespread cultural acceptance. As the historian Ingrid Tague has shown, by the beginning of the nineteenth century pet keeping was seen as a virtue rather than a vice.[10] The decades that followed saw an outpouring of pet culture – countless paintings featuring winsome children and puppies, literature that celebrated loyal dogs, moral tales offering parables on pet rabbits and even manuals with instructions on how to perform surgery on cats at home. In a period transformed by industrial, agricultural and political revolutions all across Europe, the pet revolution has largely been overlooked. Histories of home and family in the nineteenth and twentieth centuries have long charted changes in human demographics, living arrangements, ideals of domesticity and emotional intimacies. But, as the animal studies scholar Erica Fudge notes, animals are usually absent from these stories.[11] And yet the transformation of human relations with animals was radical and entirely contingent on the broader economic, social and cultural shifts of the past two hundred years. The growth of towns, the separation of the home from workplace, changing household structures, migratory patterns, rising living standards, the growth of consumerism, globalization and colonialism all worked together to make pet keeping far more accessible across the social scale, and the variety of birds and animals kept much larger. The nineteenth century also saw the emergence of a new culture of domesticity – often propagated by new forms of print culture. From the mid-century a new literature emerged that instructed people from all walks of life on the moral, social and emotional benefits of keeping pets. The word 'pet' came into use in the sixteenth century, predominantly as a derisive term for favoured animals, typically hand-reared lambs. The early nineteenth century saw 'pet' redefined to refer to a relationship with a special animal, cared for within the home.[12] It is this notion of the animal's primary purpose being one of domestic companionship that underscores most modern definitions of the 'pet'.

As the historian of medieval pet keeping Kathleen Walker-Meikle notes, 'there are no pets in nature': the pet is an artificial category.[13] Animal-studies scholars argue that the term 'pet' has not lost its pejorative meanings. To be 'a pet' is to be subjugated to another's power and to lose one's individual personhood. Many scholars reject the term for this reason, preferring alternatives such as 'companion animal', and redrawing the boundaries between humans and animals by using terms such as 'more than human' or 'non-human' to refer to animals. The challenge to nomenclature is a reminder of the power humans exert over animals. Ongoing debates over finding an appropriate language represent the continued precariousness of animals in our society.[14] Despite this, 'pet' remains the most popular term in common use for companion animals since the nineteenth century: broadly, people still refer to 'pet shops', 'pet products' and, of course, 'pet owners'. In view of this, we use the term 'pet' in this book to reflect the persistent dominance of this term in modern Britain and because the problems we associate with it – the subjugation and commodification of animals in the pursuit of human happiness – are pivotal to the story of how animals came to occupy such an important role in human lives.

This book is interested in the shifting parameters of power, intimacy and conceptions of personhood in human–animal relationships.

Historically, the creation of pets reflected both an uneven power relationship (exemplified in references to human 'ownership' of pets) and sometimes a degree of cruelty. It is impossible, for example, to think about the widespread capture and commercial sale of wild British birds without reflecting on this. While this book is not about animal cruelty (other historians have written at length about this theme), we acknowledge, here and throughout the book, the suffering that the pet trade has sometimes brought about.[15] We hope that this book will help readers think about the social, cultural and economic processes that produce pets, and the way that human imperatives and desires can contribute to animal suffering. We base our definition of 'the pet' on the criteria developed by the historian Keith Thomas for application to human–animal companionship in the past: an animal kept in the boundaries of domestic space; that was named; and that was not intentionally reared for food.[16]

Unlike most previous histories of pets before the Second World War, we address pet keeping across the socio-economic spectrum and have expanded Thomas's criteria to reflect a greater range of people and places: we include gardens and paved yards in our definition of domestic space; we recognize animals as pets where at least one member of a household named the animal; and we acknowledge that while many animals were not originally acquired for food, economic hardship sometimes precipitated a shift in an animal's status. While 'pet' is often assumed to indicate some emotional attachment to an animal, it cannot be taken for granted. The degree of human emotional investment in pet relationships differed considerably depending on context: variables include the location of pet living space (indoors or out) and time available to spend with them; the human life course (children could understand pets as siblings while the elderly might view them as friends that provided solace); and the kind of animal kept (people tended to write effusively about fur-coated animals they were used to handling yet were significantly more reticent about fish and reptiles).

Pets have been a fundamental part of British culture for the past two hundred years but the animals kept and the ways humans shared homes with them has been far from static. In Victorian Britain pets might range from birds and animals imported from new colonies and trading routes – monkeys, mongeese, parrots, bears and other 'exotic' creatures – to animals captured from the wild, such as birds, squirrels, foxes, hedgehogs, dormice and rabbits, to animals bred specifically for a burgeoning consumer market, notably dogs, but also guinea pigs, hamsters, fish, canaries and some pedigree cats. But if rising living standards meant more people could keep birds and animals in their homes for the first time, an emerging ethos of animal welfare from the middle decades of the nineteenth century meant pet keeping was increasingly regulated, shaping how people acquired animals and managed them in domestic space. From the late nineteenth century the emerging conservation movement began to encourage the idea that some animals were best left in the wild. Between the excitement a newly crowned Queen Victoria shared with her spaniel Dash in 1837 and the first foray into veterinary practice for a young James Herriot in a 1930s Yorkshire market town, pet keeping changed phenomenally: wild birds, once the most common pet in British households, were granted the protection of the law; the animal street trader gave way to the hygienic 'pet shop'; the status of cats transformed from public health nuisance to precious puss; a whole new market for advice books on how to keep animals in the home and manage everyone's emotional needs emerged alongside the exponential growth in pet products and services, from specialist foods to grooming to medicines to beds and 'accessories'; animal-welfare activists established charities to regulate and support animals in the home; veterinarians expanded their services to include small-animal practice; and pet cemeteries extended from private gardens to public mourning spaces.

Since the Second World War, many of the things we now take for granted in pet keeping were developed and refined. As the wild was banished outdoors, pets themselves were increasingly found indoors – by the 1940s it was the norm to keep dogs inside rather than chained outside the house. Pet keeping was shaped by fundamental transformations in the structure of households and families as well as the material layout of homes. The rise of the 'flat' (or apartment), which became more common in the post-war era, imposed new limitations on pet keeping, but many owners fought passionately to retain their pets, or found ways of adapting to new circumstances. By mid-century smaller families had become the norm while more diverse family formations became increasingly visible – arguably creating more room for pets, and different kinds of animal interventions in family life. As the family became less obviously patriarchal and authority-driven, animal independence and autonomy were sometimes more prized. Pet discipline became more contentious, and owners seen as more culpable in failed human–animal relationships. Social scientists began to interrogate the character of human–animal relationships and evaluate the emotional intimacies in households with pets. This new knowledge became increasingly marketable with the onward growth of the pet products sector. Legal regulations for the breeding, keeping and sale of animals were increasingly modified and adapted to changing technologies, markets and sensitivity to animal sentience; veterinary medicine became increasingly sophisticated; commercial opportunities for mourning and commemorating much-loved pets expanded considerably.

Of course, some practices were slow to change while other aspects of pet-keeping culture are remarkable for their continuity. From the early nineteenth century, dogs have enjoyed the dubious honour of being the most prized pet, partly because of their longevity and perceived empathy with their human companions and partly because of the exceptional financial outlay pedigree dogs command.[17] In the early nineteenth century dogs were often kidnapped or stolen for their financial – and emotional – value. In 2020 French bulldog puppies retailed for £10,000, people who had once run cat and dog rescue homes were prosecuted for illegal puppy farming and reports of dog theft were again on the rise.[18] In contrast, the stock of cats – widely considered a public health problem in the nineteenth century because there were so many strays – began to rise in the mid-twentieth century with the normalization of neutering and the craze for Siamese and Burmese breeds.[19] While pedigree dogs (and latterly cats) remained the most highly valued pet (emotionally and financially), birds were the most common pet for much of the nineteenth and twentieth centuries, being cheap, small, mobile and relatively easy to keep. Economics were a massive factor in shaping pet-keeping practices across our period and remain so: pets have long been commodities within a capitalist system of production and consumption; they have operated as status symbols; and they are often early casualties in the economic strife of humans. This does not thwart their importance as emotional attachments, but it does complicate it.

Adults have long drawn associations between children and animals, although the meanings and purposes attributed to that relationship have shifted. Early nineteenth-century didactic fiction encouraged children to keep pets to learn about Christian morality and human obligations to supposedly 'lower' species. From the late nineteenth century to the present, parents have encouraged children to keep pets to teach them about the mysteries of death, while learning kindness to animals is still recognized as a pathway to acquiring empathy. In the 1960s and '70s market researchers found that pets were often acquired with children in mind, and fish in particular were held to have a special educative value.[20] And yet, for all that animals were supposed to fulfil an instructive role in children's lives, Victorian artists such as Briton Rivière and Charles Burton Barber often depicted scenes of child–pet collusion in defying or disobeying an adult world of rules and restrictions, an alliance that often characterizes memoirs of growing up with pets across our time period.

One of the most striking continuities in pet-keeping culture, however, is the importance of animal companionship to those who would otherwise be lonely. The way in which owners express their love for pets has changed over time – and over the course of the twentieth century people became more inclined to speak of 'relationships' with pets. We would contend, though, that the strength and emotional depth of some keepers' commitment to pet animals has remained relatively constant. Reflections on pets as the 'lifesavers' of the COVID-19 pandemic in 2020, especially for those facing social isolation, echo the observations of social commentators, memoirists and advice writers from the earliest decades of the nineteenth century. Pets have long been recognized as essential workers in helping maintain human wellbeing, particularly where humans would otherwise live alone or contact with an outside world would be restricted by poor health. Whether this is always beneficial for pets has long been a cause for concern for animal welfare activists, veterinary practitioners and organizations geared towards supporting humans in difficult circumstances. The COVID-19 pandemic has been an exceptional moment in human and animal history, but it is also a flashpoint in bringing the longstanding relationship between humans and animals into focus.

THIS BOOK TELLS the story of pets from the perspective of the humans that acquired and cared for them, whether that was in a familial context or from a welfare or professional perspective. Inevitably, this privileges human views on pet keeping and replicates the uneven power structures between humans and animals. While we pay attention to animal behaviour when it is referenced (or implied) in records, it is human agency that shaped the archive and, therefore, human agency that directs this story. The words of pet keepers take priority. Uniquely among histories of pets, we draw on the letters, diaries and memoirs of people from across the social scale in the Victorian period and afterwards. Some names will be familiar – it is impossible to write about pets and not include Queen Victoria, Charles Dickens, Jane Carlyle, the Brontë sisters, Thomas and Florence Hardy, Edward Lear, Eliza Brightwen, Beatrix Potter, Virginia and Leonard Woolf, Joe Ackerley, Barbara Woodhouse, Barry Hines and Chris Packham. But many names are obscure, giving insights into the pet worlds of people from manifold walks of life who were undistinguished by fame or notoriety but, on some level, shared a passion for animals. To ensure representation across the socio-economic spectrum, we also draw on several collections of oral histories, the recorded memories of people born from around 1870 to working-class families, who typically left fewer written documents recounting their everyday lives. While British people across myriad occupations, geographies, sexualities, ages and incomes kept pets, the archive reflects overwhelmingly white, British-born, Protestant voices. Partly, this reflects broader trends in the marginalization of subaltern voices in archival holdings. Partly, it reflects the privileges that pet keeping demanded, notably a home and sufficient income to support animal companionship.

We complement these by engaging with the plethora of advice literature, manuals and magazines published from the mid-nineteenth century on pet keeping. Arguably, the first pet-keeping manual was *Domestic Pets: Their Habits and Management* (1851), by Jane Loudon. Loudon began her career by writing science fiction, before marrying the landscape designer John Claudius Loudon. Like many other Victorian female authors, she financially supported her family through her writing and produced a series of highly successful popular natural history books for women and girls.[21] Jane had a good eye for commercial opportunity and *Domestic Pets* was the first book in what was to become a new genre of nineteenth-century advice on how to keep and care for pet animals. Opening the book with a description of her domestic life surrounded by her pets – which ranged from affectionate cats to 'merry' goldfish – Loudon was fully aware that she was selling not just advice, but a special kind of domestic emotional world that could only be realized through animal presence. Loudon established a model that many writers followed. By the mid-twentieth century, the generic pet-advice manual had multiple spin-offs, with specialist books aimed at particular species, breeds or even pet problems: Barbara Woodhouse, who became a household sensation in the 1980s with her no-nonsense television series on living successfully with dogs, first published on dog training in the 1950s.

The records of an expanding market for pet products, services and protection provide good context for understanding the changing norms and values of cross-species companionship. Animal-welfare charities made regular interventions in the public domain, through bringing legal prosecutions for cases of cruelty or publicly campaigning to raise awareness of good practice while challenging the bad (such as leaving cats to fend for themselves while humans went on holiday or dogs tied on short chains for long periods of time). These records are essential to understanding the darker side of pet keeping. The surgery ledgers and specialist publications of veterinary practitioners demonstrate the emergence of professional pet healthcare and the changing status of pets from the indulged playthings of the rich to a mass market for animal medicine. Trade directories, shop archives and press commentary have been used to explore the expanding pet retail landscape. To understand changing trends in pet acquisition, we also surveyed adverts for the sale or exchange of pets in the periodical *Exchange and Mart* over a hundred-year period, allowing us to track the decline and rise of particular pet types. Social commentary on changing popular (and 'high') culture presents an opportunity to chart broad shifts in pet practices, while the growth of social science from the mid-twentieth century provides insights into pet keeping in relation to contemporary anxieties about changes in the family and patterns of women's work. We also turn to representations of pets in visual imagery, fiction and film as reflections of how things were or, at least, how things were imagined to be.

FOR THE FIRST TIME, this book helps us to understand the allure – and the difficulty – of inviting animals into different kinds of households by telling the story of how British pet-keeping culture came into being. It is, we argue, impossible to understand the history of home and family without bringing animals into our stories. All the contingencies that fashioned human social, economic and cultural life in the last two hundred years were factors that shaped our ability to live well with animals. More to the point, giving pets their history, and seeing them as inextricable from the human, offers an aperture onto our shared relationship with wider issues: from understanding how creatures in the hedgerow illuminate Britain's imperial project to how the pets available for sale highlight shifting global trading routes; from how tenants' legal disputes with landlords over pets demonstrate the limits of modernist housing developments to how the growth of small-animal veterinary care reveals tensions between healthcare professionals and women's struggle to access higher education and veterinary careers. Most of all perhaps, an appreciation of the changing and contested status of pets as agents in companionship and human wellbeing indicates just how mutable our perceptions of home, family and emotional status are.

Front cover of Caroline Pridham, *Domestic Pets* (1895).

ONE

Capture and Taming: Pet Keeping in a Changing World

As a powerful spring storm blew over the village of Stanmore, Middlesex, in the 1880s, a starling hatchling tumbled from his nest in the garden of The Grove, an imposing villa. The Grove's butler discovered the tiny bird and carried him to the mistress of the house. Eliza Brightwen, wealthy widow, naturalist and soon-to-be-famous author of *Wild Nature Won by Kindness* (1890) felt a keen sympathy with the infant starling, whom she named Richard the Second and made her close associate: 'He was always out of his cage whilst I was dressing, and was full of fun and play, scheming to get his bath before I did, and running off with anything he could carry.'[1] As their relationship developed, bird and woman established mutual trust. Richard accompanied Eliza outdoors, hopping on the grass or searching tree roots for tasty grubs while she read. But sharing an indoor life did not end well for the bird. One morning Eliza found him, drowned, in her domestic aquarium. Becoming tame proved fatal for Richard and the many other 'pets' that Brightwen brought indoors from their natural habitats. Eliza, a crusader against forms of animal cruelty such as falconry, the use of feathers in fashion, nesting and trapping wild birds, did not recognize taming the wild as a problem.[2] She was not alone. Domesticating wild animals was completely acceptable to the Victorians, even those that saw themselves as champions of the natural world.

Pet keeping is not static: the kinds of pets we keep, how we keep them and how we form relationships with them have changed over time. Between the early nineteenth and the end of the twentieth century the boundaries between pets and wildlife were radically redrawn. Here, we chart some of the biggest changes in pet keeping over this period, moving from the mass confinement of British wildlife (especially birds) through capture and taming to a rejection of these modes of acquisition and the rise of 'bred-tame' pets. Pet keeping did not take place in a vacuum either. Colonial trade brought larger numbers of 'exotic' species to British shores while legislation at home increasingly restricted the capture of wild birds and animals for the pet trade. But larger shifts in ideas about the value and purpose of empire as well as new ways of seeing wild animals and the natural environment also influenced the way people thought and wrote about pets and what they did with them in their homes.

In the nineteenth century people were as likely to think of a pet as a creature to be captured or tamed as they were an animal bred for domestication. Adults and children revelled in the notion of wild animals subjected to human authority. The language used to describe 'dominion' over animals echoed terms used to depict the colonization of humans and assumptions that natural resources were there for the taking. Evangelical religion was pivotal to both projects: if white Westerners justified imperialism through the rhetoric of Christianizing distant continents, they also referenced white humanity's God-given rights over, and responsibilities towards, the animal kingdom. Concepts of hierarchies, capture and taming are fundamental to understanding how people attempted to transform animals into 'pets'. Foxes, red squirrels, hedgehogs, rabbits, hares and all manner of wild birds were all seen in this way. The object in trapping such animals was not the kill, but the challenge of making a 'pet' of a wild creature. At its most benign, this rested on close observation of wild animals lured into gardens by food. For many Victorians, though, the human home was the centre of social, political and cultural life and it shouldn't surprise us that they wanted to tame and 'civilize' wild animals as part of the family circle too.

But as confidence waned in the imperial project, so too did the belief that wild animals should be captured and tamed. By the end of the nineteenth century, animal-welfare campaigners secured legislation to ban the capture of wild birds. By the early twentieth, the gung-ho attitude to the wild (exhibited *par excellence* in late nineteenth-century fiction for boys) became more muted and the protection and preservation of birds was increasingly stressed. In this new climate, Brightwen's 'rescue' of the starling would have ended with his release back into the wild. Brightwen's commitment to educating people, especially children, about the natural world remained influential throughout the twentieth century but the parameters of how this could be achieved and the ethics of domesticating animals – what species were suited to 'pet' life and from where they should be acquired – changed dramatically.

Pets and the 'Imperial Adventure'

From the early nineteenth century more and more Britons encountered a greater variety of 'wild' animals. As global trade routes expanded it became easier to transport animals around the world. From 1805 George Wombwell toured Britain with his large menagerie. The London Zoological Gardens, set up by Stamford Raffles, opened in 1828. The emergence of travelling and established menageries alongside the growth of zoos that relied on showcasing 'exotic' animals to wider publics exposed more people to 'wild' animals from overseas. Over the nineteenth century London Zoo promoted celebrity animals that captured public imagination. The display of Obaysch, a baby hippopotamus who arrived in England from Egypt in 1850, sparked a wave of 'hippomania', and when the zoo decided to sell Jumbo, a prized elephant originally imported from Sudan in east Africa in 1865, to the American animal showman Phineas Taylor Barnum in 1882, the public were outraged. As the historian Harriet Ritvo argues, British people imagined these animals as 'National Pets' – they invested in them emotionally, but they also had a powerful symbolic value.[3] Exotic zoo creatures, as well as those bred in menageries or shot and stuffed for display as natural-history specimens or trophies, were powerful emblems of Britain's dominance over colonies in India and Africa and human supremacy over animals.

From the early decades of the nineteenth century, the fantasy of the 'wild' animal tamed was accessible to adults and children alike. The lion, reputedly the 'King of the Beasts', was a mainstay of zoos and menageries. Wombwell famously had two lions – the ferocious William Wallace (a cruel irony to be named after the Scottish leader against English oppression), and Nero, a lion who reportedly lacked the brutal streak of his namesake and refused to fight. Some wild beasts might occasionally be kept more literally as 'pets' – the actor Edmund Kean had a lion in his house on Clarges Street in London.[4] A small number of specialist shops and dealers, mainly based in port cities and the London Docks, supplied naturalists, zoos and menageries for the social elite, such as the Earl of Derby, who established a menagerie at his home in Knowsley near Liverpool. But public trade in wild or exotic beasts was limited. From the 1860s dealers and private individuals who wanted to buy or sell animals advertised nationally in the magazine *Exchange and Mart*, although 'wild exotics' represented less than 1 per cent of the magazine's overall trade in animals.[5] Before 1900 parrots, some monkeys and the occasional tree frog or exotic bird appeared in the ads but were dramatically outstripped by more prosaic dogs, pigeons and rabbits. Exotic animals were relatively hard to acquire, expensive and extremely difficult to keep.

Extraordinary Victorians possessed of menageries probably did not, for the most part, think of them as pets in a domestic sense. Their focus was on keeping the animals alive (imported animals struggled in the inclement British climate), overcoming the challenge of breeding in captivity or selecting animals for their potential as exotic foodstuffs.[6] On a trip to Charles Jamrach's exotic-animal shop near the London Docks, Eliza Brightwen toyed with the idea of buying an armadillo. The proprietor, anxious to make a sale, reassured her that if it failed as a pet, the creature could be cooked instead.[7] She declined to make the purchase. Menageries also had a special aesthetic value. This seems to have been the motivation behind artist and poet Dante Gabriel Rossetti's creation of a menagerie at his home, Tudor House, on Cheyne Walk in Chelsea in the 1860s. While Rossetti formed a close relationship with Top, the wombat whose death he mourned in verse, most of his menagerie was chosen for rarity rather than a relationship. Rossetti expended little thought on making suitable arrangements for the animals: they were disruptive, noisy and sometimes escaped, causing havoc in the neighbourhood.[8] Henry Treffry Dunn, Rossetti's resident secretary and studio assistant, remarked that 'the animals could not be described as pets, as was his wont . . . it was simply a passion he had for collecting just as he did books, pictures and china'.[9]

While most Victorian homes lacked lions, tigers and the like, pet keeping and empire building were entwined. White Christian civilization espoused human hierarchies and claimed a God-given right to 'tame' colonies and native peoples: domination was couched in the rhetoric of 'civilization'. Theological frameworks also supported the human and animal hierarchies that animal-welfare charities like the Royal Society for the Prevention of Cruelty to Animals (RSPCA, est. 1824) cited as justification for the protection of animals even while taking meat eating for granted. Using biblical language, Victorian pet keepers often wrote of their 'dominion' over the animal world, which granted a degree of responsibility to animals while asserting humans' intrinsic supremacy. As 1860s editions of *The Book of Home Pets* produced by the Beeton publishing house asserted, 'we, by virtue of our great privilege, have dominion over the birds of the air, the beasts of the field, and the fish of the sea.'[10] If Beeton's mid-Victorian assurance of a human 'we' over a non-human 'them' was increasingly challenged by anti-vivisectionists and animal-rights campaigners at the end of the century, these ideas nevertheless had a long shelf life. Eliza Brightwen published books on both natural history and religion throughout the later decades of her life (she died in 1906 aged 76). Although they occupied distinct genres, the beliefs underpinning the religious books clearly shaped Brightwen's entire conception of the natural world. In 1909 bird expert Sumner Birchley continued to justify caging birds on the grounds that 'birds, beasts and flowers were sent [by God] for the use and joy of man.'

Dante Gabriel Rossetti, 'Rossetti lamenting the death of his Wombat', 1869, pen and brown ink, with brown wash.

Birchley naturalized the domestication of animals as part of an almost inevitable civilizing process: 'The cow, the horse, cat, and dog were all wild at one time, likewise our charming little bird the Canary, but all these were, by the civilisation of mankind, brought to domestication, and they seem to appreciate the kindness and consideration meted out to them.'[11]

Victorian commentators thought the human instinct towards the natural world was gendered: men sought to dominate while women strove to care and protect it. But, as the historian Diana Donald argues so eloquently in her history of Victorian women's campaigns against animal cruelty, such depictions were grounded in specific cultural contexts inextricable from other movements and ideologies, notably the rise of feminism, professional medicine and, of course, the 'new' imperialism that characterized Queen Victoria's reign.[12] During the century the imperial hunter, a swaggering figure striding through the colonial landscape 'bagging' wild animals, became an increasingly powerful symbol of a particular kind of Britishness.[13] If 'explorers' displayed the booty of empire in public spaces, including the sociable spaces of homes, the hunter rapidly found his way onto the pages of books and comics read by Victorian schoolboys too. The supposed 'Imperial Adventure' was a staple of the growing *Boy's Own* literature published in the final decades of the nineteenth century.[14] As a boy growing up in late Victorian Kilmarnock, A. V. Christie's imagination was fired by 'stories of adventure' and 'deeds of derring do on land and sea'. Tales of American Indian warfare, Buffalo Bill and H. M. Stanley's *How I Found Livingstone* took Christie and his friends far from the prosaic realities of working-class Scotland.[15] Such stories took the white British adventurer's right to conquer environments – and their multi-species inhabitants – for granted. If stories like these perpetuated jingoism and encouraged boys like Christie to volunteer for imperial wars, they fostered an assumption that wild animals were fair game for conquest too.

While overseas adventures encompassed animals that were familiar (such as horses) and exotic (the lions and tigers beloved of menageries), hunting at home mirrored the skills celebrated in imperial accounts: plotting, stalking and capture. Despite the Cruelty to Animals Act of 1835, a landmark piece of legislation pitched at ending cruel 'sports', the law excluded country pursuits such as fox hunting and shooting. Throughout the century, huge numbers of birds were bred for the sole purpose of being shot with newly available, terribly efficient breach-loading rifles.[16] The expansion of hunting, as practice and culture, influenced pet acquisition. Within children's literature, the fantasy of hunting and trapping the wild was made viable with clear instructions on how to capture animals from the more familiar 'colonies' of field and hedgerow. In a world that placed increasing social value on the symbolic performance of hunting at home and in the colonies, the capturing of wild birds and small animals facilitated a symbolic performance of masculine dominance on a modest scale. Of course, pet keeping was not about killing. But Britain's imperial expansionism and the celebration of hunting skills helps explain the emphasis on capture: schoolboys were encouraged to trap wild birds and animals in the countryside as part of an imperial fantasy.

Conquering field and hedgerow

Most authors of children's literature overwhelmingly assumed that capturing birds and animals from the wild was an activity suited to boys. Almost all manuals and magazines published for boys between 1840 and the late nineteenth century included detail on how to trap and train wild animals, especially birds, a feature glaringly absent from print literature aimed at girls. Capturing wild creatures required forethought, stalking, speed and alacrity, skills overwhelmingly associated with masculine activities in a context where idealized femininity was imagined as domestic and relatively static. The similarities between hunting creatures from the wild and the more exotic, overseas thrills of fiction and accounts of imperialist adventurers are striking. Some youths clearly did have thrilling overseas adventures capturing wild animals. Willie Wooster travelled to Australia for his health. Writing to his mother in 1882, he assured her of the fun he was having. Just the previous Sunday, he 'caught a small native bear he was about as big as a good-sized cat but about three times as strong and gave one or two of us some good scratches, he is now chained up in the yard to be tamed and made a pet of'.[17] But boys could live out adventure fantasies in the British suburbs too. A book of 'games and pastimes' aimed at boys in 1872 noted that 'tit catching' in the garden was a 'very amusing sport'.[18]

The most common wild animal captured for domestic pleasure was the bird. Most advice writers for children and adults agreed that birds made excellent companions for the home. As the journalist Henry

Mayhew noted in his ground-breaking investigation of London street folk, published in volume form in the 1860s, almost any enterprising boy could rise early and go 'hunting' for birds, either to keep for himself or to sell on for pocket money.[19] The naturalist and cleric John George Wood advised 'every boy' in multiple editions of his encyclopedia of sport and amusements, reprinted multiple times from 1856, that the 'procuring of birds' for 'amusement, curiosity or for sale' could easily 'become a passion'. He gave detailed instructions for methods of trapping birds.[20] Literature for boys often dwelt on this process. In a section titled 'The Young Naturalist', Wood gave various methods for acquiring skylarks, linnets, goldfinches, bullfinches, blackbirds, woodlarks and thrushes.[21] Beeton's *Book of Home Pets* (1861) included guidelines for 'the boy's first bird snare' as well as pegging (capturing a bird on the ground instead of in flight) and setting up decoy birds as a lure to their curious but unsuspecting feathered brethren.[22] Most Victorian writers, though, agreed that wild birds were best captured as hatchlings, straight from the nest.[23]

THE FINCHES.

CHAFFINCH AND OTHER BIRD-TRAPS.

THE trap represented in the accompanying illustration is that most commonly used by the professed "catcher." The net is a cumbrous machine fixed in a wooden frame, and hinged in the middle. Round about the net (a "snap" net it is called) are placed any sort of singing-birds in cages, or, better still, braced and attached to sticks thrust in the ground. The centre of the net is pegged securely to the ground, and the catcher attaching to the sides the strings that work the snap, retires with them out of sight, and, lying down, holds the said strings in hand as warily as does a coachman the reins of his restive horse. The tiny decoys in the cages and attached to the sticks, forgetful of their captivity in the presence of the green grass and the rustling trees, or, more probable still, joyfully hailing them as dear friends met unexpectedly, utter such glad music that all

'Chaffinch and other bird-traps', illustrated page in *Beeton's Book of Birds* (1862).

Not only did capturing wild birds cultivate hunting skills, but it had practical advantages too. To begin, as Mayhew had observed, the cost could be much lower. The Beeton manual discussed all British song and cage birds in relation to nesting and trapping, and noted for nesting chaffinches that 'A bird-dealer will ask as much as six or seven shillings for a good chaffinch; but a boy of enterprise will save his money and, at the same time derive considerable instruction and amusement in catching and training one for himself.'[24] Thirty years later, *Cassell's Book of the Household* (1893) advised readers that taking birds from the wild was preferable to making purchases from bird dealers or shops.[25] In most writers' eyes, this also circumvented accusations of cruelty: having never known the joy of liberty, birds caged from the nest could not lament its disappearance. It was also the case that animals were more likely to survive captivity and easier to tame if reared indoors from youth.[26]

From the early nineteenth century naturalist books conceded that keeping birds in the home meant depriving them of liberty. A children's book from 1824 noted with stark directness that birds and animals were right to be suspicious of human attempts to befriend them. As a clever robin point outs, boys and girls leave food for mice that kills them, tempt pigeons into dovecotes and then bake them in a pie, and cultivate pet lambs only to send them for slaughter.[27] Most writers avoided outright condemnation of capture. After all, they were advising how best to care for birds kept *in the home*. Rather, they urged readers to take birds from the nest before they became accustomed to liberty, and to allow them freedom to 'roam' from their wire 'prison house' within designated indoor rooms if possible.[28] Other writers gave advice on humane sizes of cages and tips on how to mimic the wild in a parlour or bedroom by setting up an imitation 'roosting place'.[29]

Some birds were considered more suited to captivity than others. The naturalist and gardener Jane Loudon cautioned against caging larks.[30] John Wood agreed: keeping larks caged 'betray[ed] a strange want of benevolence' given their tendency to pine and die in captivity. But he considered goldfinches 'easily reconciled to their cages', whereas confining thrushes was cruel, especially in the countryside, where they might be commonly encountered anyway.[31] By 1870 Wood had completely revised his advice on capturing birds from the wild to reject it outright: he could 'never pass the cage' of a confined indigenous bird without feeling 'sadness and regret' and longing to 'set free' the prisoner.[32] He appeared to have no misgivings, however, about imprisoning 'foreign' birds, suggesting an implicit hierarchy of concern for the freedom of domestic birds over those from overseas.

By the latter decades of the century the proliferation of bird catching by professionals and schoolboys, alongside demand from collectors for stuffed birds and eggs and, importantly, the increasing destruction of natural habitats, was enough to decimate the population of some wild birds. Legislation imposed a partial check on these activities. From 1869 a series of legal reforms offered some protection to some bird species, and the Wild Bird Protection Act of 1880 made it illegal to hunt some birds or take their eggs during nesting season.[33] But the legislation was patchy in that it only protected some species and didn't protect birds beyond the nesting season. Some advice writers continued in the 1890s to recommend taking youngsters from the nest as the best way to secure birds but introduced caveats. *Cassell's*, for instance, suggested that nesting was 'only' appropriate for country dwellers in places where birds were plentiful.[34]

Despite legislation and campaigns to leave wild birds well alone by charities such as the Royal Society for the Protection of Birds (RSPB, est. 1889), boys continued to hunt and trap feathered friends. One boy, born in 1893, got up to 'all sorts of mischief'. Having consumed the advice of countless boys' books and magazines, he and his friends constructed a 'trap cage' with a decoy bird to capture wild bullfinches and linnets. Reflecting on this in adulthood, he was appalled: what a 'barbarous', 'terrible thing to do'. At the time, though, the 'question of cruelty' didn't 'enter our minds very much'.[35] He was by no means unusual. Legislation and social disapproval didn't always dampen the enterprising boy's desire for a 'wild' adventure with tangible spoils, especially those in urban environments. In Edwardian Salford, near Manchester, a group of boys pooled resources to equip themselves with all the paraphernalia necessary to trap 'birds of all kinds'. Successful hunting meant feathered captives for each of the boys and surplus to sell to neighbours.[36] Boys might not always have understood protective legislation, especially if the print literature they consumed was out of date. Ignorance of the law was an obvious line of defence if caught capturing wild birds. One boy in Edwardian Chelmsford, Essex, was sufficiently successful in capturing skylarks that he made regular pocket money by selling his surplus 'stock' until a woman from the RSPCA threatened to prosecute him. He claimed that he and his mother didn't know about the law.[37] But for boys that were aware of the Wild Birds Acts, defiance of the law could add to the

'Teaching the "Jack" a tune', illustration in Caroline Pridham, *Domestic Pets* (1895).

thrill. Alternatively, naturalists like Brightwen inadvertently provided a justificatory 'rescue' framework for what was still, in effect, the capture of wild birds. Undoubtedly, boys might well 'find' a nest of orphaned baby jackdaws that were brought home, hand fed and tamed to perform tricks.[38] But the line between rescue and capture could be easily blurred for adults and children keen to possess a wild bird.

Birds might have been the easiest prey to capture but they were not the only wild creatures snared by eager boys. Urban children may have had little opportunity for hunting wild animals beyond the odd disoriented rabbit or mouse but (semi-) rural children could run amok in nature. Hedgehogs were a favourite of country boys, as were squirrels and fox cubs.[39] As with bird catching, capturing wild animals facilitated more affordable pet keeping: dormice could be bought for half a crown a pair but for boys 'with no money to spend', hunting the tiny creatures in the wilds of the hedgerow provided adventure and pets for free.[40] As with birds, however, some writers were mindful of the cruelty of removing animals from their natural habitats, although this didn't equate to condemning the practice. Observing that country lads were fond of hunting for squirrel nests, John Wood urged his 'good young friends' to at least give the captured creature 'elbow room!' Like birds, they should be taken from the nest when young and taught to 'forget' their native woods by 'the freedom you give him in his prison'.[41]

Again, by the final decades of the century some writers expressed disquiet about removing animals from their natural habitat. It is notable, however, that these authors tended to be women who urged a different model of human–animal interaction to the boys' adventure writer. Posing as a friendly advisor on domestic animals, Caroline Pridham noted the drawbacks of keeping hedgehogs as pets (indoor hogs had a high mortality rate) but stopped short of criticizing people who did.[42] The children's story *The Tale of Mrs Tiggywinkle* was based on a wild hedgehog the author and illustrator Beatrix Potter had tamed. But Potter conceded that 'the long course of unnatural diet and indoor life' were fatal to hedgehogs; if anything, it was a 'wonder she has lasted so long'.[43] Another children's author, Emma Davenport, related how a hedgehog kept in the kitchen to manage the black beetle population fell 'victim to his own greediness' and was found dead 'amidst a heap of the slain'.[44] Better to blame the hog than chastise the human for keeping the wild animal captive in the first place. A compromise that was often recommended for birds was to try and cultivate a relationship with an animal while permitting it to remain outdoors. Even this was precarious. One Lambeth ironmonger's son had outdoor 'pet' hedgehogs in the spring of 1874, although he liked to pick them up and weigh them. One died within a fortnight while the other, more fortunate perhaps, escaped from the garden.[45]

If capturing hedgehogs seemed a little tame in the adventure stakes (hedgehogs tend to stand still, curled into a ball, when sensing a predator), it is notable that they were often associated with younger children, girls or women. Not only did girls' literature eschew instructions for capturing wild animals, but some writers thought wild animals unsuitable companions for nice girls. Mrs R. Valentine, author of *The Home Book of Pleasure and Instruction* (1867), advised that outdoor 'pets' were best left to servants and that while some 'town' girls might keep squirrels or mice indoors, this was 'not very desirable'. Her objection rested on these animals' resistance to taming. Biddable creatures were far more appropriate as girls' playmates and Valentine thought birds – pretty, mostly pliable and purchased from reputable dealers – best suited to growing girls. If boys' literature encouraged hunting skills, girls' texts counselled nurture and kindness: Valentine thought capturing wild birds was cruel but suggested girls might rescue 'orphan' fledglings or those 'taken captive by village boys'.[46] 'Village boys' probably referred to the sons of agricultural labourers who, as the rural author George Bourne reflected, would derive pleasure from watching a dog worry a hedgehog but treat an animal who had *become* a pet with great tenderness and 'gentle hands'.[47] For Valentine, then, cruelty was about gender and social class: it was the refined girl's place to rescue innocent creatures from abandonment or ignorant boys' adventures.

Of course, prescription didn't necessarily map onto experience and while many girls' leisure, especially in working-class families, was curtailed by domestic chores, girls could – and did – participate in capturing creatures from the wild. A boy growing up in Edwardian Oxford might prefer 'village boys' for comrades but be willing to include the 'girls next door' in hunting adventures.[48] The curate Francis Kilvert, fond of rambling through fields, playfully cautioned a group of girls out looking for birds' nests not to steal any.[49] This was several years before the 1880 Act but the girls were indignant, possibly taking umbrage at being thought as low as boys, or possibly objecting to the curate's interference in their game (Kilvert was fond of little girls). Nevertheless, here were girls actively looking for birds' nests, and who was to say how much effort they put into determining the difference between fledglings that were *really* orphaned and those that the girls desperately *wanted* to be orphaned?

Taming pets

Intrinsic to the adventure of capturing – or 'rescuing' – a wild bird or animal was moving beyond mere possession and attempting to train it. This was partly what transformed wild creatures into pets. Indeed, it wasn't only concern about cruelty that prompted advice writers to encourage the capture of birds and animals when young: it was easier to tame and train the young into responsive practices and performing tricks. This was especially the case with birds snatched from the nest, although even then taming demanded patience and persistence. Taming was a civilization process that fostered a supposedly reciprocal relationship, emotional rewards (for humans) and endless entertainment. Bullfinches, for example, could be trained to sing using a human whistle or a bird organ. Part of the pleasure was the challenge: as John Wood warned, this was a 'lengthy and arduous business'.[50] *Cassell's* believed birds to be a 'real boon' to a young person but warned that training required 'some sacrifice as to sleep and general comfort for a week or two'.[51] Larks could be trained to eat from the hand or table while an attentive child could teach a goldfinch to imitate death, draw water or fire a small cannon.[52] Native 'talking birds' such as starlings and jackdaws could be taught to mimic sounds. Ravens provided 'infinite amusement' for their 'trickiness, intelligence and retentive memory',[53] although they also, as Charles Dickens's beleaguered wife would have attested, caused domestic havoc. Dickens's ravens (there were several over the years) could 'say anything' but their antics provoked 'mingled sensations of horror and satisfaction', a 'kind of awful delight' as they variously swallowed door keys, buried household goods in the garden or attacked the butcher. All of them had a fatal predilection for smashing windows and eating putty and paint.[54]

Like Brightwen's ill-fated starlings, many birds – ostensibly tamed – were simply not suited to domestic or family life. During the early 1840s Dickens kept a 'pet' eagle that, not surprisingly, disliked household chaos and numerous children. The bird wasn't freed but moved into a calmer environment with the artist Edwin Landseer after 1845.[55] Documented antagonisms and fatalities did little to deter earnest bird enthusiasts from trying to domesticate the wild. Even in the 1870s, as agitation to prevent the capture of wild birds was gathering pace, people continued to attempt to keep birds of prey as pets, despite the manifold challenges of taming them to meet human domestic expectations. This was evidenced by the havoc wreaked by Ruth, a pet owl forced to spend the night in a London hotel when the two women she lived with missed their last train home to Wales. A nocturnal creature in any case, Ruth escaped from her basket and flew about the hotel room hooting in panic all night, frightening a chambermaid 'to death' while a waiter was dispatched on a fruitless endeavour to find mice to placate the traumatized owl.[56] Bestowing a human name on a wild bird might signal possession and the desire to tame, but animal behaviours were unpredictable and far from tractable.

For some people, though, the sheer difficulty of taming the wild was what made it compelling. Squirrels were widely acknowledged as difficult to tame, requiring a 'great deal of method'. But if successful, the rewards were great. John Wood kept a squirrel named Jacob who would 'play us many a trick', diving into pockets for nuts, jumping over sticks, turning head over heels and leaping distances for a walnut.[57] Hedgehogs could be trained to respond to their name call.[58] Authors disagreed over whether mice were tameable. Wood thought only white mice could be domesticated while Valentine insisted the common brown mouse was 'more tractable and intelligent', 'easily tamed by patient kindness'.[59] Rabbits were also adaptable to human demands, being walked on leads, toilet trained and capable of performing tricks.

Depictions of birds interacting with humans – especially starlings and ravens that might be given the run of the house – gave the sense that birds actively participated in these games. Brightwen claimed her first starling, Dick, took great pleasure in learning to 'talk' and visiting the dining room after the evening meal, where he would hop among the used dessert dishes, 'stopping with an emphatic "Beauty dear!" at the sight of some coveted dainty, to which he would forthwith help himself liberally'.[60] But there was a fine line between teaching tricks and practising cruelty. Brightwen was uncomfortable with birds being taught to draw their own water and suggested that food rewards be used in training as positive reinforcement.[61] Yet, like many of her contemporaries, Brightwen's approach to birds and animals was deeply contradictory. She insisted that no free adult bird be captured, though they could be 'rescued' and subsequently tamed. She condoned taking one or two nestlings (apparently the parent birds would find it easier to care for their reduced family!) but urged against raiding nests. She presented taming as an act of kindness when pursued with patience and framed her interactions with the natural world in theological terms: 'No cruelty of any kind should be tolerated for a moment in our treatment of the tender dumb creatures our Heavenly Father has given us to be a solace and a joy during our life on earth.' Humans had responsibilities to the natural world but this granted them the power to expect 'solace and joy' from them, to determine where an animal or bird's interests lay, to interpret their behaviours and subject them to human control. Many of Brightwen's 'tame pets' did not fare well. The first three pet birds mentioned in her book – Dick, Richard the Second and Verdant – all died because they had been brought into domestic environments, the first two drowning in water containers and the third flying into a plate-glass window at high speed.

Critics of capturing wild birds and small animals encouraged children and natural-history enthusiasts to pursue adventures of a less destructive kind: to tame wild animals while permitting them to remain at liberty. Pitched in terms of kindness and requiring longer stints of patience, this activity was associated in the first instance with girls and women who were discouraged from engaging in a 'capture' culture. Mrs

Valentine urged girls to establish friendships with birds in their garden: feeding wild birds regularly would create 'a family of pensioners' and generate 'much insight' into individual birds and their 'special characteristics'.[62] In *The Picture Book of Mabel May* (1868), the little girl protagonist learns 'feelings of kindness towards dumb animals' by cultivating four 'quite tame' garden sparrows that 'never failed to present themselves' for breakfast every morning. Mabel named each bird after its characteristics (Frisky, Merry, Jumping Dick and Wagtail) and liked to believe that they recognized their names, although the author suggested this was 'mistaken'.[63] Cultivating relationships with garden creatures was best when it affirmed boundaries between species. Henrietta Wilson's *Chronicles of a Garden* (1864) advocated taming birds in the natural world: blackbirds and chaffinches were described as 'pets' that formed a 'friendship' with humans in the protected space of the garden.[64] She called these 'sky pets', distinct from 'pets properly called', which were defined as domestic animals and included caged linnets and chaffinches.[65] 'Sky pets' were a substitute for captive animals but they did represent Wilson's willingness to imagine a pet–human relationship that went beyond capture, domination and containment. For Wilson, the wildness of 'sky pets' was integral to their appeal: they were always slightly out of reach.

The relationship between humans and 'sky pets' went beyond middle-class fantasies of the rural garden. Feeding wild birds became more common in the late nineteenth century: a range of commercially produced bird tables and feeders appeared on the market, and in the cold winters of the early 1890s, when the ground froze, there was a newspaper campaign to encourage people to feed birds.[66] According to the naturalist and bird expert William Henry Hudson, working people were drawn daily to The Dell in Hyde Park to feed the birds there: 'I call these my chickens and I'm obliged to come every day to feed them,' an elderly man 'in the shabbiest clothes' told Hudson.[67] In 1903 the popular illustrated magazine *Living London* celebrated the ubiquity of bird feeding across the capital.[68]

But encouragement to tame the wild wasn't restricted to birds. The children's author Emma Davenport narrated the story of a hedgehog, Pricker, who lived in the garden of a suburban house. The resident children made a 'pond' of milk in the lawn for him and, over time, Pricker let the children stroke his feet and face and would run about on the grass 'as if he liked our company'. Pricker did sometimes take trips into the kitchen and nursery, where he would roll up, apparently in sleep, for an hour or so (though possibly he was just very afraid of the alien environment).[69] From Davenport's perspective, this was a happy compromise between permitting the hedgehog to remain at liberty and taming him sufficiently to establish a cross-species relationship. Henrietta Wilson noted that almost any garden creature could be tamed outdoors, even those 'generally considered disgusting', like toads, newts and lizards.[70] On holiday in Cornwall in the summer of 1870, Francis Kilvert remarked on his hostess's 'pet' toads living in the stump of an old garden tree. She fed them breadcrumbs everyday and they made a 'funny little plaintive squeaking noise' when she called them.[71] Cultivating wildlife outdoors could generate rewards without the expectation of reciprocity. When a little girl in 1890s Devon made a garden pond from a bowl discarded by her mother, her pleasure was in watching transplanted tadpoles 'come on to frogs'.[72] Even at this simple level, cultivating a 'tamed' environment for wildlife outdoors provided hours of fascinated entertainment.

Partly on account of welfare legislation to protect birds and the increased activities of animal charities in schools (the RSPCA began to work with schools from the end of the nineteenth century), notions of capture increasingly gave way to the rhetoric of simply cultivating friendship with animals who remained at liberty. But, as with 'rescuing' baby birds from nests, the boundaries of how friendships were cultivated were often blurred. If simply feeding garden birds was at one end of a friendship spectrum, Eliza Brightwen's 'rescue' of Richard the Second and his subsequent residence indoors was another. *The Field*, a country sports magazine for adults, regularly carried 'Notes and Queries' on wild animal 'rescues', demonstrating the range of differing outcomes. In January 1902 a correspondent noted that he regularly took breakfast with a squirrel that, although 'never' having experienced 'confinement', was perfectly 'tame', coming into the house of its own volition, tempted by tasty morsels of proffered food.[73] Another correspondent contributed his experiences. He had 'rescued' a hare in October 1901 when it was just four weeks old. Unlike baby rabbits (kittens), young hares (leverets) are independent early on. But instead of being released back into the wild, four months later the hare remained indoors – apparently thriving on a regime of carrot tops and sticks, parsley, bread, milk and water. The hare had a box for its bed and had become 'very tame', sitting on different family member's laps, eating from their hands and stretching out leisurely in front of the fire in the evenings. Despite scratching the wallpaper and chewing the hearth rugs, the hare made a 'delightful pet' and the family 'are very proud of it'.[74] Thoroughly 'rescued' from self-sufficiency, this hare was unlikely to return to the wild.

Beatrix Potter, at this time farming in the Lake District, read the letter with 'great pleasure' and wrote in with her experiences. As a girl she was 'always catching and taming mice'; she found 'common wild ones' were 'far more intelligent and amusing than the fancy variety'. As a young woman in the 1890s, Potter had rescued a rabbit – 'regular vermin' – caught in a snare. She couldn't bear to see wild animals 'mauled about' and took the rabbit home to tend its wounds, wash it, warm it by the fire and relieve it of fleas. Potter thought the wild rabbit had more character than the 'idiotic hutch' creature bred for docility (though if taken in hand early, a shop-bought rabbit could become intelligent). Wild rabbits could be 'easily trained to cleanliness' and taught tricks like ringing a bell and playing a tambourine, although few could be 'broken' of the nibbling habit. Despite the plus points of the wild, though, Potter's rabbit rescue ended with her releasing it, not least because it was incompatible with her long established, shop-bought rabbit, Benjamin Bunny.[75]

Taming, then, might acknowledge an animal's ability to thrive in its natural habitat, and even a recognition that it should be returned to it. But for many Victorians, taming continued to mean bringing wild animals indoors and, often, keeping them there. After all, it was the appeal of the idea that wild birds and animals were ready to respond to human 'friendliness' that made Eliza Brightwen's *Wild Nature Won by Kindness* such a bestseller in the 1890s. According to Brightwen, 'truly to know and enjoy the society of a pet creature you must make it feel that you are, or wish to be, its friend, one to whom it can always look for food, shelter, and solace; it must be at ease and at home with you before its instincts and curious ways will be shown.'[76] Taming wild things was not a straightforward process and required 'a large fund of patience', daily interaction with animals over many months and in some cases, such as the nursing of young fledglings, very early rising for feeding. An emphasis on taming, especially animals who remained at liberty, drew on a different rhetoric from the instructions issued to boys on capture. It demanded different skills, notably patience, and a willingness to accept that not all animals were biddable (or at least easily tamed). For some authors, it also required a modification of assumptions about human privilege to enable birds and animals to remain at large in their natural habitat. What remained constant across capture and taming narratives was a taken-for-granted belief that white Westerners had every right to exercise power over the natural world and that civilization was, in and of itself, a worthwhile endeavour.

The rise of the 'bred-tame' budgie

In his 1915 book *Birds and Men*, the naturalist William Henry Hudson wrote:

> I am not an admirer of pet parrots. To me, and I have made the discovery that to many others too, it is a depressing experience, on a first visit to nice people, to find that a parrot is a member of the family . . . When I am compelled to stand in the admiring circle, to look on and listen while he exhibits his weary accomplishments, it is but lip service I render: my eyes are turned inward, and a vision of a green forest comes before them resounding with the wild, glad, and mad cries of flocks of wild parrots.[77]

Hudson had been brought up on a ranch in the Pampas in South America in the 1840s and '50s, where he roamed freely and developed a passion for wild birds. After travelling around the world as a naturalist, he arrived in England in the 1870s, exhibiting a keen interest in the countryside and its birdlife and writing popular natural history books that celebrated the English landscape, its flora and fauna. By the early twentieth century Hudson's books enjoyed considerable popularity and he was one of a growing number of people who recognized the value of leaving birds in natural habitats.[78] Parrots in cages depressed him because they were never meant to be indoor birds. These new ideas redefined the boundaries of pet keeping, challenging and shifting the predominant Victorian view that people had a right to take pets from what were increasingly viewed as wild natural environments. Instead, pet keeping was increasingly grounded in the consumption of birds and animals bred as domestic creatures. As Hudson's distaste for the caged parrot demonstrates, though, this shift didn't address whether it was ethical to keep birds and animals as domestic pets at all.

The RSPB (it received the royal charter in 1904) and its campaigns led to the 1896 Wild Birds Protection Act, which permitted county councils to apply for orders to protect areas or species. Subsequent acts in the 1900s permitted the confiscation of illegally acquired birds or eggs and forbade some forms of trapping.[79] By the end of the nineteenth century the SPB had 25,000 members and ornithology was becoming a widespread public pastime.[80] From the early twentieth century, as Diana Donald has shown, the SPB worked with Hudson on the 'Bird and Tree' initiative for primary schools, a pioneering educational campaign that encouraged children to go outdoors and observe nature for themselves.[81] As Hudson remarked: 'the existence of a strong and widespread public feeling in favour of the preservation of our wild birds has of late shown itself in many ways, especially in the unopposed legislation on the subject during the last few years.'[82]

This shift coincided with a falling off in the public trade in British birds. In the 1890s *Exchange and Mart* was filled with adverts for blackbirds, bullfinches, goldfinches, linnets, thrushes and skylarks. These rapidly diminished in the twentieth century, and marketing rubrics reflected growing disapproval of capturing wild birds for sale. Blackbirds offered in 1910 were described as 'brought up from the nest' and a bullfinch was advertised as 'hand reared'. It was a selling point that the birds had been nurtured as fledglings rather than snatched from natural habitats. British birds represented 10 per cent of *Exchange and Mart's* pet trade in the 1880s and '90s, but by the 1920s this had fallen to around 2 per cent.[83] Writing in the mid-1920s, the environmentalist and ornithologist Edward Max Nicholson believed that the activities of bird catchers had been curtailed.[84] Even so, the trade did continue in some quarters into at least the 1930s.[85] In 1919 *Aviaries, Bird Rooms and Cages* still offered advice on what to do with 'freshly caught' birds,[86] and, as we will see in Chapter Two, wild birds continued to be sold at bird markets in the 1920s. But – increasingly – campaigns by charities like the SPB made capturing and caging wild birds unacceptable. The Protection of Birds Act of 1933 made it illegal to sell any live British bird (this included 66 species) unless it had been bred in an aviary or cage, although implementation of the legislation was not straightforward.[87]

An early sign of this shift in attitude lies in the publications by Robert Baden-Powell, founder of the Boy Scout Movement. *Scouting for Boys* (1908) addressed animal tracking and stalking skills but avoided giving instructions on capture and killing: increasingly sophisticated and lightweight cameras meant photography could be used to acquire trophies without causing damage. Baden-Powell urged boys to become 'ornithologists' – to take a keen interest in bird life – but the scout 'does not, like the ordinary boy, want to go out and rob them of their eggs'. Scouts were encouraged to be sensitive to the natural world. Baden-Powell referenced the author Mark Twain's emotional account of unthinkingly killing a blackbird in boyhood, acknowledging that the story moved him and including Twain's response in his handbook: 'I couldn't see nothing for the tears.' And yet Baden-Powell's book retained a degree of ambiguity.[88] His quotation from Twain adds colour to the account, using the story to bring the consequences of bird killing to life. Yet his shift to a different, American, voice slightly distances the reader from the message. Perhaps the idea of shedding tears over a blackbird was still a little too much for the stiff upper lips of English imperialists. After all, capture and collection were not quite outlawed in 1908. A microcosm of abstruse legislation, *Scouting for Boys* referenced doing the right thing but came close to looking like lip service. The book still hinted that birds and animals might be studied at home, although Baden-Powell urged boys who did collect from the nest to restrict themselves to a single egg. Restraint wasn't out of keeping with other dimensions of a scouting culture that cultivated a new kind of imperial masculinity in the wake of successive Boer Wars. Even allowing for ambivalence, the tone of Baden-Powell's book was different to Victorian *Boy's Own* literature. Partly, this reflected a shift in Britain's position in the world and increasing anxiety about the success of the imperial project. There was a difference between producing adventure stories intended for escapism or manuals that celebrated imperialism unequivocally and marketing an organization and ethos intended to actively train boys – especially working-class boys – to be dutiful and responsible citizens.[89]

Baden-Powell's token sensitivity towards the natural world also reflected a contemporary trend for pet advisors and specialists to express increasingly mixed feelings about bird capture, especially when writing for children. *Pets for Boys and Girls* (1914), for example, emphasized the moral importance of keeping 'aviary-bred' birds rather than trapping them.[90] By 1922 *The Boy's Own Book of Pets and Hobbies* took a harder line: 'There is a good deal of feeling nowadays against keeping birds in confinement, but in this little book I shall deal with such as are bred tame [including canaries, budgerigars and parrots], and therefore have never known liberty, or can be let out safely.' Captured wild birds were not included in the author's definition of pets, although even here ambiguity remained, with reference to clipping the wings of magpies and jackdaws to prevent them flying off.[91] A later edition of *Pets for Boys and Girls* (1923) did not include wild birds and animals in its list of pets and stated: 'there is no need to impose the slightest punishment on the wildings of the countryside.'[92] This repudiation of capture in children's books on pet keeping coincided with a changed attitude towards military heroics in British culture – the catastrophic loss of life on the battlefields of the First World War dealt a damaging blow to the jingoistic imperialism of previous decades.

Bird specialists and fanciers increasingly favoured British birds that were 'bred tame'. Sumner Birchley recommended that nightingales, linnets and finches should be bred like canaries and pigeons.[93] According to John Robson's *Popular Cage Birds* (1924), breeding hybrids – mixing so-called foreign birds with British stock – had become a popular although challenging hobby. The goldfinch–canary hybrid was recommended for 'its perky, happy-go-lucky nature, bright disposition and cheerful song'.[94] Would-be bird owners with qualms about confining British birds had other options. Canaries were imported and bred in Britain in larger numbers in the nineteenth century, especially in working-class households in Leicester, Norwich and London, and were often favoured by pet advisers because they circumvented the moral unease occasioned by the caged wild bird. Instead, civilization was bred into these pets.

In the 1920s the 'bred tame' canary had a new rival. Small Australian parakeets known as budgerigars were reputedly first sold in England by Charles Jamrach and bred in small numbers in the second half of the nineteenth century.[95] But it was a small and specialist market.[96] When sky-blue budgies were first exhibited in 1910 they became wildly popular: between 1925 and 1927 they fetched from £125 to £175 a pair thanks to demand from the Japanese market (although prices rapidly fell when the Japanese banned imported budgies in 1927).[97] The Budgerigar Society, founded in 1925, had around 2,000 members by 1929.[98] Despite being relatively expensive to acquire, numbers rocketed in the 1930s and budgies accounted for 7 per cent of the pet trade in *Exchange and Mart* by 1940.[99] The brightly coloured birds were easy to manage and could be fed at a relatively low cost. *Your Pet Budgie* (1955) noted a further 'astonishing' surge in budgie ownership in the seven years after the Second World War.[100] By the 1950s a pair of budgies could be bought for £2 and the cost of food was within the average child's pocket money, which meant, according to *Pet Birds for Boys and Girls*

(1954), that you 'should be able to do it all by yourself without bothering mother or father'.[101]

Despite being 'bred tame', budgies were popular because of their special capacity for interaction with humans. Although taming wild animals was now considered outré, people still wanted to build relationships with pets through training. If acquired at an early age, budgies could, in the right circumstances, be trained to talk. According to William Glanville's *Cult of the Budgerigar* (1935): 'There are today in houses all over the world Budgerigars which can talk with marked ability, perform little tricks for the enjoyment of families and visitors, and which have become so tame and friendly that no pet could be more admired or be a greater source of delight.'[102] Pre-trained birds were hard to come by and budgies were attractive partly because of the time and effort required for training. According to Andrew Wilson, the author of *Talking Budgerigars and How to Train Them* (1936), this was a difficult process: kindness, patience and at least six months of daily sessions were usually required to get a bird to speak. The rewards, however, were great: 'To no other bird does a family become so deeply attached.'[103]

Many budgie owners wrote of the pleasure these small, feathered pets brought to their lives. For Glanville, 'it was indeed a fortunate day for me when I was persuaded by my wife to buy two pairs of Budgies. It brought a new joy into my life.'[104] In 1937 Jennie Gauntlett Hill, a young middle-class woman living with her parents in rural Hampshire, gifted two budgies to her mother, who was 'delighted with her Easter present of the birds'.[105] When her mother went to Eastleigh to choose a new cage for the budgies, she was as 'pleased as [a] child with [a] new toy'.[106] During the Second World War thousands of budgies died during air raids or from starvation due to lack of seed.[107] But people also found solace in these pets. Andrew Wilson reported seeing an older woman in a London air raid shelter clutching 'her greatest treasure', 'Wee Joey', on her lap.[108] As Britons adjusted to post-war life with ongoing rationing, housing shortages and a recalibration of Britain's place in the world, the budgie supplanted the captured wild bird to become a domestic fixture, bringing colour, movement and song into millions of British homes. By the early 1960s, according to the naturalist and broadcaster Katharine Tottenham, a nationwide survey identified 11 million caged birds in Britain, while the number of dogs and cats had fallen to half this figure.[109]

The wild outdoors

If birdlife was secured from the pet trade by legislation and awareness raising, this shift in attitude had implications for other wildlife too. Natural history books of the interwar years increasingly placed emphasis on 'taming' wild animals while leaving them in the wild. For some authors, these relationships still counted as 'pets'. Gilbert Fisher, a naturalist and broadcaster known popularly as 'Hut Man', created an educational children's radio series in the 1930s and a book (1938), aimed at eight- to thirteen-year-olds. Fisher wrote about 'Field Folk', his outdoor 'small neighbours' and the pleasure of getting to know their habits. Anthropomorphism enabled him to combine the naturalist's knowledge with narrative interest, rendering animals as persons. He even claimed that 'Old Brown the Tawny Owl' first suggested the series, the Field Mice agreed and Jenny Wren applauded. Reflecting that pets were typically associated with animals that children could 'stroke and fondle', Fisher made a case for considering pets creatures of 'fascination' as much as affection. He found spiders to be 'amazing little people'. Fisher's project was less about domesticating wild animals (although he claimed to allow field mice living in his cupboard to remain) than observation of 'companions' and, by learning about the natural world, to develop an understanding and respect for wildlife: to 'be gentle, kind and sympathetic to all creatures smaller and weaker than ourselves'.[110]

Much of Fisher's material drew on the same spirit of adventure and derring do that Victorian authors appealed to, and there remained traces of imperialism. Notably, Fisher's black-and-tan cocker spaniel was called Mowgli, after Rudyard Kipling's character in *The Jungle Book* (1894). The book ended with the dog wishing readers 'good hunting', even though that meant something different in the mid-twentieth century.[111] What made Fisher different to John Wood, or even someone like Eliza Brightwen, was a much clearer sense that although birds and wild animals could be imagined as pets, they were to be left firmly outdoors. Yet even here, capture hadn't entirely disappeared from the story. Now, there was a hierarchy of species. If birds and small mammals were off limits, insects appeared exempt from notions of cruelty. Thus, Fisher kept 'pet ants' that he had gone 'hunting' for and 'captured' to keep in a formicarium as pets. He couldn't stroke or fondle the ants but this counted as pet keeping because there was pleasure – and a relationship of sorts – based on watching the 'wonderful' life and community of the ant colony.[112]

Even so, Fisher's endeavour represented the emergence and coalescence of new sensibilities about leaving wildlife in its natural habitat. The relationship between British people and the immediate outdoors – and perceived boundaries between the home and the wild – were shifting. From the early twentieth century, there was an increasing recognition that spaces and habitats for wildlife needed to be preserved. Some of this work was carried out by the National Trust (empowered by the National Trust Act of 1907) while the Society for the Promotion of Nature Reserves (founded 1912) raised awareness and, from the 1920s, a growing number of local trusts worked to build enclaves to protect wildlife.[113] As part of the drive for reconstruction after the Second World War, National Parks were created.[114] The changing attitude of the public and successive governments to animals in the wild played out in pet-keeping practices too.

For many people in interwar Britain, the outdoors had come a little closer too. New homes – state-planned municipal houses as well as semi-detached suburban houses – came with reasonably generous gardens and by the 1950s, if placed alongside parks and playing fields, accounted for a third of the area of British towns and cities.[115] These new spaces allowed certain birds to flourish – even small gardens, when placed together, encouraged blackbirds, blue and great tits, song thrushes and dunnocks, and chaffinches and wrens were to be found in larger gardens.[116] The idea of the garden as a wild space that could fascinate and enthral adults and children recurred throughout inter-war advice manuals on domestic life and pet keeping. *Pets for Boys and Girls* (1923) stressed the value of studying birds that had been attracted to the garden by bits of food.[117] A piece on 'Nature in the Garden', meanwhile, in *The New Home Encyclopaedia* (1932) waxed lyrical on the potential for friendship with animals in the natural world, recommending the acquisition of a bird bath and suggesting that relationships could be established with free-roaming squirrels.[118] The 1920s and '30s also saw books published that celebrated adult relationships with garden wildlife, including Viscount Grey's *The Charm of Birds* (1927), which tracked changing birdsong in the garden throughout the year, and the artist Claire Leighton's *Four Hedges: A Gardener's Chronicle* (1935), which devoted a chapter to plants and birds in the garden during each month.[119]

For some, the garden was best enjoyed when wildlife intermingled with creatures imported for sale from overseas or bred for a pet market. One notable enthusiast of garden wildlife was the political activist, publisher and writer Leonard Woolf, who invested considerable time and effort in creating a garden at Monks House in Rodmell, the Sussex home he shared with his novelist wife Virginia. The combination of shop-bought and wild inhabitants in the garden was important to him. In 1937 three tortoises were installed in the lily pond although, as Virginia noted, they were 'so active we can't keep control of them. I am perpetually being sent up the road in pursuit of the father tortoise.'[120] There were two ponds (the second a 'folly', according to Virginia) where Leonard anxiously watched over fish, removing them to a special indoor tank when they became ill. These creatures lived alongside the garden's natural residents and Leonard took measures to treat both if they were unwell or in danger. In July 1940 an unsympathetic Virginia noted 'A large hedgehog was found drowned in the lily pool; L[eonard] tried to resuscitate it. An amusing sight.'[121]

For all the tragedies of garden life, engaging with wild visitors to gardens could bring emotional rewards. In the late 1930s birds provided company for lonely housewife Betty Shadbolt, married to a dentist and living in a suburb of Newcastle-under-Lyme in Staffordshire. Taking full advantage of her new garden, Betty cultivated pigeons and other wild birds. She built a house from a grocer's box and fixed it under the eaves of the garage. When four pigeons moved in, she named them and fed them breakfast. The birds responded to her when she 'cooed'. At the same time, she fed sparrows and thrushes in the garden and noted how 'tame' they were.[122]

In this context, even species considered wild – including those acquired from shops – were increasingly only acceptable if accommodated out of doors. If squirrels and hedgehogs were to be kept at all, they should be housed in the garden. In 1937 the magazine *Ideal Home* recommended that hedgehogs be given open hutches: 'When properly domesticated, the hedgehog may be given the freedom of one's garden.'[123] Some authors still discussed squirrels as pets but only if they were kept in a 3-foot-long (1 m) hutch out of doors.[124] By the 1950s hedgehogs and squirrels still featured in discussions of more unusual pets, but it is clear that they were no longer bought in large numbers, nor was it seen as appropriate to keep them in captivity. In 1955 the pet specialist Thomas Sidney Denham suggested that squirrels and hedgehogs could be tamed, but only if they had been acquired as babies.[125] Others stressed that they should not be caged, unless a very large aviary could be provided in a garden.[126] Many people, it seems, were happy to 'tame' from afar. Living in a glamorous apartment in Versailles, the author Nancy Mitford was not, perhaps, an obvious animal enthusiast but she did include 'natural history' reports ('which may bore so I'll cut it short') in letters to her sister Debo (the Duchess of Devonshire) in the 1960s. Despite going 'slightly off' hedgehogs since reading that their 'brain development is very low' (the 'brilliant genius' she thought she was cultivating turned out to be 'two half-wits'), Nancy sought to make her two garden visitors 'more comfortable' and provided them with milk. She was diffident about her apparent fascination with the animals ('Really, I [could] write a volume . . .') and wondered if Debo could recommend a book that 'might throw light on their eccentricities'.[127]

One couple that bucked the trend for enabling wildlife to live wild were Doreen and Charles Tovey, middle-class professionals who lived in a cottage in rural Somerset in the late 1940s. Doreen was later to become president of the Siamese Cat Club but, at this point, a squirrel named Blondin dominated their lives. Seemingly unaware of contemporary advice on squirrel keeping, the couple briefly attempted to keep Blondin in a cage before giving in and allowing him the run of the house and even Doreen's office.[128] Tellingly, they had not bought Blondin but found him helpless and injured after falling from his drey. Like Brightwen some sixty years earlier, they had restored the creature to health but failed to release him back into the wild. After his death in the early 1950s they were baffled by the apparent impossibility of purchasing a replacement: 'we trudged the town pet shops, enquiring above a murderous cacophony of yelping puppies, mewing kittens, screeching parrots and glugging goldfish, for a simple, ordinary little squirrel, it was obvious that the proprietors thought we were mad.'[129] Squirrels were now outside the normal boundaries of pet keeping.

For every home naturalist who respected wild animals' need for a natural environment, albeit with some human assistance, there did remain those that continued to assert the dominion of the human over the animal world. When naturalist and broadcaster Katharine Tottenham wrote *The Pan Book of Home Pets* (1963), she disapprovingly noted that a recent national survey had identified 'tens of thousands of people' that kept 'uncommon tame animals'.[130] While she was reasonably enthusiastic about squirrels and monkeys, other 'wild' animals – badgers, foxes and otters – were, she argued, extremely unsuitable pets. 'In recent years bottle-reared young badgers have been offered for sale in ever increasing numbers; yet any animal less suited to life as a family pet would be hard to find.' The concern was twofold: while wild animals were always best left to the wild, badgers were simply unsuited to domesticity because of the havoc they wrought on human homes: adults could weigh up to 18 kilograms (40 lb) and were violent and destructive. But the worst animal to keep was the fox: 'the animal remains what it is, a wild creature of the woods whose forebears have been hunted and persecuted by man since time immemorial, and however tame it may become on the surface, the fox remains a highly strung animal, very liable to bite if accidentally frightened, and with naturally extremely dirty habits. In short it is not in the least the pretty little dog it appears to be.'[131] As Tottenham's exasperation shows, there were still some people attempting to keep wild animals as pets but they were being written out of the main pet-keeping narrative, increasingly seen as delinquents.

A resurgence of the wild

Between the early nineteenth century and the mid-twentieth there were significant changes in the kinds of animal people kept as pets and the imagined boundaries between domestic pets and nature outdoors. In the mid-nineteenth century pet advisors had been happy to recommend the capture of all kinds of British wildlife, but by the early twentieth century they had become more circumspect. In 1953 the Wild Bird Act, tidying up complex and contradictory legislation, finally outlawed the capture of all British birds. Squirrels and hedgehogs were no longer viewed as animals that could be unproblematically introduced to the home. Yet Victorian ideas continued to influence how humans related to the animal world.

Taming, although loaded with notions of capture, cruelty and dominion, was also about care. Katharine Tottenham's 1963 book expressed the view that the wild should be kept firmly out of doors but there were still some important exceptions. The final section included a short note on the Wild Bird Act: 'While the Act protects healthy wild birds from trappers and egg collectors, it does not prevent the humane care of crippled wild birds or the rearing of orphaned young ones.'[132] The book also included a section on what to do with wild bird casualties that were increasingly found due to the growing amount of motor traffic on roads.[133] As late Victorian writers like Eliza Brightwen would have recognized, the key words here were 'orphan' and 'injured': human intervention and capture was still acceptable in the case of vulnerable animals – especially fledglings – and, again, nineteenth-century ideas about the nursing and 'bringing up' of pets lived on.

Yet even as the boundary between the domestic and natural appeared to harden, some people continued to fill their homes with creatures of all kinds. While keeping wild animals as pets became increasingly censured, collecting natural-history 'specimens' remained an accepted childhood pursuit for most of the twentieth century. The natural-history writer Peter Marren, writing about butterfly collecting in his youth in the 1950s and '60s, identified himself as belonging to 'the last generation that could set out on foot, or on a bike, with a net and satchel without feeling self-conscious'.[134] For some enthusiasts, the appeal of wild pets never went away. Recent arguments over culling badgers have brought this animal back into the limelight. In 2013 Owen Paterson, then environment secretary of the UK, defended the cull, drawing on stories of childhood pet-keeping to claim empathy with the animals. Wildlife campaigner Chris Packham, opposed to the badger cull, condemned the romanticization of badger keeping too. Growing up in the 1960s, Packham also had a brief spell of badger keeping, which he remembered with 'fondness', but also noted that the badgers were destructive and had to be quickly returned to the garden. The 1973 Badger Act made keeping badgers illegal, and as Packham concluded, 'The badger's place is in the wild.'[135]

Since the 1970s a raft of legislation has been introduced to protect British wildlife, and the Wild Mammals Protection Act of 1996 outlawed killing or injuring all wild mammals.[136] Keeping foxes as pets has never been illegal in Britain, although the RSPCA strongly advises against it: 'because foxes are wild animals and do not fare well as domestic pets, they should not be kept as such.'[137] Despite this advice, the organization reported a rise in keeping foxes as pets in the 2010s following the social-media sensation of popular Instagram foxes Juniper, Penny and Winchester (around 1 million followers in 2016).[138] It is no longer an activity associated with schoolboys or empire, although the legacies of a muscular Victorian imperialism clearly haunt our relationship with the natural world. For some, the fascination of taming the wild continues, despite incontrovertible knowledge of the damage involved.

TWO

Building Trust and Buying Love: Shopping for Pets

Strolling through stalls selling cheese, meat, fish and fresh produce, the visitor to Leadenhall Market in Victorian London would soon be assailed by an altogether different kind of product: live animals. By the 1860s the market was one of the most important sites in London for purchasing all kinds of pets: birds, fish, guinea pigs, squirrels, rabbits, cats and dogs. Customers varied from children desperate to exchange pocket money for birds to well-heeled ladies perusing pedigree dogs. But the market's appeal to shoppers keen to bag a bargain was matched by some commentators' suspicion that the animal goods on sale were of dubious provenance. As one late Victorian journalist noted of the excellent dogs for sale at Leadenhall, some prices were just too good to be true.[1]

By the time a young Queen Victoria bolted down the corridors of Buckingham Palace to share the thrills of coronation with her spaniel Dash, the parlours of Britain were well stocked with pretty songbirds, white mice and affectionate dogs. Even artisans and clerks kept birds and terriers to reproduce the 'simple pleasures' of the countryside in their 'city-pent' lives.[2] Victorians celebrated the idea of capturing pets from the wild but increasingly urban lives meant that, for many, securing a wild pet was a fantasy rather than a practical reality. There were, though, other ways of obtaining wild companions, especially birds. Consumer demand drove a trade in live birds that saw 'catchers' travelling to rural districts on the new railway network to secure birds for sale in the city. There was also, increasingly, a lively trade in animals bred for the pet market – especially dogs, rabbits and canaries. The purchase of pets was beset by fraud and risk, from dealers selling stolen goods or cheap birds disguised as expensive 'exotics' to issues of poor hygiene and animal welfare. Faced with spectacular growth in the choice of live animals in retail, finding creatures that might make long-lived pets was a challenge for consumers.

The growth of the pet market in the nineteenth and twentieth centuries had important consequences for animals and humans. It depended on an increase in animal capture, breeding and transportation as pets, whether bred for a domestic market or imported from overseas, were sent across the British Isles via the new rail network. It brought increased possibilities for human emotional investment in pets but often contributed to animal cruelty and suffering too. In this chapter we uncover the economic trends and traders who created this new market, as well as thinking about why shopping for pets was different to acquiring other kinds of commodities. We examine the perils of buying pets and the measures traders took to win consumers' trust. Traders had to work hard to promote their credentials as honest merchants who treated animals with care and they increasingly prioritized the emotional connections between people and their pets in marketing as part of this initiative. The emotional value of pets – and the need to promote pet wellbeing and *joie de vivre* – lay at the heart of a whole new pet industry that, by the mid-twentieth century, had come to focus on building relationships. Yet retailers' emphasis on emotion and a rhetoric of care continued to eclipse issues of animal suffering and provenance. Pet purchase remained an awkward process, with the animal caught somewhere between consumer good and emotional subject.

Victorian pet shopping

By the start of Victoria's reign, animals were core commodities in domestic and international trading. Merchants like Gilbert Pidcock and, later, Charles Jamrach ran flourishing 'animal menageries' in London that operated as retail and entertainment businesses. Pidcock had a kind of warehouse-showroom in Exeter Exchange on the Strand in London where exotic creatures could be viewed at one shilling a room. By the middle of the century traders in provincial port cities had established what were often called 'wild beast shops', stocking animals such as monkeys, lions, tigers, marmosets and brightly coloured birds. Typically, though, 'exotic' animals were not intended as domestic pets. Dogs were not obviously 'exotic', but for the über fashionable, imported dogs carried a certain cachet and reflected Britain's place in the world. Poodles could make a 12,000-mile trip from China to the lush drawing rooms of Sussex country houses while spaniels and miniature greyhounds might be shipped from homes in the Netherlands and Italy respectively to the boudoirs of grandes dames in the northeast of England.[3] These dogs were usually acquired either through personal networks – the borzoi, a Russian hunting hound, arrived in Britain in the late nineteenth century largely due to connections between the English and Russian aristocracy – or via commercial connections.[4] The rising popularity of the Pekinese in Britain matched the increasing presence of British banking and commerce in China.[5] Home markets for these dogs would emerge once British-based breeders started to produce lines from imported stock.

For Britons who enjoyed global travel or worked at sea, a fancy dog – or bird – was an interesting souvenir to bring home from a tour. Travelling through New York in 1842, Charles Dickens enjoyed 'parties, parties, parties – every day and night' and guided tours of prisons, workhouses, hospitals and police stations. But the highlight of his trip, surely, was the gift of a Havana spaniel pup, originally called Boz but renamed as Mr Snittle Timbery or Timber to intimates, that accompanied the novelist home to England and, later, on Dickens family jaunts across Europe.[6]

By the late nineteenth century London department stores began to boast 'zoological departments', refined versions of Jamrach's and Pidcock's 'wild beast' showrooms. A catalogue from the landmark department store Whiteley's in 1885 included listings for a 'Zoological Department' where 'every description of domestic pets will here be found'. The range was extensive: 'foreign birds, German Tree Frogs, Salamanders, Lizards, Tortoises (land and water), white mice, dormice, white rats, rabbits, goats, cats, dogs (pet, sporting and watch), squirrels, monkeys, marmozets, goldfish'.[7]

Although there was a trade in pedigree cats, the generic puss had little market value, not least because so many strays populated towns and cities. Authors of home-advice manuals were much more likely to discuss how to dispose of unwanted kittens than how to acquire a cat.[8] Most felines were obtained from friends and acquaintances (those unwanted kittens) or by offering food to strays, either from kindness or to recruit a cat to help control household vermin.[9] Grace Platt (later Foakes), who grew up in a tenement flat in Wapping in the early twentieth century, thought cats were important community members, providing playful companionship to children and helping manage rats and mice. There was no shortage of supply and a youthful Grace was much exercised by neighbours who turned out old cats or unwanted kittens to fend for themselves (she wanted to open a cats' home when she grew up).[10]

There was a much broader market for exotic birds, which could be purchased through people trading as 'naturalists' who sold live birds, birdcages and food from a warehouse or shop while providing other services like taxidermy to preserve specimens for keen ornithologists and collectors. The overlap between these trades made sense given the popularity of natural sciences in the early decades of Victoria's reign and, somewhat more gloomily, the high mortality rate of imported birds and animals. 'Foreign' birds were the most common imported pet in Victorian Britain and parrots were particularly attractive (the African grey was apparently the most popular import before 1930).[11] Canaries were shipped from Tyrol in Austria, a region known for high-quality birds. But there was also a substantial homegrown market. According to the historian Ingrid Tague, the eighteenth century saw the 'transformation of canary birds from exotic imports to common pets, thanks to the rise of large-scale breeding'.[12] By the 1830s 'Canary Finch Societies' were dotted all over London, with showrooms in coffee-houses on Cockspur Street, Great Queen Street and Rathbone Place as well as 'various respectable public houses'.[13] The societies were largely hobbyists and fanciers, but there was crossover with the pet market, with suppliers geared towards both competitive breeders and 'parlour pets'.

Birds were available from less auspicious premises too. In Dickens's novel *Martin Chuzzlewit* (1844), the sparrow-like Poll Sweedlepipe conducts a thriving – if somewhat smelly – trade in birds and rabbits from his 'easy-shaving' barber shop.[14] By the 1860s the bird shop was increasingly common in towns and cities across Britain, although many traders still operated under the label of 'naturalist'. Trade directories in London show animal and bird dealers steadily expanding – clustering around the site of the long-established Sunday bird and animal market at Club Row near Spitalfields, in the streets around Leadenhall and in the West End before spreading south of the river and into the new suburbs. By the end of the nineteenth century bird fanciers bred and sold distinctive regional types such as 'Norwich', 'Yorkshire' and 'Lancashire' canaries. In 1902, for example, the self-proclaimed 'Bird Specialist of Norwich' sold 'Norwich Canaries direct from their native city', boasting they were 'the cheapest and best in Great Britain'.[15] Bird shops were often small and, while birds represented the staple commodity, they could trade in other small animals too.

Trade-directory listings for dealers in live birds and animals peaked at almost 120 in mid-1890s London, a trend broadly replicated in the provinces. In 1890s Newcastle, bird dealer and taxidermist ('stuffing a speciality') Joseph Harris boasted a double-fronted 'Zoological Grotto' selling British and 'Foreign' birds and goldfish.[16] The grotto mimicked a bazaar, with caged birds piled high in the shop windows alongside taxidermied birds and small mammals while manifold live birds trilled from cages hooked onto the shop's exterior. To a point, these smaller shops borrowed the aesthetic of larger concerns. By 1900 William Cross's fantastic animal menagerie in Earle Street, Liverpool, repre-sented the spectacular pinnacle of bird shop traders in the city. Visitors to the city could stroll through multiple markets with bird and small animal traders but Cross's menagerie was a tourist destination in its own right.[17] In nearby Manchester, where bird and animal shops appear to have enjoyed similar success to those in London, 85 per cent of animal traders dealt in birds.[18]

For all the fantastic shop displays, genteel commentators viewed animal shops with suspicion. In the final decades of the nineteenth century well-heeled people often visited London's East End, sometimes offering help or religious guidance but often as tourists eager to witness a way of life depicted as depraved in the print media of the day. The animal and bird shops on and around Sclater Street in Bethnal Green were an established destination for these visitors. James Greenwood was a pioneering journalist and social commentator whose 'slumming' adven-tures (disguised as a pauper) revealed the secrets of London's workhouses to a bourgeois readership. In the 1870s he visited Sclater Street, one of the streets where the Club Row market took place, and was dismayed. He described 'dark and foul little shops' in which '"rats for the pit" . . . fancy mice, pigeons, chickens, hedgehogs, and ferrets' were rammed together in tiny cages stacked to the ceiling and blocking the light. The place had a horrible smell and 'what composes the floor it is impossible to say, for it is covered some inches deep with dirt, seed husks, and the droppings of the birds'.[19] The animal shops based around Seven Dials came in for similar criticism. When they appeared in the contemporary graphic press they were often rendered picturesque but potentially sus-pect, showing animals packed tightly together in grubby backstreets.

'The Morning Toilet, Seven Dials', *Illustrated London News*, 5 September 1874.

While much of the criticism of animal shops in this period was undoubtedly rooted in class-based suspicion, this wasn't without foundation. Browsing outside a 'charming bird shop' in Portsmouth's High Street in November 1882, a youthful Beatrix Potter noted two cages crammed full of adorable mice. Knowing her natural history, Potter was doubtful these substantial creatures were 'dormice' as advertised; they were three to four times bigger than they should have been.[20] Worse, some shopkeepers treated stock with cavalier disregard. Around England, the RSPCA repeatedly pursued prosecutions against shopkeepers like Richard Wilson who, in 1878, went on a drinking spree for several days, leaving the birds in his Liverpool shop without food or water. Found guilty, Wilson was fined £15 plus costs.[21]

Shopkeepers, then, had to struggle against this image of dank and smelly cruelty to tempt customers onto their premises. In the latter decades of the century, good reputations for animal or bird shops rested on an establishment's longevity and loyal patronage by customers. By the 1890s the Towell family had run a bird dealership from premises in Manchester's city centre for almost four decades. Established by husband and wife George and Caroline in 1860, the business survived George's premature death in 1869. By the 1870s adverts in the *Manchester Guardian* suggest that Caroline occasionally traded in 'thoroughbred' dogs too and by the 1880s, she was employing her four eldest children as 'assistant bird dealers', although, mindful of the nuances of social class in these things, they also used the term 'Naturalist' when it suited. When she died in 1886, Caroline's personal estate was worth £1,000. Her eldest son, George, took over the shop.[22]

Despite the growth of bird and small animal shops, throughout Victoria's reign large numbers of pets – dogs, birds and other small animals – were acquired through transactions in the street. Towns and cities teemed with street sellers of live animals. Women and child street traders typically sold food, flowers and matches but the animal trader was overwhelmingly male. Most common was the bird seller. Henry Mayhew notes that sellers were usually also catchers, who disposed of around a tenth of their hoard on the streets (of the remainder only about 50 per cent made it into shops, as the mortality of captured birds was high).[23] A picturesque figure, bird sellers stood at the corner of busy thoroughfares with cages of mostly British birds displayed artfully on the pavement. No one grew rich from bird selling but this was offset by its relative independence. The disabled bird seller might sit with two bird cages by his feet, appealing to punters' compassion as much as their desire for a bird. More able-bodied sellers tied their cages to railings or placed them on a wall to catch the eye of passers-by. The most ambitious borrowed a barrow to display their wares or knocked on doors in the hope that clamouring children would persuade beleaguered mothers to treat them. In the 1850s and '60s, the bird sellers' target market was the artisan family that had a little money to spare and, as the journalist Henry Mayhew observed in his study of street selling, the 'intelligence' to seek something of the countryside in their urban digs.

After birds, the biggest 'animal' street trade was in goldfish. By the 1860s three wholesale dealers in London supplied almost two-thirds of their stock of gold and silver fish to street sellers, some of whom adopted the guise of travelling salesmen, stocking so-called medicines, confectionary and fancy goods alongside the fish. This was nice summer work, moving from town to town, following fairs or travelling shows. Other street sellers had more comprehensive stock, placing small animals like mice and rats in cages while squirrels, rabbits and foxes were better displayed on leads. The most ambitious street sellers traded in dogs. Henry Mayhew estimated there were around 25 dog traders in mid-century London, most of whom worked prosperous areas – Regent Street, West End squares, Charing Cross, the Royal Parks and the Serpentine, and by the Bank of England and Royal Exchange.[24] On sunny days, they might be seen on street corners with dogs 'yelping' about their feet and 'little shaggy heads peeping forth from their capacious pockets'.[25] Over half their trade was in spaniels, the lapdog *par excellence*, while the remainder were mostly terriers with a smattering of pugs, poodles and French bulldogs.[26] Some enterprising traders employed a fellow to patrol thoroughfares wearing a sandwich board advertising where dogs for sale could be inspected at leisure.

Some street sellers rented pitches in market halls and squares, generating multiple 'Leadenhall' experiences across the provinces. At Lancashire's Preston market, pet stalls mingled with those selling livestock, flowers, fruit and vegetables, meat and dairy produce.[27] In nearby Bolton, the first-floor gallery of the indoor market was dedicated to stalls selling cats, dogs, birds and small mammals.[28] London's Leadenhall Market was a little 'shabby' by the 1860s but still boasted 'extensive' pet stock. Amid fancy pigeons and turkeys (destiny: dinner) there jostled decorative birds, a 'proud and gorgeous peacock', 'pet rooks, ravens and owls'. The market traded in 'every animal whom it is possible to make a pet': 'common favourites' like rabbits, mice, guinea pigs and squirrels rubbed shoulders with ferrets, badgers, foxes and even moles. The resourceful stallholder stocked aquatic and reptilian species while the 'Place of honour' was reserved for dogs. Stalls boasted all canine breeds but especially those favoured by ladies and children – from smaller types like 'Scotch' terriers, poodles and spaniels to the gentle large varieties such as St Bernards and Newfoundlands. Although cats, viewed as mousers by most householders, were much less commodified than their canine cousins, 'thorough bred' or 'fancy' felines could be bought at markets, some commanding as much as ten shillings.[29] As one cat lover stated, 'there are cats and cats.'[30]

Working-class families in London and the provinces frequently shopped for pets from street sellers and markets in the middle decades of Victoria's reign. The lack of commercial overheads meant costs were low, even compared to small-scale shops. By the end of the nineteenth century bird stalls had 'pretty good stock'.[31] Prices were reasonable, although sellers could not guarantee that parrots, cockatoos and parakeets wouldn't swear like a sailor once ensconced in some respectable parlour. Birds were relatively cheap to keep and, by the latter half of the century, within the reach of most families with regular wages. Huge provincial towns like Manchester and Liverpool boasted dedicated bird markets catering for a variety of pockets and interests: pigeons for fanciers' coops, colourful imported birds from warmer climes and tiny British birds aimed at children eager to spend pocket money.[32]

Some markets were more informal. Bird fairs were popular in parts of the metropolis by the 1860s and '70s, often taking place on Sunday mornings.[33] Bird seller 'fancy carts' and stalls lined Bethnal Green's Sclater Street on Sundays, prompting one wag to rename it 'Birdcage Walk', since an avenue of birdcages blocked the view of shop windows where established bird dealers traded in slightly more expensive and, in some cases, exotic goods. The market was a continuation of the well-established bird and animal market at Club Row, which had long been noted as a curiosity by London sightseers. The market remained a hub for bird and animal sales well into the twentieth century. Kerb hawkers spilled into the roads, packaging their feathered wares in paper bags as if they were 'a penny bun'. Bird-fair activity peaked between noon and 1.30, when the hum of humans contracting business was complemented by the trilling of 'myriad canaries'. Nestled in between the bird and bi-cycle market was a small 'dog market' where dealers paraded baskets of puppies and all manner of pedigrees.[34] Rat sellers regularly attended dog markets too, although these were not the white rats beloved of children but brown specimens destined for 'sport' with dogs (according to one bemused reporter, a lively canine could kill an estimated one hundred rats in an hour).[35]

The Artful Dodgers of animal trade

Buying from street traders was ostensibly cheap and accessible. But it was risky too. Street selling had all kinds of negative connotations for Victorian consumers. In the moral imagination, the crowded street was a place of pickpockets, sex workers and shoddy goods. The very idea of street dealers evoked a squalid character to most genteel Victorians keen to distinguish between respectable merchants with quality stock and sleazy traders selling adulterated goods of dubious provenance. Associated with the poorest class of traders – costermongers, hawkers and tinkers – street trading was pitched at those whose income levels limited how picky they could be about produce. It shouldn't surprise us, then, that those who could afford to shop elsewhere viewed street dealers in birds and animals with suspicion. Some of the caution was well founded.

Street purchases of birds were notoriously fraught with risk. By the 1870s ownership of a caged bird lay within the reach of most families with relatively stable income. But however pretty the bird or tempting its song, street-bought birds were a poor investment. First, their survival rates were appalling. *Cassell's Household Guide* noted that hardy birds, likely to survive confinement, were never cheap.[36] Most bird catchers sold the best of their stock to bird shops and then took to the streets with the leftovers, partly explaining why street birds had higher mortality rates than shop-bought stock. Surveying the bird market in the late 1850s and early '60s, Mayhew noted that the linnet was cheap in retail value (just three to four pence) but captivity often proved fatal and few even made it to the homes they were intended to beautify. At the other end of the market, the bullfinch cost up to three shillings. Given their tendency to live only a few weeks in captivity, the expenditure was a luxury to be enjoyed so long as it lasted. Among non-songbirds, the sparrow was by far the most popular and affordable type, costing as little as half a penny, but the fragile lives of these feathered wallflowers rapidly ended when purchased as 'playthings' for children.

Second, street sellers might have regular pitches but given the 'vagrant' character of the trade, there was no guarantee that sellers were traceable. The street was the natural roosting place of the trickster. Bird dealers were notorious for conning consumers with what Beeton's *Book of Home Pets* (1861) called 'fraudulent machinations'. Some sellers passed off pale-feathered greenfinches (retail: threepence) daubed with paint as 'some curious foreign bird' (retail: three shillings). Bird dealers 'play[ed] off innumerable tricks' on 'inexperienced' youths, who were advised to take someone who knew what they were doing when going to purchase a bird.[37] Like other 'how to' guides, Beeton's gave a full description of popular birds so that consumers might dodge 'some curious bird' by knowing exactly what they were buying.[38]

The most extravagant 'duffing' concerned blackbirds sold as parrots, their beaks and legs painted and varnished as well as their feathers. Sellers dressed as sailors lent an air of authenticity to the swindle, claiming they must sell the bird before their ship sailed again. Sales techniques – 'Oh you mustn't touch; it's timid with strangers!'– completed the fraud. How common this was is debatable. According to Mayhew, this kind of shamming had 'seen its best days' by the 1850s.[39] Even so, urban myths on 'duffing' operated as a kind of advice telegraph that pursed-lipped authors reproduced in prescriptive guidebooks. In London's Bethnal Green, the Sunday Club Row market had a reputation for attracting less desirable elements of the working classes.[40] Even the small bird shops on Sclater Street were criticized for being 'rough'. A visitor in the 1880s suspected that recent legislation to protect wild birds from being sold had little impact on the bird dealers – street- and shop-based – in Bethnal Green. Echoing the complaints of James Greenwood ten years earlier, J. Ewing Ritchie's *Days and Nights in London* lamented that animal dealers were 'unwashed', their shops were 'dirty', the air was 'bad' and an 'uncongenial fog' of immorality hung about them.[41]

Suspicion regarding the dubious morals of working-class traders wasn't restricted to bird sellers. An *Illustrated London News* sketch of 1885 showed a mild-mannered grandpapa with little 'Tommy' being sold a 'wery genteel' pet monkey. Of course, the monkey exposed his 'true' character once ensconced in the refined home of his new guardians: chaos ensued.[42] Likewise, advice writers warned shoppers that placid, 'wonderfully tame' animals nestled in a street dealer's elbow had probably been sedated. They would likely die or regain their natural ferocity once established in the home.[43] Shamming was less common in the purchase of goldfish but, then, their mortality rates were unpredictable at the best of times. Home-advice manuals encouraged children to see the purchase of fish as a 'last resort' over 'collecting for yourself'.[44]

By far the biggest risk, in that they represented the most substantial outlay, was the street purchase of dogs. Dog sellers were a different class of dealer altogether. Associated with 'low life sports' (such as dogfighting and rat catching), dog stealing and trade conducted in public houses, dog selling had a squalid reputation. Advice writers were unequivocal: the dog dealer was to be avoided at all costs. Popular illustrations of the dog dealer depicted a seedy, out-at-elbows kind of fellow with all sorts of dogs stuffed about his person. Commentators' suspicions that some dealers' prices were too good to be true frequently proved accurate. Trial reports from the Old Bailey and in newspapers indicate that victims of dog theft often made markets, such as Leadenhall and Club Row, their first port of call in the search for lost companions.

An epidemic of 'dognapping' – the theft and holding to ransom of a much-loved canine companion – in the early century had become such a problem that new legislation in 1845 reclassified dogs as property. Until then, thieves were more likely to be prosecuted for the theft of a dog collar than for the dog wearing it. Increased recognition of the sentimental value of dogs as companions inflated their economic value, both in terms of original purchase price but, more particularly, in ransom value. Dog

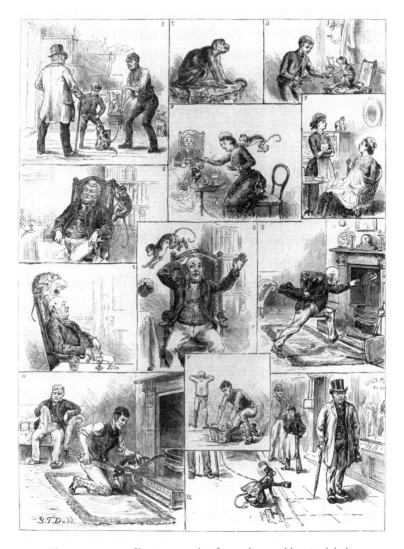

The consequences of buying a monkey from a disreputable animal dealer:
"'That Monkey!'", *Illustrated London News*, 4 July 1885.

thefts affected everyone whose affection for their dog was matched by the depth of their pockets. Or so dognappers gambled.

It was big business. At its height in the 1840s, organized gangs could make almost £1,000 over two years.[45] Much depended on the resale value of the dog, the tractability of the owner and the willingness of nappers to be flexible. Ransom demands for 25 guineas could – with bartering – be settled for eighteen. According to figures from the government inquiry into dognapping in 1844, the average ransom was around £12 per dog, but individual sums varied greatly. Sir Robert Peel secured the return of his dog for just £2, the Bishop of Ely almost £5 and a whip-maker named Mr Thorne £15, while the Duke of Cambridge laid out £30 on the restoration of his. The danger for owners was that if they had paid a ransom once, nappers were more certain of their attachment to the dog. One woman had spent a staggering £50 on ransom for her dog at various times.[46]

The poet Elizabeth Barrett was greatly attached to her spaniel Flush (her 1843 poem 'To Flush, My Dog' details just how much she adored him). During the 1840s Elizabeth and Flush were victims of dognapping three times and on the third occasion, when her brother baulked at paying ransom yet again for the little dog, the supposedly invalid Elizabeth rose from her sofa and ventured forth into the dognappers' den to retrieve her beloved Flush. As it turned out, this act of defiance was a prelude to Elizabeth arranging a romantic 'napping' of her own as she fled to Florence, Italy, with lover Robert Browning. Naturally, Flush was in on the plan and accompanied his mistress into married life on the continent, far removed from the overbearing Barrett paterfamilias and metropolitan dog thieves.[47] Jane Welsh Carlyle, inveterate correspondent and thinker (and married to the historian, essayist and biographer Thomas Carlyle), got a little dog named Nero in December 1849. Just two months later he went missing. As she noted in a letter recalling the incident, 'dog-stealing' was a 'regular trade' in Chelsea. When her husband inquired what she would be willing to give to secure Nero's return, Jane said she 'answered passionately with a flood of tears "my whole half-year's allowance!"'. Happily, Nero escaped (if, indeed, he had been stolen) and returned home the next day but, as Jane ruefully observed, this willingness to hand over all one's available income was a 'fine way' to be in.[48]

There were different roles in the dognapping game. First, 'street roughs' espied wealthy homes with canine inhabitants, learned the walking routines of the dog and executed the dognap. Then, there were negotiators, known as 'restorers', who would liaise with owners over the price for the return of their pet. Dog 'finders' claimed to have bought a dog in good faith but agreed to return it to its original owner for mon-etary compensation. Some owners refused to play ball, especially if they had been targeted numerous times, and pooches left to their fate would be sold on. It was these dogs that commentators feared made their way into street sales.

Yet dogs were expensive, and if a pretty spaniel could be got at a good price on the street, was it all so bad? Despite the risks attached, even reasonably affluent families traded with dog dealers. And for all the negative commentary on doggy lowlife (human), not all street sellers were reprobates. As Henry Mayhew acknowledged, there were 'honest' street sellers too. Their principal markets were well-heeled children whose longing for a pretty dog meant they could only be hauled away from the seller with their mother or nurse having given the seller an address, promising that the 'dog man' could call on them at home that evening. If dealers had the shifty and mean demeanour of the Ratcliffe Highway criminal, the honest seller was respectable in manner, smart in appearance and modulated his speech without being comical. He had the confidence to follow through and deal with a father on the family doorstep.

Even so, dog thefts remained a problem. As late as the 1890s, *Cassell's Book of the Household* warned dog owners to beware of letting their canine companion 'romp' in the streets 'lest he be stolen'.[49] The advice was well founded. James Goode, a 'well known dog dealer', maintained the appearance of a legitimate business in Red Lion Yard in London's Clerkenwell. But when the police visited his premises in spring 1885, almost all the forty to fifty dogs on the premises turned out to have been stolen.[50] In 1890 William Clements, aged 65 and a known dog dealer, and Minnie Handley, aged 34, appeared at the Old Bailey charged with having 27 stolen dogs in their possession. Giving evidence, one of their victims, Isaac Leadam, a barrister, stated that this was the second dog in as many years stolen from him. Another witness for the prosecution stated that he 'always looked to Clements' if a dog had been stolen.[51] While many dealers offered perfectly legitimate canines for sale, then, some operated within more flexible moral boundaries to peddle dogs that had been 'got' by more mysterious means. The novelist Joseph Stamper, writing of his Edwardian Lancashire boyhood, recalled 'Uncle Sil', the very likeness of ruddy-cheeked John Bull with no children but a house and garden 'saturated with dogs, all kinds, all sizes'. Uncle Sil acquired all sorts of animals from dubious sources to sell on but, aside from a few small fines, always managed to evade the law. Stamper didn't really see the harm: Uncle Sil undoubtedly 'took his cut' from selling ill-gotten goods but, then, so did the 'original Robin Hood'.[52]

Breeding trust

How, then, were consumers to judge between the honest and unscrupulous dealer? As advice authors were keen to highlight, dog purchases should have been the safest exchange. Canines benefited from expert breeders who staked their public reputation on the quality of their dogs and for whom selling was secondary to the interest in cultivating dogs for show. Selective breeding had long been practised with regard to sporting dogs to encourage excellence in the field but, from the 1850s, was increasingly applied to domestic dogs. The quality of a dog rested on the reliability of the breeder. Measures of trustworthiness took into consideration the dog's parentage, the hygiene of breeding kennels and the breeder's reputation. For the first half of the nineteenth century, there were two distinct cultures of dog fancy: the patrician and the plebeian. Dogs purchased from the kennels of country estates were de facto good dogs, their pedigree guaranteed by human gentility and the pastoral idyll. The other 'fancy' was rooted firmly in working-class ideas of canine 'beauty' and ratting contests held in pubs for sporting entertainment. This dog fraternity carried the taint of lowlife activities, epitomized by disreputable fictional 'doggy' men like Dickens's Bill Sikes.

From the 1860s the social profile of dog breeders expanded as the merchant and professional classes sought to reform the working-class fancy, gain kudos with the landed elite and, in some cases at least, transform the sport-based dog show into something more entrepreneurial. For the genteel breeder, sniffy about enterprise at the best of times, there was little to distinguish the wealthy merchant who bred pedigree dogs (and sold them) from the seedy dog dealer of London's East End. Defendants claimed that so little money was made from dog breeding that it sprang 'as much from a natural love for animals' as from any material gain.[53] Incredulous speculations in 1870 as to what anyone would think of an archbishop who set up as a dog dealer (would his poor curate set up as a rat catcher?) had been replaced by the 1890s by a degree of acceptance that clergymen, lawyers and medical men all might breed and sell dogs without their morals going to the wall.[54] After all, dealers made a living from buying up (or stealing) dogs at low prices to sell on, hardly the same as engaging in the science of studs.[55] Despite these tensions, the increasing popularity of dog shows from the 1860s onwards democratized dog breeding. One of the purposes of the Kennel Club, founded in 1873, was to act as a kind of product guarantor: dogs secured from club members commanded a premium. By the end of the century, domestic-advice literature urged potential consumers to write to the secretary of a 'good' dog show to get a list of respectable breeders.[56]

Purchases could also be made through advertisements in the sporting or, increasingly by the late nineteenth century, 'doggy' press, such as the *Kennel Gazette* or *Our Dogs*. James Hutchings, an Exeter solicitor, ran a successful dog-breeding business as a sideline to his day job. Having begun breeding mastiffs in the 1870s, by the mid-1880s he employed a full-time kennel man to oversee his thirty-plus dogs and was judging classes at the annual Birmingham dog show, one of the biggest shows in the country. Hutchings sold dogs via the doggy press and his clients ranged across a broad social network, from clergymen to members of the executive committee of the Kennel Club, civic dignitaries to editors of periodicals, naval and military men to other solicitors.[57] For families who wanted the very best, breeders were the go-to sellers, even for dogs intended as pets rather than show specimens. Emily Rathbone, doyenne of the extraordinarily wealthy Liverpool Rathbones and certainly able to afford pedigree prices, drove a hard bargain to secure a 'beautiful' and 'clever' Pekinese at less than half the going rate because he was intended 'only' as a pet.[58]

If a dog was to be a companion for children and pedigree didn't matter so much as temperament, families could place a sixpenny advert in one of the sporting newspapers, or in one of the journals specializing in commercial exchange, such as *Exchange and Mart*. Trading animals through the 'exchange' press became increasingly popular from the middle decades of the century as buyers learned to be suspicious of street transactions. These sales were supposedly secure, with editors holding onto purchase money until both buyer and seller were satisfied.[59] In practice, the frequency with which mail-order frauds appeared before the Old Bailey in the latter decades of the nineteenth century indicate that the 'exchange' press offered little security if strict guidelines weren't followed.

Some crooks exploited sellers' gullibility by requesting goods 'on approval' with payment promised if satisfied (and the goods returned if not). Too often, sellers sent stock on approval to an address that had been rented for one or two days and never heard of the buyer again. When Sarah Morris, John Davis and John Onley were tried at the Old Bailey in November 1881 for stealing birds and dogs, the prosecution presented copies of *Exchange and Mart* found at their lodgings with their victims' adverts circled, damning evidence of their intention to defraud the people bringing the prosecution.[60] The frauds could work the other way too, with consumers sending advance payment for, say, a canary or puppy direct to the seller without ever receiving their goods, or receiving goods that were not as advertised: as in one Old Bailey trial, the customer paid over seven shillings for a canary only to receive 'common birds, just as Mr. Cross of Liverpool sells two for 2s'.[61]

Social and family networks could be as important as professional sellers. Many dogs were given as gifts or to cement friendships. Charles Dickens was the recipient of numerous canine presents over his career and had to periodically refuse offers of dogs from admirers. He often bred from those he kept, though, gifting the offspring in turn to his children and friends.[62] But for many would-be dog owners, buying from a breeder remained a hallmark of quality well into the twentieth century. In the summer of 1935 Leonard and Virginia Woolf acquired a new dog, Sally, a cocker spaniel.[63] This important purchase took place at Swakeleys Farm in Ickenham, the home of Mr Lloyd, a breeder and 'great expert' according to Virginia. The trade in dogs was clearly lucrative and Lloyd had made 'a very snug place for himself out his passion for cockers'. The dog was expensive: 'She cost £18 – dear me.' But such was the price of pedigree and they hoped to get some money back: 'Still as we say, it's nice to have a good dog. And we shall breed from her. She is very distinguished looking.' Sometimes, social networks and pedigree breeding happily collided. When Alan Withington, a well-off trainee businessman, married his wife, Morag, in 1933, they decided against getting a pet. But Morag was related to a family with a long pedigree in the dog fancy and a few weeks later, when her uncle came for dinner, he brought an unexpected present: 'lo! And behold! Soon after my return this evening on the 4 o'clock, in he came being dragged by a tiny Cairn bitch on the end of a lead.'[64] Initial misgivings were soon cast aside and the couple welcomed the little pup, and all the chaos she entailed, into their lives.

Buying from a breeder was also becoming more important in the cat world, as the first decades of the twentieth century saw a boom in the pedigree feline market. Ordinary cats seldom made it into *Exchange and Mart* but by 1910 breeders from London, Reading, Hull and Widnes were all advertising Persian cats. Siamese cats, an exotic rarity in the late nineteenth century, were increasingly bred for sale too. After the First World War, when many people abandoned breeding and shows were suspended, there was a further upsurge in breeding and selling Siamese.[65] From 1924 the Siamese Cat Club held an annual show that saw a steady increase in exhibitors.[66] Until the 1960s the show had 'selling classes' so that the public could take kittens home. In 1946 more than 8,000 pedigree Siamese were registered with the Governing Council of the Cat Fancy.[67] As Kit Wilson, vice-chairman of the Governing Council and Siamese Cat Club Committee member, put it in 1950, to own a Siamese when the club was founded was like possessing 'a Corot or a Ming Vase. Today, the Siamese is found in every home from castle to cottage.'[68]

This was an exaggeration, but by the early 1950s the Siamese craze had hit rural Somerset. After their unsuccessful search for a replacement squirrel, Doreen and Charles Tovey decided to get a cat (Blondin, the squirrel, had been an excellent mouser). The couple were mulling things over when 'one fateful Sunday morning' they met Mimi, a young Siamese queen recently acquired by a neighbouring family.[69] Doreen was enchanted, thinking her 'the loveliest animal I had ever seen'. A short time later the couple visited a local breeder with a litter of Siamese kittens, among which was Sugieh, a tiny blue point: 'She sat there on the hearthrug like a small girl with her suitcase packed to go on holiday – her eyes screwed up tight with anticipation, her paws pounding up and down like little pistons.'[70] And that was that. According to Doreen, Sugieh chose them, rather than the other way around.

Of course, not all pet people wanted pedigree. From the end of the nineteenth century some animal shelters attempted to rehome stray cats and dogs (which otherwise would be euthanized). Pedigree dogs, which had some financial value, were easier to rehome than mongrels or stray cats and, until the interwar period, less than 10 per cent of dogs in shelters were rehomed while figures for cats were negligible. But for labouring people, animal shelters could be a cheap way to acquire an attractive pet (especially after the introduction of the annual five-shilling dog licence in 1867).[71] After the First World War shelter staff worked increasingly hard to promote rehoming, whether the animals were pedigree or not. The Mayhew Home in London sought to rehome all its animals, claiming that no animal in decent health was ever destroyed. Figures for animal shelters on Merseyside between the 1920s and 1940s show a growing push towards the rehoming of cats and dogs, although variations in success rates indicate that much depended on the energy and determination of those (usually women) running the shelters. But these early indications of an 'adopt don't shop' movement were entirely in keeping with growing awareness of animal sentience and welfare, campaigns that increasingly impacted upon commercial pet acquisitions too.

Shopping for love, happiness and welfare

By the turn of the twentieth century some pet sellers began to take a new approach, establishing their trustworthiness by addressing critics' concerns head on. Victorian commentators had long castigated street and shop dealers for the poor conditions in which they kept birds and animals, evidenced through the high mortality rates of creatures that never made it out of dealers' premises. But cavalier approaches to animal welfare made little business sense either, as the value of animals was written off if they died. Increasingly, animal and bird sellers promoted their services by advertising their investment in animal welfare, not least through attention to hygiene.

Much like their early nineteenth-century forebears, large animal shops in Edwardian London and the provinces continued to advertise as tourist destinations, trading on their established names, celebrity clientele and well-known locations. By the end of the nineteenth century, large dealers in exotic animals, like Charles Jamrach's famous animal shop based close to the London Docks, or William Cross, whose animal emporium on Earle Street in Liverpool boasted the Prince of Wales, most of the crowned heads of Europe and countless aristocrats among its customers, exploited print media to establish their enterprises as the go-to places for animal purchases to suit all pockets, from tiny birds and hamsters for small children to more outlandish creatures destined for country-house menageries. The *Illustrated London News* and *The Graphic*, image-laden magazines with national circulation, featured Jamrach's shop as a tourist site for spectacle and display as well as a destination for animal purchases.[72] In Liverpool, William Cross's shop featured as a 'must see' in printed travel guides to the city.[73]

But while spectacle and exoticism were thrilling and large menageries carried a certain cachet as landmark stores, they weren't exempt from criticisms about hygiene and high death rates among animals. One of the most discussed aspects of any animal shop was the physical and material conditions in which animals were kept. In the 1890s Augustus Zache, a Prussian-born bird dealer, established a new, large-scale animal emporium in Great Portland Street, London. The shop sold foxes, rabbits, guinea pigs, mongooses and pugs. By 1902 it was such an established part of the London landscape that it featured in the popular series *Living London*, a journal that promoted key sites in the capital to readers across Britain.[74] So far, so predictable. But Zache made key innovations that

'At Jamrach's, The Dealer in Wild Animals, East London', *Illustrated London News*,
19 February 1887.

over the next fifty years became standard in pet shops across the country. Importantly, by 1903, he was claiming to have the 'cleanest hygienic shop in London'.[75] Zache had taken one of the key criticisms of the animal shop – that it was dirty – and turned it on its head.

Yet promoting hygiene and its bedfellow, welfare, as positive selling features was slow to catch on. In the 1920s advice manuals such as *Pets for Boys and Girls* still warned against bad bird shops or the 'ordinary general dealer' with 'little interest in his stock beyond its capability of making a profit'. A 'bad' shop meant birds 'huddled into totally inadequate cages, too often filthy for lack of proper attention'. Such dealers weren't the exception, but 'widely scattered throughout our large towns'. 'Good' dealers' premises were different: 'A clean, well-lighted and well-ventilated shop, fitted with comfortable, roomy cages' that were 'occupied by sprightly birds constantly hopping from perch to perch, with frequent visits to the seed hopper'.[76]

Department stores, which increasingly stocked pet animals from the late nineteenth century, were also influential here. By the interwar period, the Army & Navy Stores, Harrods, Selfridges, Gamages, Derry & Toms and Peter Jones all had animal sections. Some stores' catalogues, such as Whiteley's of Regent Street, had featured 'Zoological Departments' from the late nineteenth century but by the 1920s, department stores placed strong emphasis on the hygienic modernity of these premises.

Glossy marketing materials transformed pet selling from a suspect activity, with animals squashed into cages in darkened shops, to a modern vision of light and roomy shop floors, with pets housed in spacious (relatively speaking), healthful and hygienic conditions. The animal showrooms in these elite stores became the preferred destinations for well-heeled pet shoppers over the course of the twentieth century – notable patrons of Harrods' 'Pet Kingdom' included Ronald Reagan (who bought an elephant) and Noël Coward (who was gifted an alligator).[77] But their influence went far beyond the elite world of exotic pets.

Smaller traders soon appropriated the display strategies of department stores. The 'Zoological Grottos' aesthetic of the 1890s was, by the mid-twentieth century, replaced with streamlined window dressing and display styles. When Pathé Pictorial launched the short-film series *Dave and Dusty* (1946), following the adventures of a ragamuffin boy and his dog, the opening film focused on the pet shop where the two friends meet. Strolling down the street, Dave sees a small Sealyham puppy in the window of a pet shop where puppies, kittens and birds are arranged in clean straw for the perusal of passers-by. He enters the shop, where more cages of puppies and birds are neatly arranged for inspection. The floor is clean and female shop assistants wear crisp cotton frocks and aprons. As if to confirm that this is a 'nice' pet shop, Dave's purchase is subsidized by a smartly dressed woman in the process of scrutinizing a pup for herself.[78]

Thoughtful display was increasingly linked to welfare standards. Leading conservationist Gerald Durrell is best known for his semi-fictional autobiography *My Family and Other Animals* (1963), detailing a boyhood spent on Corfu with an ever-expanding collection of animals. But on the eve of the Second World War the Durrells were based in London, where animal-mad Gerald, aged fifteen, found a job in a pet shop known as 'The Aquarium'. While not intentionally cruel, the shop owner lacked imagination and 'did not quite know what the form was'. Luckily, precocious Gerald was at hand to wheedle the shopkeeper into varying the diet of his stock, modifying their accommodation and letting his juvenile assistant redecorate the large fish tank in the shop window: 'I worked on the giant tank with all the dedication of a marine Capability Brown.'[79]

By the 1950s advice for pet shopkeepers stressed the need to pay attention to presentation (the emergence of a pet trade press also testified to the respectability of this retail sector). According to F. W. Jefkins, writing in the *Pet Trade Journal* in 1954, 'Pet traders need to win the trust of the public, and this they can do through the right sort of display which suggests that the stock is kept under tip-top conditions.' The shop should be well equipped, organized, 'neat, clean, bright and airy' to create the impression that the shop was 'reliable'. The shopkeeper could mitigate suspicion about their personal integrity through appropriate dress: 'The personal appearance of the shopkeeper is also part of the display and he should be dressed to give the right impression – a clean overall rather than a grubby suit.'[80]

If one innovation of the twentieth century was to promote hygiene and animal welfare as marketing tools, another was a small but significant shift in nomenclature. Again, Augustus Zache was ahead of the curve. Unlike other large-scale animal dealers, Zache exploited the word 'pet' to sell his wares. Although Victorian culture had increasingly celebrated pets, animal dealers were slow to capitalize on the term. But from at least 1903, Zache billed himself as a 'bird and small pet dealer', advertising the shop's 'many varieties of children's harmless pets',[81] a strategy that tapped into the emotional value particular prospective consumers invested in animals.

This strategy was the beginning of a larger trend. Although references to 'bird' or 'zoo' shops persisted into the 1940s, traders' willingness to engage with a language of 'pets' over 'livestock' or 'animals' served the dual purpose of exploiting the potential emotional value of animals to owners while indicating the seller's cognizance of animal sentience, a technique that discriminated between the caring pet seller and the dodgy dealer. The Post Office Directories for London, which businesses used to advertise their services to consumers across the capital, record just one pet shop in London in 1927, 'Camberwell Pet Stores' in the suburban southeast, but by 1959 there were 73 listed 'pet shops' or 'pet stores'. It was happening in the provinces too as enterprising shopkeepers branded their stores 'pet shops' and promoted the emotional rewards of pet ownership. In April 1924 the *Derbyshire Advertiser and Journal* promoted a 'New Pet Shop' in Derby's Babington Lane, promising pets as 'ideal gifts' and recommending that buyers 'give your friend or child a sensible gift this Easter . . . Nice puppy. Parrot and cage. Tame mice. Garden aviary'.[82] Promoting animals as 'pets' to specific markets, notably children, was becoming an established strategy for shop and business owners.

Yet for all shopkeepers' improvements in hygiene and welfare, the dog market remained hard to crack. Dogs, the pet that people invested in most (both financially and emotionally), epitomized the awkwardness of marketing animals as sentient stock. Advice manuals such as *Pets for Boys and Girls* (1923) continued to disdain shop-based dog dealers as dirty and disease-ridden and still urged would-be dog owners (children and their parents) to approach well-known breeders instead.[83] Distaste for shop-bought dogs encompassed practical worries about provenance, care and disease but extended to ideas about cross-species relationships too. Human–dog relations enjoyed a long-established status as special; it was an individualized relationship that could not, and should not, be reduced to a financial transaction. Increasingly, the emotive human–pet dynamic inflected advice on acquiring dogs. As *Ideal Home*, offering readers advice on dog purchases, noted in 1925: 'A dog is a person, not a piece of merchandise to be bought over a shop counter. Go to a breeder, if possible; choose your dog from the home in which he was reared, observing closely the conditions he had known 'til now.'[84] Here, dogs were viewed as prospective friends and family members. As such, it was important that they came from a good home. This harked back to Victorian fears concerning social environment, parentage and disease

Herbert Ashwin Budd, *The Bird Shop*, c. 1920, oil on canvas.

but the distaste for grubby commerce had morphed into something more emotive. The impersonal nature of over-the-counter purchases reduced the acquisition of a dog to a monetary exchange and limited owners' ability to gauge canine character, essential if they were to truly understand – and connect with – their pet.

Some owners were reluctant to present the moment when their pet had come into their lives as a financial transaction, which may explain why so few wrote about it in letters, memoirs or diaries. The writer and editor J. R. Ackerley, who immortalized his dog Queenie in the memoir *My Dog Tulip* (1956), presented pet acquisition as a rescue mission rather than a purchase. Ackerley obtained Queenie when she was eighteen months old from 'some working-class people who, though fond of her in their way, seldom took her out'. Queenie had been left alone in a yard during the daytime and was sometimes disciplined violently: 'It was from this life, when she was eighteen months old, that I rescued her, and to it that I attributed disturbances of her psyche.'[85] Since she was a valuable pedigree dog, it is likely that Ackerley paid Queenie's first family in order to acquire her but he makes no mention of this, preferring to present her arrival in terms of liberating her and the intense relationship they forged afterwards.

Pet shops had to work harder, then, to develop strategies that overcame these anxieties, especially regarding the sale of dogs. From 1900 James Willson traded from 37 New Oxford Street in London. He specialized in foreign birds but stocked dogs, poultry and Persian cats too. He put most of his marketing resource into advertising dogs. A 1916 advert offset consumer fears about 'shop' dogs' poor health: adult dogs were sold on fourteen days' trial and could be exchanged, while 'all our dogs are inspected daily by a Qualified Veterinary Surgeon.'[86] This extended beyond addressing welfare concerns. Willson tried to counter the perception that dog purchase was impersonal. A more explicit ad in *Ideal Home* in 1922 promised that owners could 'personally select their dog' and it could be swapped for another if it proved unsuitable.[87] Willson even promised to exchange the animal until the customer was 'satisfied'. This swap-it-if-you-don't-like-it strategy might seem counter-intuitive when promoting the specialness of human–dog relationships but Willson recognized that people wanted their dog to *fit* with the family. Much like dating, canine looks might be deceiving and it could take time to establish the possibility of a more meaningful bond. If the relationship wasn't going to be successful, better to end it and try again.

Other traders peddled a more romantic, if clichéd, idea of emotional connection: eyes locked through a shop window could signal the start of something beautiful. In his memoir of Yorkshire veterinary practice in the late 1930s, James Herriot tells the story of local misfit Roland Partridge, a reluctant farmer turned artist who lived alone and found great solace in his relationship with Percy, his small, shaggy white mongrel: 'Mr Partridge, looking through a window of a pet shop in Brawton about five years ago had succumbed immediately to the charms of the two soulful eyes gazing up at him from a six-week-old tangle of white hair and had put down his five bob and rushed the little creature home.' While the pet shop had identified Percy 'somewhat vaguely' as a terrier, his questionable parentage gave much amusement to local farmers who referred to him as a 'tripe 'ound' or 'mouse 'ound'. Herriot thought Percy rather attractive, 'having never had much time for the points and fads of dog breeding'.[88] But Roland's impulsive love-at-first-sight purchase of Percy underlined his separation from the rest of the small market-town community that believed he'd been had and that he should have gone to a breeder.

After all, falling in love through a shop window was exactly what children did, which was why shop owners put their most winsome specimens in full view. The first instalment of the 1940s *Dusty and Dave* films traded on this. When Dave sees Dusty through the pet shop window, he recognizes a kindred spirit that will partner him in mischief and wonder. As the narrator reflects, don't we all remember seeing our animal soulmate dolefully staring back at us through a pet shop window? *Mr Finch's Pet Shop* (1953), a children's picture book, epitomized the perfect marriage of welfare, love and happiness. Lost or stray animals arrived independently at Mr Finch's and grew contentedly fat under the avuncular shopkeeper's care. Mr Finch developed such strong attachments to each animal that he never wanted to part with them. Shopkeeper and children united, then, in understanding the unique privilege – beyond any commercial transaction – of pet happiness, welfare and affection.[89]

Pampered pooches and the pet economy

If pet shops increasingly peddled animals as emotional companions, they had long exploited people's affection for animals by encouraging them to spend money on pet products. Accoutrements and equipment for pet needs were big business from the beginning of our period: London trade directories show large numbers of birdcage makers operating in the East End from the 1840s. In the 1850s Mayhew interviewed street sellers hawking dog collars and leashes fashioned from a variety of materials while offering bespoke services such as engraving.[90] Surviving dog collars from the mid-nineteenth century indicate the ability to personalize products, partly as insurance against loss or theft. Emily and Anne Brontë's dogs, a bull mastiff named Keeper and a smaller spaniel named Flossy, both wore adjustable brass collars with decorative padlocks engraved with the family name and address.[91] From the 1860s there was a rapid increase in manufacturing aquaria and associated paraphernalia for fishkeeping.

Over time, though, the range of services on offer for pets, especially dogs, expanded, not least because of the commercialization of dog shows from the 1860s and all the attendant paraphernalia that went alongside caring for, grooming and displaying 'fancy' dogs (even those that would only ever compete for attention in the family parlour). By the start of the twentieth century the dog press carried advertisements from specialist providers of collars, leashes, kennels, beds and grooming services. Some metropolitan businesses were sufficiently successful to enable proprietors to register in trade directories exclusively as 'dog collar' manufacturers.

By the twentieth century providing services for precious dogs was a commercial enterprise with markets beyond the dog fancy. In the 1940s and '50s new categories of pet services appeared in London trade directories: 'Dog Requisites', 'Dog Stripping and Trimming' (what we would call 'grooming') and 'Dog Hairdressers'. In 1959 there were six London shops that dealt exclusively in dog paraphernalia; they were concentrated in the West End, including the Kensington Dog Shop, Deva Dog Ware and Brookwick and Bliss & Co. Outlets for dog stripping and trimming – which jumped from three in 1949 to thirteen in 1959 – were also high end, including Poodle Parlour on King Street (w6), Town and Country on Sloane Street and Pets Parlour on Chiltern Street (w1), although Heidi's Dog Bath and Parlour – listed at 221 Holloway Road – was a bit more downmarket. By 1959 there were also three dog hairdressers operating in the capital, including Shampoodle in St John's Wood and Dog Baths and Requisites on Beauchamp Road (sw3).

While many of these outlets were clearly aimed at well-to-do clientele and the 'fancy' market (many of them also had stalls at Crufts), the pet economy expanded at a popular level too. From 1927 new licensing laws created a record of traders operating at the Sunday morning market on and around Sclater Street.[92] As well as animal sellers, there was a significant trade in pet-related goods including birdcages and appliances, bird seed and 'condition food', dog medicine and powders of various kinds, dog collars and leads, 'discs and name plates for dogs' and dog brushes. In 1928, 120 licences were granted to sellers of animals or animal-related goods in the area, indicating just how substantial the pet economy was.[93] By the 1960s Boots chain stores were marketing a 'Meet the Scamp' range – including conditioners, wormers, shampoo and ear canker powder – competitively priced for a mass market.[94]

While cats had a smaller share of the service market, there was a significant shift in the marketing of food for both cats and dogs. Increasingly, manufacturers promoted the notion that products or special foods for loved animals didn't just secure health and sustenance but a new kind of human–animal relationship too. Early advertisements used

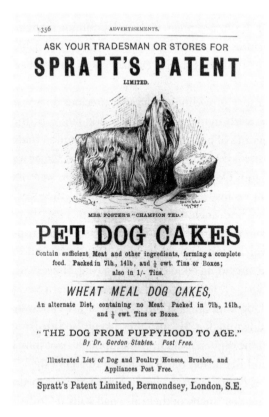

Advertisement for Spratt's Patent Pet Dog Cakes, in Gordon Stables, *Our Friend the Dog* (1884).

winsome images of pets to sell their wares, but in the twentieth century pet food advertisers took a new approach. From 1919 the dog-biscuit manufacturer Spillers launched a new advertising campaign in the *Daily Mail*. Buying Spillers was no longer just about improving canine health – it was an expression of love: 'Pet him by all means but make your fondness *practical* by giving him Spillers Victoria.'[95] Soon, pets purportedly began to speak for themselves in advertising bylines and images. In a 1930s Spillers campaign for 'Shapes' biscuits, a begging Westie demands, 'Pen and Ink Please! I'd fill in the coupon myself if I could! GET ME A BAG TODAY!'[96] The tinned dog food Pal, marketed from the 1950s, evoked companionship simply through its brand name. Dog-food manufacturers were no longer advertising on the basis of physical health benefits alone but on a pet's quality of life: owners were told that they could buy emotional wellbeing for their pets. In the 1960s the evocatively named Ful-O-Pep promised not just 'perfect health' but to 'help your dog really LIVE'.[97]

The cat food market took a similar tack. In 1939 Spratt's, a reputable dog-food brand, advertised their cat food with a winsome photograph of a tabby kitten, pointing out that 'Spratt's make food for me too.'[98] Tinned food for cats appeared from the early 1950s. In a 1950 Kit-E-Kat ad, readers were confronted by a cartoon black cat speaking highly of the new food: 'We black cats are lucky – if we are fed on KIT-E-KAT . . . Look at my lovely shiny coat. They say my eyes are bright and clear, and I'm certainly as lively as they make 'em. It's all due to Kit-E-Kat.' Health was still paramount but advertisers tapped into the idea that pets had personalities and preferences independent of their humans: 'I hear the family say that Kit-E-Kat is good for me, but believe me, it's the smell and taste *I* love.'[99] For a mere 10½ pence an owner could buy their cat's love on a plate. By the early 1970s market researchers segmented the cat-food market according to 'owners' personal involvement with the cat'. 'Cosseters', those who treated their cat 'almost as a child substitute', were most likely to feed their pet a high-quality, varied diet and have lots of questions about processed foods, while 'accepters' (who viewed the cat as a family pet but within a human–animal hierarchy) and 'resenters' (who kept the cat for children) were more convenience-oriented.[100]

Trust triumphant?

Despite the efforts of pet-shop traders, suspicions about their practices never entirely went away and calls for the regulation of shops and market stalls persisted well into the mid-twentieth century. Between the 1920s and the 1930s the National Canine Defence League campaigned against the 'cruelty' and 'roguery' of 'Crooked Dog Dealers'. Posing as a potential customer, one League member uncovered a 'guilty' minority of London traders, from the small shops of the East End to the fancy stores of the West, that cared little for the wellbeing of their merchandise: dogs were afflicted by sickness or skin complaints and kept in uncomfortable conditions, some had their tails docked and an Alsatian at one shop had pieces of leather glued to the inside of his ears to make them stand erect. The genealogy of some 'pedigree' dogs 'did not bear investigation'. The public were apathetic 'mugs' while pet-shop owners 'waxed fat and rich'. In the face of animal-welfare legislation that churned too slow, the foolish public had to wise up and request health certificates, ask for dogs to be examined by veterinary surgeons before paying the full amount or take experts with them – advice that would have been familiar to Mrs Beeton's readers or Leadenhall Market sceptics almost eighty years before.[101] A chapter on birds and animals in *Introduction to Police Duty*, a guide for police constables produced in the 1940s, highlighted ongoing problems with dog theft and resale.[102]

But while dogs remained a particular concern because of the expenditure and expectations invested in them, agitation for pet welfare increasingly ran across species. After a long-running RSPCA campaign for an 'Animals Charter', the Pet Animals Act of 1951 brought the inspection of pet shops onto the statute books. Proprietors of shops, stalls and barrows were obliged to obtain a licence, animal accommodation and food was to be regulated, and pets could no longer be sold to children under twelve. The act responded to a growing sense of public disgust at the conditions in which some pets were sold but it was also fundamentally shaped by social class. MPs permitted a number of exemptions from the Act: animals sold by 'pedigree breeders', traders who sold animals from home and sellers recognized by 'registered clubs and societies'. In effect, therefore, the Act presumed that the only animals susceptible to mistreatment were those handled by 'trade'. As R. S. Russell, Conservative MP for Wembley South, put it, it was poorly kept shops that were the problem. Some were obvious: 'one shop looked as if it had not had the floor washed for a year, its only blind was a dirty piece of sacking over the door with nothing over the window.' More insidious were the wily owners who presented a good shopfront but let welfare slip in the hidden places. As Labour MP for Accrington H. Hynd declared, legislation needed to 'deal with the cases that could not be seen in public, the cellars, the back shop and under the counter'.[103] The shopfronts of groups exempted from protective legislation, their upper-middle-class credentials, were above scrutiny.

Evidently, trust had to be hard won and problems with fraud, theft and poor hygiene continued throughout the whole period despite the best efforts of legislators, police courts and cautious consumers. While the majority of shopkeepers traded within the law, there were some who would always cut corners to save money or who saw animals purely in terms of commodities rather than sentient beings, whatever their advertisements might say. Likewise, the high retail value of pedigree dogs and cats means that theft and trading in stolen cats and dogs remains a problem well into the twenty-first century. The COVID-19 pandemic that emerged in 2020 saw an exponential rise in pet ownership in response to families spending more time at home. This was accompanied by a spike in cases of pet theft. Again, dogs were the animal most at risk of being stolen.

While new legislation in mid-twentieth-century Britain promised to sweep away the illicit pet trade by licensing shops and market stalls, the RSPCA and the police continued to work side by side to enforce the law. But by the late twentieth century illicit bird trade on Sclater Street, the locus of Victorian bird fairs and shops, had moved from the streets into the pubs. When police raided the Knave of Clubs on Club Row in 1977, they and the RSPB found the two bars 'crowded with caged wild British birds'.[104] By now this kind of trade was subject to widespread public disapproval, but some people must have been prepared to buy these birds for it to take place. At the other end of the scale, the trade in exotic pets was curtailed by the Endangered Species Act of 1976, which prohibited the importation and sale of animals specified as endangered species, including tigers, crocodiles and boas. Elite emporiums such as Harrods' Pet Kingdom now had to stock more mundane creatures. But even the sale of ordinary pets remained contentious. In 2018 new legislation came into effect that banned pet shops or licensed dealers from selling puppies or kittens under six months old, partly to try and combat the huge growth in farms where pedigree dogs and cats, kept in cruel conditions, are used as breeding machines until their reproductive usefulness is spent. Related to this, animal charities began to lobby for legislation to check the growth in third-party and unregulated pet sales online. In 2018 the animal charity Blue Cross estimated that a minimum of 40,000 puppy sales a year were through unregulated third-party sales.[105] Not unlike shoppers strolling through Victorian London's Leadenhall Market, consumers at the start of the twenty-first century are warned to check the provenance and welfare of animals they buy, to be mindful of where they buy them and to remember that making pets into commodities comes with responsibilities. Shopping for pets, it seems, remains an activity fraught with potential fraud, deception and animal cruelty.

THREE

Rules Made and Broken: Pets at Home

The late Victorian and Edwardian author and dramatist George R. Sims was well known for his love of animals, particularly dogs. Journalists who interviewed Sims in his grand home overlooking the duck pond in Regents Park marvelled at the sheer amount of stuff he collected: dolls of the world vied for space with Turkish pipes, rugs, wall hangings and slippers; Charles Dickens collectibles nestled among souvenirs of horrible crimes; tin soldiers waged war on oriental tea sets; cats sculpted from lava played hide-and-seek with casts of Napoleon among the cabinet sprawl of glass and porcelain; Louis Wain sketches and animal-themed memorabilia provided the backdrop to games of battledore and shuttlecock. Amid all this, Sims's pets 'bounced' and 'scrambled'. If human visitors were nervous of crashing into something valuable, the household's 'lively' animal residents (at one point, Sims lived with fourteen dogs, numerous cats and birds) had no such qualms. They 'made friends' with interviewers' feet, friendship being conditional on approval, sat on fine chairs in the drawing room, lay across Sims's desk and followed him about the house 'like a shadow'. Sims even commissioned an illustration of his animal companions fortified with napkins and cutlery, seated at his elegant dining table enjoying a hearty Christmas dinner.[1] The household was entirely in keeping with Sims's public persona: subversive, chaotic, gregarious and sentimental. Most journalists commented that Sims, twice widowed and childless, was childlike. The insinuation was clear: Sims's anarchic household arrangements were not those of a responsible paterfamilias and, certainly, no wife would have tolerated such disorder.[2] They had a point.

'Christmas Day with his favourite companions', illustration in Arthur H. Lawrence, 'Christmas –Then, and Now! Mr George R. Sims at Home', published in *The Idler*, XII/5 (December 1897).

The growing enthusiasm for pets sat side by side with an increased commitment to home life in the Victorian period. How and why people kept certain animals was closely connected to how they saw their homes and the values they hoped to inculcate, but, as we show in this chapter, the relationship between pets and homelife was far from straightforward. The Victorian commitment to creating ideal homes left many households juggling astonishing amounts of clutter with highly regulated rules and boundaries to maintain order and propriety. In the nineteenth century those with money to spend increasingly lavished it on the home, introducing new household technologies, regularly redecorating, buying yet more furniture and a plethora of ornaments. Material display was accompanied by a new moral emphasis on the home. It was seen as the engine of Victorian social values, where husbands provided and wives nurtured and trained the next generation in virtuous Christian behaviour. Introducing animals into this moral and material mix was a challenge.

Animal companionship brought different expectations and challenges in homes across the social scale. Sims was an eccentric exception to most affluent Victorians, who treated their household gods with reverence and care. Wealthy Victorians, despite inhabiting impressive villas or large terraced houses, were restricted in their use of space by the sheer volume of furniture and decorative goods it had become customary to display. These houses were filled with humans too: in the mid-Victorian period it was normal to have lots of children, extended family and servants living together. Lower down the social scale, gradual improvements in housing stock and sanitary infrastructure made keeping birds and cats viable for many working-class families. Dogs were more challenging to accommodate in small homes alongside children, china and the stuff of everyday life. Regardless of size and space, humans hoped to be able to bring companion animals into their homes and retain both unbroken china and reasonably orderly domestic lives. But animals, unaware of the nuances of social hierarchy or morality, tended to disrupt households and constantly test the boundaries of human expectation.

Pet keepers had to negotiate the physical and material structures of the home, which often limited or restricted numbers and types of pets. The home environment changed over time – and pet keeping evolved alongside new kinds of living spaces. In the twentieth century it became more acceptable to keep dogs and cats indoors. But it didn't necessarily become any easier. Housing stock changed to meet the perceived needs of modern life, but pets weren't factored into new designs for the home. If the large gardens of interwar suburban estates met with pets' approval, the trend towards small kitchens created a constant indoor battle for houseproud humans against mud, the pungent aroma of wet animals and moulting hair. Worse, if purpose-built 'new model' tenements were a novelty in the late nineteenth century, the low- and high-rise flat became an increasing emblem of urban modernity as the twentieth century ticked onward. Flats, pet people generally agreed, were not conducive to keeping animals and exacerbated the challenges of maintaining domestic order. And yet, for all the potential disruption of animals indoors, increasing numbers of people throughout the nineteenth and twentieth centuries invited animals to share their homes.

Outside and inside the Victorian home

For the Victorians, the most straightforward way of accommodating animals while maintaining human domestic boundaries was to keep them outdoors or in outhouses. Some animals, especially those tamed from the wild such as squirrels or mice, probably preferred outdoor cages over the stifling heat and stuffiness of the domestic hearth. There was also a trend for aviaries in both large and small gardens.[3] The game-keeper at Kinnaird House on the Duke of Atholl's estate in late Victorian Scotland kept a pet fox chained to an outdoor kennel, where it fed upon porridge and terrorized passing hens for six years.[4] Rabbits and guinea pigs adopted by affluent families could be homed in nurseries or chil-dren's bedrooms, although household guides like Beeton's *Book of Home Pets* (1861) considered outdoors the most hygienic place to keep small animals. The rabbits and guinea pigs kept by working-class children were often housed in hutches or cages in paved backyards. Beatrix Potter didn't consider cats suitable for domestic environments at all, but most cats occupied a liminal position in households, moving between domes-tic interiors – especially kitchens and spaces with high incidences of mouse or rat intrusion – and the outdoors.[5] Nevertheless, some com-mentators thought the 'large, sleek fireside cat' imparted an 'air of homeliness', while nothing adorned a drawing room quite like a 'fluffy' Persian, not least because, if dogs were the companions of man, cats were the 'chosen allies' of woman (though evidently not Beatrix Potter!).[6]

Most dogs were homed in outdoor kennels, especially overnight, when their keen hearing and supposedly intrinsic desire to protect their human family could provide home security. Taking possession of his country home, Gad's Hill Place, in 1856, Charles Dickens immediately contracted the local carpenter to make a dog kennel.[7] Fifty years later, even George Sims still kennelled his dogs at night, despite his relaxed attitude towards animals in the home. Some dogs were intended as watchdogs, so it was appropriate that their place was outdoors. Small watchdogs – typically terriers – could guard the house from indoors, always 'giving notice' when anybody stepped over the boundary into the property.[8] While large and occasionally terrifying breeds (Sherlock Holmes met his fair share of fierce mastiffs) were bred for utility, in the idealized family setting the watchdog was both careful gatekeeper and friend. In *The Picture Book of Mabel May* (1873), a children's story about learning to accept responsibility, the family dog Brutus, named after the Roman senator for his legendary honesty and courage, is of 'such a size' that even when seated on his haunches he 'quite looked over' the infant Mabel's head. Capable of deadly ferocity (Brutus had once held a house-breaker by the throat), the dog was in the bosom of the family: his trustworthiness extended from protecting them from danger to acting

Advertisement for
Boulton & Paul,
in Gordon Stables,
Our Friend the Dog
(1884).

as pony for the toddling Mabel. Yet despite being 'dearly loved by the
entire family', his story took place wholly outdoors.[9]

By the late nineteenth century most household guides carried advice
on kennel design and location, taking for granted that dogs – and certainly larger dogs – would be housed outdoors. Caroline Pridham,
author of *Domestic Pets* (1893), suggested that all large dogs should be
kept outside and given their own kennels or sheds.[10] John Maxtee's
Popular Dog Keeping, a kind of bible for dog owners first published in
1898, laid some ground rules – kennels should have light, ventilation,
good drainage and no draught.[11] The best kind of kennel came with an
outdoor run attached, as this 'has the advantage that the dog need not
be chained – which breaks their coat and spirit'.[12] Manufacturers were
quick to capitalize on the increasing popularity of dog ownership and
marketed purpose-built kennels towards the end of the nineteenth
century, although many kennels remained homemade, as the fashion
or necessity for Victorian DIY prompted an outpouring of 'how to' guides
on building a castle for man's best friend. Lapdogs were an exception

to the outdoor rule, their assumed role as some daughter or widow's darling assuring them a plush bed to call their own or, better still, a place on the pillow beside their loving mistress.

The anxieties of middle-class Victorians over creating the right kind of domestic environment encouraged the construction of external accommodation for pets. Building garden lodgings for favourite animals extended the boundaries of home and family, and humans applied a language of domestic comfort to animal dwellings. Beeton's *Book of Home Pets* (1861), discussing rabbit hutches, stressed that the 'first care' in providing 'lodgings' for rabbits was to make them 'comfortable'.[13] The Rev. John Wood clearly had this concern in mind when he constructed an elaborate outdoor house for his cat Pret on the family's relocation from central London to Kent in the mid-nineteenth century. Wood devoted pages to describing 'Pret Villa', originally fashioned from a box but later made more substantial in brick with a slate roof. The recreation of the ideal bourgeois home for the cat extended even to garden features: according to Wood, 'Pret is mightily fond of his own villa residence, and since I planted a row of laurels in front of his porch, has been quite proud of it.'[14] Rather more prosaic, at Clifford Priory in Radnorshire, cat-loving curate Francis Kilvert found a 'dear delightful' pussy chained to 'a little kennel' in the strawberry garden while three more cats were chained to kennels by the back door. These cats were probably intended to keep birds and mice at bay but they were clearly familiar with human companionship, rubbing their bodies against human legs and climbing readily onto Kilvert's lap.[15]

Some pets were allowed indoors, and might enjoy more access to high-status areas of the home than some human household members. Middle-class homes typically had a parlour or drawing room, used for entertaining guests and off limits for children. By the middle of the nineteenth century these special rooms – usually where the best furniture and textiles were on display – often accommodated some kind of animal companion. Best known was the fancy 'parlour dog' of notable pedigree, but, as advice writers noted disapprovingly, these animals had a tendency to be overfed and spoiled. Writing of 'Cat and Dog London' in 1901, Frances Simpson lamented the fate of pugs and spaniels whose lives were shortened by the perils of living in 'too luxurious' homes with 'high-born dames'.[16]

From the mid-century onwards aquaria brought the living natural world into Victorian homes and provided striking decoration. According to one 1850s commentator: 'Gold and silver fish can hardly be termed Pets.' Rather, they were 'live ornamental objects, and may be ranked with china, glass and other similar articles, the value of which consists in the pleasure they may afford the eye'.[17] Drawing rooms and bedrooms were also commonly adorned with elaborate cages for exotic and song-birds. Even when families had the resource to invest in an aviary, most would retain caged birds indoors too. Birdcages were available in cane, iron or, more expensively, gilt. On warm, sunny days, delicate birds might be allowed from the confines of stuffy boudoirs and drawing rooms to be hung outside window frames in the fresh air.

Pets brought beauty, life and movement into the static world of the Victorian interior – but above all they were prized for their emotional contribution. Pets made a house a home. In the 1850s Jane Loudon, author of what was arguably the first pet-keeping manual, *Domestic Pets: Their Habits and Management* (1851), celebrated the pleasure of being surrounded by pets at home: 'and with my favourite dog lying at my feet, a cat purring on a sofa at my side, and two goldfish swimming merrily about a vase before me, I sit down to write about the animals I am so fond of; and which, fortunately for the interest of my book, thousands of other people are equally fond as myself.'[18] *Domestic Pets* was the first book in what was to become a new genre of nineteenth-century advice literature on how best to keep, and care for, pet animals. Opening her book by describing domestic life surrounded by her pets – from affectionate cats to 'merry' goldfish – Loudon was aware that her book was selling a special kind of domestic emotional world realized only through animal presence.

Owners of different stripes depicted pets as essential to the harmonious and homely atmosphere of home. Staying with friends in Cornwall in 1870, Francis Kilvert appreciated the 'soft sweet deep cooing' that swept through the house from a pair of doves kept in the kitchen.[19] Kilvert kept a cat, Toby, who offered tactile reassurance on 'wild rainy' nights and liked to greet Kilvert with 'his funny little note of affection'.[20] Retrospective accounts of both middle- and working-class homes in this period tend to point to the presence of animals as reassuring and cosy. The heart of Grace Platt's Edwardian tenement in London's East End was the living room where seven people cooked, ate and worked. It was crowded but warm and, well, 'it was home', not least because this was where Mother could always be found. The other mainstay of the living room was the cat. She had a special box that slid out from underneath a cupboard but liked to 'snuggle down' in father's chair, the only comfortable chair available, by the cooking range, or to play with the younger children.[21] The cat was a source of emotional and physical comfort and Grace couldn't imagine home without her.

Alongside this idea that pets could be fundamental to home was a growing sense of the home as a site of cruelty if pets were mistreated or neglected. Advice literature urged child pet keepers to provide safe and comfortable homes for their charges. The RSPCA, founded in 1824, began to include domestic animals in its campaign – issuing its first tract covering dogs, cats and even hedgehogs – in 1857.[22] In the first decades of operation, the society targeted popular cruel sports and working animals, including horses, donkeys and cart-pulling dogs, rather than pets behind closed doors. As the historian Diana Donald points out, inspectors had no right of access to private property and tackling animal abuse among the wealthy would have meant challenging the social hierarchy.[23] Nonetheless, by 1886 there were eighty RSPCA inspectors operating in Britain and some pet owners were brought before the courts for neglect.[24] In 1883 the RSPCA magazine *Animal World* reported that as a result of its efforts 4,481 people had been convicted of animal cruelty that year. The vast majority of cases concerned horses, but 77 had involved dogs and 65 related to cats.[25] Some of this cruelty took place on the streets (where, for instance, animals were made to fight); some were victims of children or drunken adults. But there were cases where the courts intervened directly in the way pets were kept in the home: eight dog owners and one cat owner were charged with 'withholding food'. Proceedings were also taken on behalf of pet birds – there were five prosecutions for 'breaking the wings of a tame blackbird' that year.

The cruelty of caging birds indoors was an ongoing theme in debates about animal welfare throughout the century. To many, the practice of caging any bird was intrinsically cruel, even more so when cages housed too many birds. But this was weighed against their emotional value, especially in poorer homes. When Henry Scherren lamented the practice of caging birds in working-class homes, he offset the cruelty with the 'brightness' these 'petted little prisoners' brought into otherwise 'dull grey human lives'.[26] This was a theme sometimes picked up in working-class memoirs: pets lifted the spirits. Harry Burton recalled his childhood as an 'uninspiring time' where horizons were 'so small' and 'our tastes so mean'. Yet this did not amount to 'depressed' lives: 'happiness' was achieved through family togetherness in an overcrowded but 'comfortable

Walter Howell Deverell, *A Pet*, exhibited 1853, oil on canvas.

homely home' (his emphasis). This family scene included the cat, 'sitting on the table's edge facing the fire', purring as Burton's mother stroked its head on her way towards the kettle.[27]

The pretty caged bird, trapped by the suffocating elegance of domesticity, also operated throughout the century as a metaphor for women's imprisonment in domestic space and double sexual standards. Walter Deverell's *A Pet* (1853), a pastel-coloured painting depicting a young woman poised in the doorway of a glasshouse with a dog sleeping at her feet as she leans in and almost kisses a birdcage, was originally displayed with a quotation asking what kindness made a pet of a volatile creature. It was deliberately ambiguous who the creature at stake was: the woman, the bird or the dog. Even relatively anodyne paintings of women and birds seemed to hint that, however pretty the cage, it was an unnatural entrapment. In Henry Tonks's *The Birdcage* (1907), a young woman reaches towards a caged bird with a cup. The shimmering sunlight falling into the room, the flowers awaiting arrangement, the yellow of the canary and the white frou-frou of the woman's gown suggest lightness and frippery. But nothing is entirely natural: roses grow about a cane, the woman looks like a painted doll, the plucked flowers must wither and the poor bird is trapped inside its tiny cage. John Byam Liston Shaw's *The Caged Bird* (1907) took this to its logical conclusion, picturing a woman seated outdoors as she watches her caged bird fly free. Her face, full of wonder, is the more haunting because the viewer knows the woman cannot mimic the bird and must remain in her gilded cage.

In many Victorian homes, though, enthusiasm for pets – kept both outside and inside – overrode nascent worries over animal wellbeing. In an 1878 book of 'anecdotes' about 'little toys' (an alarming if revealing term for children's pets), the children's author Emma Davenport sketched one household's arrangements for a variety of animals, noting the porous boundaries between wild and tame, outdoor and indoor animals. The children's first rabbit, Moppy, was purchased off the street and lived in a packing box in the 'empty garret' at the top of the house, being carried to the nursery when the children wished to play. Moppy was superseded by Bunny, a baby rabbit rescued from the wild that lived initially with the cook in a box by the side of the fire in the kitchen. Slowly, Bunny pushed the boundaries of permitted space and soon enough had the run of the nursery, sitting room and all the bedrooms. All of this was fine, but Bunny also had a fondness for the cellar where he dug the soil from in between cellar stones. Attempts to prevent this were unsuccessful and he was eventually released back into the wild. The canary and songbird's cage rested on the window seat or the table of the nursery with occasional excursions to the drawing room. Subject to all the windows and doors being closed, the birds could fly about the nursery, drawing room and, sometimes, the staircase. The parrot lived in a cage in the sitting room, although for a short while she slept in an older girl's bedroom. A jackdaw, meanwhile, had its wings clipped and lived in the garden, although he was allowed to visit the dining room and kitchen. A hedgehog lived outside but was permitted trips to the kitchen and nursery before the family terrier killed it, testifying to the perils of letting animals loose in

John Byam Liston Shaw, *The Caged Bird*, 1907, oil on canvas.

domestic space. Humans sought to transform animals into pets by inviting them to share homes and gardens but, even in homes like that of George Sims, where the anarchy of interspecies living was celebrated, the ensuing chaos could test the boundaries of companionship and prove harmful to the animals.

Domestic order . . . and disorder

The Victorian middle-class home was, ideally at least, a carefully ordered world in which separate spaces were created for husbands, wives, children and servants. There was usually a timetabled domestic routine with times for rising, meals, family prayers, social activities and domestic work. As evidenced by the spaces set aside for pets, animals were expected to fit in and even contribute. According to an 1854 advice manual: 'If trained when young a dog can be trained to do almost anything. Above all, humans should insist on good dog manners – to be silent when required, or to lie down, not to leap into the laps of visitors or others and to conduct himself submissively.'[28] According to *Popular Dog Keeping* (1898), the well-trained canine occupied a predetermined space in a given room: 'They should be taught their place in the room, and if this be pointed out to them a few times, putting them, if need be, in the desired spot, they will recognise what is required of them, and act accordingly.'[29] Dogs were even expected to participate in domestic rituals – the same volume supplied advice on tricks, including welcoming the man of the house on his return from work by removing his hat and fetching his slippers.[30] The Victorians were also fond of moral tales featuring notable pets who helped uphold domestic order. Thomas Jackson's *Our Dumb Companions*, published in the 1860s, was filled with exemplary animals including Tiny – a small dog who reputedly stood at the word 'Amen' during family prayers.[31] There were also stories of cats who could ring bells, knock at doors or capture burglars. Dickens apparently owned a deaf cat who in the evenings would often put out a candle with its paw, to prevent Dickens from reading and therefore secure his attention.[32]

Despite social commentators generating moral panics about perceived depravity, most working-class households strove to run along ordered lines too. One magazine article on London's pet birds noted that most labourers' dwellings had some kind of small and containable pet, from the solitary goldfish to guinea pigs or rabbits.[33] The most common pet was the caged bird because it was easy to keep in small

'Dickens's cat putting out the candle', illustration in Caroline Pridham, *Domestic Pets* (1895).

interiors but, even here, some ingenuity and flexibility might be required. In one Bolton family at the start of the twentieth century, Dad kept pigeons in the back yard but hung his 'lovely birds' in cages in a downstairs alcove while others shared a bedroom with his young son.[34] Where space really was at a premium, or the collection of birds outgrew the interior, cages might be fixed on the exterior walls of a house stretching up to first- and second-floor windows.[35]

Standard working-class homes had two rooms downstairs: a living room with a cooking range and a parlour reserved for 'best'. Many families liked representations of animals in their homes: china dogs on over-mantels or dressers were popular, as were sentimental images of cats, dogs, birds and other animals depicted with faithful human companions.[36] But, aside from birds and fish, sentient pets, especially dogs, were less common in the nineteenth-century working-class interior as they represented potentially smelly, disruptive members of small, busy houses. Even in families with slightly more space, hard-earned higher standards of living could render dogs unwelcome indoor guests. Having only one child, a middle-aged manual labourer and his wife enjoyed the unusual luxury of space in their terraced house in late Victorian Lancaster. But even here, dad kept his much-loved dog kennelled outdoors in a shared yard.[37]

Pets could uphold order in the home by contributing to pest control. The abilities of cats and dogs as mousers and rat catchers are well known. The cats around Grace Platt's tenement block feasted fortnightly

'Caged', photograph from Henry Scherren, 'Bird-Land and Pet-Land in London', published in George R. Sims, ed., *Living London* (1902), vol. II.

when the emptying of the building's rubbish chute released large quantities of rats and mice.[38] Mice occupied an interesting territory between housewife's scourge and schoolboy's joy – these 'pests' were sometimes transformed into pets.[39] Some smaller inhabitants of the home that never made this transition were the small insects that plagued both working- and middle-class households – bed bugs and black beetles. In the case of the latter, help was at hand from a surprising ally – the hedgehog. Black beetles often besieged kitchens. Hedgehogs ate the insects with speed and efficiency and were in demand as a result. Beeton's *Book of Home Pets* (1861) related the acquisition of a hedgehog called Peter, acquired by the family after a particularly arduous struggle with black beetles, even though neighbours warned that hedgehogs were difficult to keep alive. Peter quickly ate the black beetles, but he became emotionally significant in the household too, forming an attachment to a daughter of the house who took responsibility for feeding him. Once the family worked out that Peter ate meat, he seems to have stayed with them for a long period of time, even surviving a near blinding from a rat.[40] Of course, pets with pest-control functions were not immune from contributing to the interspecies mix with fleas and other assorted vermin of their own.

While Victorian homes were supposed to run along ordered lines, pet advisors acknowledged that animals often had other ideas and human families could struggle to contain them. In the late nineteenth century the declining popularity of monkeys as pets was blamed on their capacity for domestic destabilization. A monkey-keeping advice manual from 1888 urged that domestic monkeys must be kept in cages: 'The right place for a monkey, in civilised society, is in a cage; here the once pest of everybody becomes everyone's pet.'[41] Henry Scherren's survey of London's 'petland' in 1901 claimed that although the monkey remained the 'king of pets', this might well refer to their imperious temper rather than their popularity. London Zoo, joked Scherren, was the capital's penitentiary for naughty monkeys.[42] Caged birds, whose movement was restricted, were less of a problem, but grouped together the noise they made could shatter a quiet Victorian drawing room. 'It is impossible to read aloud, or to converse with animation', warned *Timbs' Manual* in 1847, in a room where parakeets are 'confined'.[43] Caged birds might be permitted liberty to fly about rooms under certain conditions, but there was always the risk of escape if a thoughtless person (children usually blamed servants) left a door or window open. More perilous to the winged pet, whether caged or in drawing-room flight, was the 'tragic' presence of a cat.[44]

Again and again, advisors urged that pets should be kept in their place. The constant repetition is a strong indication that this was difficult to achieve. John Maxtee, author of *Popular Dog Keeping*, was optimistic on this front and issued a list of dos and don'ts for domestic dogs. Protecting furniture was crucial: 'Dogs should not be allowed to sit on chairs, as they would cause no end of damage to furniture coverings and the like, as they are obviously unable to differentiate between wet and fine weather.'[45] If dogs could not discriminate, many owners appear to have been powerless to assist. In 1854 the writer Jane Carlyle turned down the opportunity to 'rusticate' in Lord and Lady Ashburton's country pile while the owners were away because she was 'always afraid of my dog's making footmarks on the sofa or carpet'.[46]

Although Beatrix Potter found dogs belonging to the aristocracy 'behaved as badly as plebeian dogs',[47] problems of pets disrupting domestic calm were amplified in working-class homes where space was at a premium. The labour involved in keeping small homes clean was phenomenal, especially if husbands were employed in 'dirty' trades (mining was the worst). It shouldn't surprise us that women were rarely keen to let dogs indoors, viewing them as unhygienic, labour-intensive and, given their appetites, the enemy of thrift.[48] One woman had been in service before marriage and expected her tiny Edwardian terrace to outperform the hygiene standards of her erstwhile employers, despite having five children. Although the budgie and cat were allowed indoors, the poor dog never got a look in.[49] Movement in working-class living rooms, according to one Glasgow resident, represented a 'constant dodging of the sharp corners of the furniture and evasion of unexpected chairs'.[50] Adding medium or large animals into the mix was, for some families at least, unthinkable. In a late Victorian 'two up, two down' in Lancaster where eight children lived with their parents, a mother compromised with her older son: his dog could stay indoors overnight provided he tied it to the table leg to prevent it wandering about the house and wreaking havoc.[51] Other families waited until older children moved out or the family relocated to larger premises before they acquired indoor pets.[52] Cats, relatively independent residents, could represent additional labour and sources of infection to houseproud women: one little girl wept bitterly when her mother refused to let their cat use the younger children's pram as her bed.[53] Even birdcages needed to be cleaned.

Status-conscious Victorians often displayed their newfound wealth in parlours and drawing rooms. The mid-Victorian home was awash with small ornamental tables, strategic drapery and precariously balanced ornaments – all vulnerable to paws and tails. Roughie, a badly behaved Skye terrier belonging to the Rev. John Wood, was responsible for much damage:

> That tail of his quite ruined the breakfast-room paper, for Roughie had a habit of sitting in the mud until his tail was wet, and then running over the house and switching that muddy member against the walls, so that they were streaked as if with dashes of a painter's brush; not to mention printing off accurate impressions of his feet on the stair-carpets.[54]

Even reasonably well-trained animals could be destructive. Peter, the beetle-eating hedgehog, also liked 'foraging for bed clothes – stealing all the stray towels, house-flannels, and pieces of cloth and carpet which fall his way'.[55] Occasionally pets were seriously destructive. *The Book of Home Pets* (1861) gave details of a delinquent raven who 'new pointed the greater part of the garden wall by digging out the mortar, broke countless squares of glass by scraping the putty away all around the frames, and tore up and swallowed in splinters the greater part of a staircase of six steps and a landing'.[56] Benjamin Bouncer, Beatrix Potter's tame jack hare, might well have scuppered her artistic career, such was his appetite for 'certain sorts of paint'.[57] In 1892 the artist Louis Wain produced a full-page cartoon, 'Other People's Pets', for the *Illustrated*

Louis Wain, 'Other People's Pets', *Illustrated London News*, 10 December 1892. Wain's cartoon explores the variety of ways in which pets wreaked havoc in the home.

London News. Featuring marauding monkeys, biting parrots, dogs destroying clothing and cats digging up garden beds, the images were a comic reminder that domestic destruction often spilled over into neighbouring homes.

But even exasperated anecdotes relating to animal chaos were often suffused with humour and grudging admiration for animal cleverness. Benjamin Bouncer had a 'volatile temperament', was 'vulgar', 'shallow and absurdly transparent', rocketing from amiable affection to behaving like a 'demon', upsetting jugs or teacups, 'throwing himself on his back, scratching and spluttering'. But this behaviour was what Potter found 'so delightful'.[58] Some pets upset domestic order by bringing their animal instincts into dialogue with human practices. Potter took delight in the story of a gentleman who taught his cat to sit at the dinner table, 'where it behaved very well', appreciating the scraps master put onto its plate. The picturesque scene took a gruesome turn when the cat arrived for dinner slightly late one evening dragging two dead mice in its wake, carefully allocating one mouse to each plate.[59]

Some pet people even seemed to revel in domestic disarray. Cats slept amid the clutter of George Sims's desk while the dogs – bulldogs and terriers – either followed their master from room to room or crashed about the house to find him.[60] Alarmed at how little regard the dogs (and Sims, who liked to play shuttlecock amid dainty china) showed for household clutter, one bemused journalist was told that 'Things must take their chances.' All in all, Sims embraced the happy chaos that animals brought, claiming that – all things considered – his pets were 'exceptionally well-mannered animals'.[61] If there was any slight on the manners of human visitors intended here, journalists failed to note it. This cheerful insouciance was also found in the Hardy household at Max Gate in early twentieth-century Dorset. Here, literary visitors were confronted by Wessex, Thomas Hardy's much-indulged terrier, who sat on the dining-room table at mealtimes and took umbrage if not provided with a share of the repast.[62] Among the ladies disgusted by this spectacle was Lady Cynthia Asquith, who visited the Hardys in 1921, and described Wessex as 'the most despotic dog . . . not under, but on, the table, walking about quite unchecked and contesting with me every forkful of food on its way from plate to mouth'.[63] In such circumstances, it was difficult for orderly dinners to take place, although the Hardys clearly considered human notions of order at table to be overrated.

Thomas and Florence
Hardy with their dog
Wessex.

Cats were wont to steal fish and meat not intended for their consumption while other animals transgressed forbidden spaces with myriad
consequences. A wild rabbit taken in by Grace Platt's tenement neighbours was 'full of mischief': he climbed into the oven and almost got
roasted, attempted to climb the chimney and dislodged clouds of soot,
and tried to make himself comfortable in the marital bed before becoming trapped and tangled in bedclothes.[64] While these anecdotes added
humour to a memoir of hard toil and relative poverty, they also suggested
that animals in domestic space brought chaos and represented matter
out of place. Even cages were unreliable. The religious periodical *The
Quiver* related the story of a sailor trapped at home by his squirrel, Jack,
who would fret if left alone. Having been bullied into leaving Jack to
go to church, the sailor returned to find the squirrel escaped from his
cage. Only after a heartrending search was Jack found cowering in the
oven in terror. The sailor declared that henceforth he would happily
stay home with Jack.[65]

Worse, despite the expectation that dogs would guard the home,
there were many exceptions. While the Rev. Wood praised his exemplary
watchdog Apollo, his other dog, Roughie, fell well short of the required

standard. Hopes that the Skye terrier would prove a staunch defender of the home were quickly dashed:

> I never made a greater mistake in my life. Roughie was quite charmed with the beggars, and positively welcomed them as he saw them coming. Instead of barking and snarling, as he ought to have done, and so calling our attention, he only rolled over on his back, and invited the intruder to a game of play.

Oblivious to nineteenth-century human hierarchies, the friendly canine welcomed all comers, much to the disgust of his upper-class owner: 'He really seemed to have no powers of discrimination, and was ready to play with anyone who happened to approach. Man, woman, or child was equally welcome, and he seemed as glad to see the most repulsive tramp as myself or any other of the household.'[66] Roughie had failed on two counts – to protect the home and to uphold his master's idea of the social order.

More seriously, in the final decades of the nineteenth century it became seen as a matter of civic duty to keep dogs within domestic limits. Stray dogs were perceived as a major social and public health problem, not least because people feared catching hydrophobia (rabies) from dog bites. How far rabies threatened public health was a hotly contested, deeply emotive issue. Even so, the Metropolitan Street Act of 1867 expanded the powers of the Metropolitan Police Act of 1839, enabling the police to fine owners of unmuzzled dogs (this Act also introduced the flat-rate dog licence).[67] From 1871 the Dangerous Dogs Act allowed owners to be brought before a magistrates' court if accused of owning a dangerous dog, where they were subject to fines, control orders and even orders of destruction. Elizabeth von Arnim, a writer and the English widow of a German nobleman, fell foul of the dog laws when she settled in North Devon in the early twentieth century.[68] Elizabeth rented a house that came with a canine occupant, a black dog called Prince. One day, the dog escaped and worried some sheep in a neighbouring field. Unused to English law, Elizabeth was shocked to be brought before the local magistrate (who was part of her social circle) and fined. Even more upsetting was the fate of Prince, who was sentenced to death. Elizabeth, deeply shaken by the verdict, vomited on the spot, while the magistrate politely looked the other way.

Modern homes: a place for pets?

In the early decades of the twentieth century it was becoming more widely accepted that pets would live indoors. Core shifts in home building and design, the increasing professionalization of animal training and the expansion of small veterinary practice made keeping pets inside increasingly viable for a broader range of families, especially regarding cats and dogs, and promoted the idea of the pet as companion and friend. Bringing animals indoors reflected a changed perception of their role. When John Maxtee's *Popular Dog Keeping* was reissued in 1947, the book made clear how much had changed since the previous century, noting that 'These are the days when the companion dog, however large, usually has the "run of the house" by day and indoor sleeping quarters at night.' Hardier breeds might still be kept outside, but it had become the norm to keep dogs indoors for the benefit of both parties, especially if the objective of dog ownership was companionship: 'constant contact' with the family 'develops the dog's intelligence and adds amazingly to the interest and enjoyment to be derived from its society'.[69] But these shifts were not straightforward and changes were far from uniform. And of course, animals continued to behave independently, and sometimes in direct opposition to their human keepers.

Shifts in home design and norms of pet keeping had significant impacts on human–animal relationships. Crucially, in the first half of the twentieth century, new forms of housing changed the way that people lived: some offered new opportunities for pet keeping while others complicated it. The boon for pets was the growth of suburbia, often facilitated by expanding rail and bus networks and, steadily, the growth in car ownership. Model villages from the late nineteenth century established core principles of blending new housing design with the benefit of the countryside. Suburban developments from the end of the First World War tended to extend these principles with roads built in curving sweeps and gardens for all. Between 1919 and 1934, 2,459,000 houses were built in England and Wales. Sixty-nine per cent of these were built privately and aimed at the expanding middle and aspirational working classes that were able, thanks to building societies, decreased building costs and falling house prices, to own their own homes for the first time.

The most popular suburban developments were characterized by new terraced and semi-detached houses, often in the 'Tudorbethan' style. These homes were lighter and had larger rooms and more outdoor space than Victorian terraces. They were also planned differently. Kitchens were on the ground floor, adjacent to the dining room, rather than in the basement, not least because servant labour was less readily available after the First World War. Municipal developments mirrored these principles, relocating housing to the outskirts of towns and cities, and planning houses with gardens and ready access to green spaces. In theory, these developments were ideal for pet keeping. But as families across the social scale settled into their bright, modern homes, the flaws of suburban development became increasingly apparent. Women in particular reported feeling isolated and removed from the social networks of long-established communities. Pets in these homes could be freighted with additional emotional and practical responsibilities as they became the everyday companions of housewives.

One of the inhabitants of this new suburban world was Betty Shadbolt, who lived with her husband, a live-in maid, a large Airedale and four pigeons on a street of large, detached suburban homes in the late 1930s.[70] Betty took part in a Mass-Observation Survey, so we know quite a lot about her daily life. As a housewife, her main task was to manage the home. Although she had the help of a maid, Betty undertook cleaning and cooking herself, as well as shopping for the household – a not inconsiderable task in the 1930s, when separate high-street shops had to be visited individually. Betty never named her Airedale dog, but her account reveals how far he was entwined in her daily life. The dog came into the dining room at breakfast and was brushed as part of her morning cleaning routine, and he accompanied Betty feeding the pigeons outside. While she changed to go shopping, the Airedale waited patiently at the bottom of the stairs (he was apparently too big to be allowed in the upstairs rooms). The dog then accompanied her to the cake shop (a feisty cat had to be removed before they went in), the 'foreign' meat shop, the stationer and the library, where he was offered treats and much petted. Betty's writing suggests that she found the housewife's role frustrating and sought intellectual solace in amateur history. She was sometimes bored and lonely. In sharing everyday errands and the monotony of domestic chores, her dog made all the difference to Betty's ability to survive the suburban housewife's lot.

Fond as Betty was of her Airedale, the dog still spent some of its time chained up outside the house – this was still routine in the 1930s. But the practice was being placed under more scrutiny. Since the early 1900s the RSPCA and National Canine Defence League had identified keeping dogs chained outdoors as cruel: it made dogs 'cowed', 'dejected' and 'sullen', and rendered them 'useless as companions'.[71] In August 1922 the RSPCA's *Animal World* reported on a man brought before the bench in Kingston for causing 'unnecessary suffering' to a dog by 'omitting to provide it with proper care and attention'. The dog 'was chained to a kennel and could not move a distance of more than four feet, the chain being not quite two feet long; the place was deep with filth'.[72] In September the same year a woman from Basingstoke was found to have starved and neglected her dog – a brown mongrel kept on a chain of about '3ft. 6inches long' for six months.[73] The length of the chain, which severely restricted the animal's movements, was of particular concern. Both charities lobbied for more people to use runs or, where possible, to take dogs to work with them. Acknowledging that some households could not leave dogs indoors, the Canine Defence League marketed a 'post and wire' system that enabled dogs to be chained for safety but have freedom to run up and down the wire. This wasn't perfect but it was 'better'.[74] As the animal historian Hilda Kean has shown, these changes were strongly encouraged by Colonel Edwin Richardson, who trained dogs to perform military support tasks in the Great War, and Arthur Croxton-Smith, chair of the Kennel Club from the late 1930s to 1948. Croxton-Smith also argued that if there wasn't room in the family home for a large dog, smaller breeds should be considered instead, rather than keeping the animal outside.[75]

RSPCA records show that modern housing, while offering more space for pets, also provided a new means to conceal animal cruelty. In February 1935 *Animal World* reported on 'cruelty to twenty-three dogs', mainly greyhounds, kept together in a garage in Chelmsford without proper food, ventilation or sanitation.[76] The garage – a new, large, windowless and potentially well-insulated space – allowed animal abuse to take place unobserved.

Despite the emergence of the 'modern' house, many people were still making the best of keeping pets in difficult conditions. Alongside the Tudorbethan suburbs, new purpose-built tenement flats and out-of-town housing estates, many families and animals continued to live in older housing. Yet people who wanted pets continued to find ways to keep them, despite difficult domestic situations. Sidney Day, a labourer's son, grew up in a family of eight who shared the ground floor of a terraced house on Balmore Street in Highgate in the 1910s and '20s. The small house teemed with human and animal life – there were indoor birds, an aviary, rabbits and chickens in the backyard. Somehow the family always had at least three dogs, who slept outside. During the war years, flying in the face of practicality, Dinah, Sidney's mother, adopted yet another dog – a whippet – found wandering during an air raid. The animal became a cherished pet and joined her in bed, where it curled around her nightly, acting as a 'hot water bottle'.[77] Both animals and humans in the Day household were living in close conditions with limited resources, yet there was a great deal of affection. Growing up, Day spent much of his time roaming nearby parks and Hampstead Heath, accompanied by his favourite dog, an Airedale named Babs: boy and dog swam in the ponds on the edge of the Heath.

During the Second World War the widespread disruption of people's domestic lives and damage to their homes had a powerful impact on pet keeping. Hilda Kean has written about the impact of the war on relationships between humans and pet animals. She shows how the war changed people's everyday routines in the home as the night blackout was introduced, shelters were built and precautions were taken against fire. These took the form of buckets of sand that were, according to Kean, sometimes 'misinterpreted' by cats. Evacuation, too, caused large-scale domestic disruption. Children removed from the city wrote home longing for their pets, and some people took their animals with them.[78] Then there was the actual destruction of homes caused by bombing from the Luftwaffe. While the rescue of plucky dogs from the rubble made good headlines, many pets were killed in the Blitz and in the early days of the war a significant number of owners euthanized pets in the belief that they might not survive the bombing. Kean argues, though, that overall the war strengthened the bond between humans and pets as the shared experience of sheltering in times of danger drew the species together.

The challenges of pets in flats

Alongside the sprawl of suburbia, the other major housing development following the First World War was the expansion of low- and high-rise flats. Again, this housing was available across the social scale, from the relatively small flats built by municipalities to the rather grand, self-consciously modern developments inhabited by the likes of Bertie Wooster in P. G. Wodehouse's novels. For some families, developments in veterinary technology, especially surgery to neuter toms, made keeping cats in flats far more viable, particularly for pedigree breeds that were considered suited to indoor living. While some vets had performed this operation in the late nineteenth century, and many owners had taken matters into their own hands, the expansion of small animal practice in the 1920s made veterinary treatment available to a wider range of pet owners. Safe and humane neutering was becoming more accessible. By the 1950s it was accepted that a non-stud male cat should be neutered.[79] Neutered toms were known to grow to a large size, and were generally thought to be gentler. Importantly for anyone who wanted to keep them indoors, they were less likely to mark their territory by 'spraying' – a practice that encouraged earlier generations to keep them firmly outside.

For owners who kept cats exclusively indoors, the impact on domestic life could be dramatic. Tory MP and writer Sir John Smyth and his wife Frances acquired two Siamese cats, Pooni and Tomkin, in the early 1950s. The arrival of the animals transformed the couple's smart flat. Pooni, who came first, demanded access all areas and, after a battle, was allowed into the Smyths' bedroom at night.[80] While Frances initially held out against cats on the breakfast table, here too there was capitulation: 'she could not resist, any more than I could, the sight of Tomkin with his head in the milk jug when he was a kitten.'[81] But the real challenges emerged in relation to the flat's location on the eighth floor of the building on London's Embankment. When they discovered that Tomkin was able to escape from the dining-room windows Frances had every window fitted with flat nylon curtains pulled over brass bars (an expensive innovation).[82] Perhaps the greatest sacrifice was Frances's balcony garden – a flower-covered enclave from which the couple, pre-cats, had enjoyed a view of the Thames. Not only was it necessary to enclose the balcony with wire mesh to prevent the cats from falling out, but the delicate plants did not survive the onslaught from the Siamese. Despite the demise of their view (which they had waited years to obtain), Smyth remained sanguine, writing that he would not be without the two cats.[83]

As the Smyths' experience indicates, flats were far from ideal environments for keeping pets. As early as 1901, commentators were advising against keeping cats in flats where they could not access gardens.[84] Despite such concerns, working-class people had long kept cats in flats converted from large houses. Robert Tressell's protagonist, Owen, in the novel *The Ragged Trousered Philanthropists* (1914), lived with his wife and child in a three-roomed flat on the top floor of a three-storey house. Despite these living arrangements, Owen rescued a stray kitten to be his son's companion, turning an old toy box into a cat bed with rags.[85] This is a metaphor for the socialism of the novel: Owen is a decent man who cares for the weak and defenceless, even when such arrangements are far from straightforward.

Despite the relative unpopularity of flats in the UK (a Mass-Observation Enquiry into People's Homes in 1943 found 'flats are unpopular among the vast mass of people'),[86] and the assorted challenges of living in them, increasing numbers of people did live in purpose-built flats by the 1950s. Many of these residents kept pets. Contemporary commentators thought the rising number of small urban dwellings accounted for the decline in popularity of some dog breeds. Ownership of St Bernards, Newfoundlands and Great Danes, the darlings of Victorian middle-class homes, was waning by the interwar period. While there is little evidence to suggest that homes were actually smaller, the shrinking gap between working- and middle-class incomes after the First World War and the gradual demise of servant labour contributed to a sense – expressed by some members of the middle classes – that the large Victorian home (which in addition to family members, servants and a plethora of domestic goods apparently had room for the odd Great Dane as well) was a thing of the past.[87] According to dog expert Percy Soderberg, 'few houses to-day are suited to really large dogs while comparatively few men, on the other hand, are attracted to the really small breeds.'[88]

One answer to this problem was the medium-sized dog – large dogs would no longer fit in the home, while diminutive 'toys' were feminized. As early as the 1920s, Robert Leighton singled out the 'small companion dog' as the best for city living, citing the terrier, which could be 'equally a man and woman's dog' and was 'pure British', as the ideal.[89] Other recommended small- to medium-sized dogs included the dachshund, Pekinese, Pomeranian, Yorkshire terrier, Maltese terrier, Australian terrier and miniature poodle. According to advice writer Valerie Higgins, these little dogs were 'ideal to keep in a flat, [and] carry on the tops of buses or in the Tubes'.[90]

The realities of the situation were more challenging. As John Smyth had noted when deciding to acquire Siamese cats: 'Some people in our block of flats do keep dogs, which involves much going up and down again in the lift for (canine) purposes of nature and trailing them along the Embankment on a lead.'[91] One man who faced up to the challenge of keeping pets in a modern flat was Frederick Archer, who kept a dog and a cat in a Brighton flat in the late 1930s. As staff reporter for the Brighton area for evening and morning newspapers in London, Frederick's central location was crucial: he, his wife, a large white cat and a small fox terrier bitch (chosen perhaps to suit flat living) lived in 'Five rooms, well-furnished, all modern conveniences except hot water. All electric save for gas cooker and geyser.'[92] Keeping animals within a relatively confined space could be tricky: the window box outside Archer's study was desecrated by the large white cat, who liked to sit there and chew the plants. Negotiating between the animals could be difficult. Archer described how, when preparing breakfast for himself, his wife and the animals (prawns on toast – fresh from a newly acquired refrigerator), the cat and dog had to be kept separate so the large feline would not gobble up the little terrier's share. After some careful negotiation and much opening and closing of doors, the animals breakfasted and the household settled down to enjoy the day in peace.

Increasingly, however, many flat dwellers were denied the opportunity to keep pets at all or given ultimatums on account of the perceived incompatibility of their animal's behaviour and proximity to other dwellers. Few architects designed flats with the needs of animals in mind. For sure, rabbits, guinea pigs and cats could be trained to empty bowels and bladder in suitable receptacles but dogs presented greater challenges. Joe Ackerley mused (at length) on the challenges, and unexpected joys, of training his Alsatian, Queenie, to use his flat's balcony for her toilet needs, although he suspected that she was always sheepish about this on account of knowing Ackerley liked to sit there in his leisure.[93] Given that Ackerley swilled her urine with buckets of water, this can't have been too pleasant for the people on the balcony below either. Certainly, flats were never intended to serve as whelping kennels. Queenie gave birth in Ackerley's bedroom but, as her eight puppies grew more independent, he transformed his dining room into a puppy pen and fenced in the terrace to prevent them careering 18 metres (60 ft) to their deaths. Aside from the exhaustion of living – quite literally – alongside the puppies, Ackerley's flat looked and smelt 'like a stable'. It wasn't long before other residents complained to the landlord and Ackerley was given an ultimatum: get rid of the puppies or leave at once.[94]

In 1953 *Pets and Aquaria* magazine reported that many landlords had implemented a 'no pets' rule due to worries over noise, the fouling of public areas and the potential menace of cat colonies created by unwanted kittens. Post-war housing shortages left people with less choice over where they lived; 'in these days, many people are caused unhappiness and denied the companionship of pets because of the completely inflexible rules.' During the 1950s the loss of space for pets was also recognized as one of the problems faced by working families who were moved into flats as part of 'slum clearance'.[95] While not all councils and boroughs forbade pet keeping, it was relatively common among local authorities and private landlords.

Pets and Aquaria urged a rethink, suggesting neutering cats to deal with the kitten problem and allowing budgies, canaries and fish. The pet-less flat, the article concluded, was a joyless thing. The piece ended with a poem lamenting the loss of 'the scuffle of paws in the hall' and 'old slippers that are never brought'.[96]

Yet many flat dwellers felt strongly enough about their pets to defy the rules, and some were even willing to come before the courts in a bid to keep companion animals. In 1929 the Canine Defence League intervened with the London County Council on behalf of tenement tenants given an ultimatum to get rid of their pets. Admitting that the rules clearly stated 'no pets', the League thought 'harsh rules of this kind were made to be broken.' The League reached a compromise with the Town Clerk and the tenants were allowed to keep their pets on the understanding that they would not replace them once they died.[97] In 1947 the *Daily Mail* reported a test-case decision in which a magistrate issued possession orders against four tenants of London County Council flats in Euston who had defied the council's ban on pets by retaining their dogs. The council for their defence, instructed by the Canine Defence League, argued that it would be 'an exceptional hardship' for these tenants to give up their dogs. The Magistrate said that he was obliged to uphold the order but was clearly sympathetic, as he told the LCC to hold off evicting them for thirty days to give them chance to appeal the decision.[98]

Wealthier flat dwellers were not immune from these problems. In June 1950 tenants in one of London's biggest blocks of luxury flats, Du Cane Court in Balham, were up in arms over the landlord's demand that thirty dog-owning tenants get rid of their animals or quit the building. The tenants came together to oppose the move and help was sought from the Canine Defence League, who referred them to a solicitor. The CDL commented that 'There have recently been a number of similar complaints. People have had to have their dogs destroyed or leave their homes. Some of them are elderly women who feel that they must have the dogs for protection. Others have been robbed on several occasions.'[99] Despite the social and practical problems involved in keeping dogs in flats, this was a right that pet owners were prepared to fight for.

Pets in the 'ideal' post-war home

After the Second World War, home and domestic life took on new importance as governments and people sought to rebuild their lives. Home life acquired a new symbolic significance in the reconstruction, a rebuilding programme saw the modernization of many homes and there was a new emphasis on domestic leisure – watching television, gardening and DIY. In 1957 the RSPCA released a short film, *Cats on the Hearth*, harnessing the celebration of domesticity to draw attention to the need to care for cats. Since at least the 1890s campaigns by animal-welfare groups had argued for humans to take more responsibility for cats, seeing them less as independent animals and more as domestic pets. From the 1920s, the Liverpool RSPCA printed information leaflets about cat care in Chinese to extend the reach of feline welfare campaigns to diverse communities.[100] *Cats on the Hearth* opened with a cosy scene in which a middle-class white family of four sat together on a winter's evening – the father with his paper, the mother knitting and two boys avoiding bedtime. But the camera then panned to 'the fifth member' of the family, a tabby cat ensconced beside them on a comfy chair: 'And as she lies there, at peace with her little world, [she] is a symbol of contentment and calm'.[101] In the film the cat is cast as a valuable contributor to post-war domesticity, helping foster the tranquillity that was surely an emotional goal of the post-war home.

There were of course limits to the realization of this cosy vision. Despite all the new housing built in the mid-twentieth century, old and unsuitable accommodation remained – and remains – a real problem for poorer families. And the suitability of any house, old or new, often depended very much on the distinct qualities of human and animals. As animal-welfare campaigners would continue to argue for the rest of the century, some people were simply not fit to keep pets, regardless of their housing. Although it was impossible to keep more than one Alsatian in his London flat, Joe Ackerley was bitter with self-recrimination for giving one of Queenie's puppies to an Irish labourer whose home he viewed as 'poky', poor, full of children and 'no place for a dog', especially not a large one.[102] RSPCA prosecution figures between the nineteenth and twentieth centuries show an overall decline in prosecutions for animal cruelty but the figures reflect the diminishing use of working animals. Prosecution figures for mistreatment of dogs and cats remained relatively steady, and even increased in the 1950s, presumably as the organization was now able to pay closer attention to them. Positive steps to educate the public in how to keep animals in the home became a more overt part of the organization's campaign.

For migrating families who arrived in Britain from the West Indies and South Asia from the 1950s, the idealized home was even harder to obtain. The photograph opposite, from the Jewish Museum, shows the Isaac family, a Jewish Indian family who moved from India to London in 1957, with two monkeys and three parrots who sit comfortably with them, one parrot nuzzling Miriam Isaac's shoulder. The accompanying oral history does not mention the animals, but pet keeping would have been difficult in the Jewish shelter that the family lived in when they arrived.[103] Migrants often struggled to find accommodation in the face of landlords who racially discriminated when they let properties. To cope with this situation, South Asian migrants often lived in shared rooms in shared houses and might have little space or time for pets. Sometimes there were cultural reasons for avoiding certain pets – contemporary commentators thought Muslim populations treated cats with care but were likely to reject dogs on the grounds that they were seen as ritually impure in Islam. But there were also situations in which pets could help migrants settle. For Sikh migrant Chana Joginder, who arrived in Plymouth in 1956, walking neighbours' dogs was a means of finding human and animal friendship within a new local community.[104] For others, pets provided much-needed companionship in otherwise hostile localities. In 1934 the Canine Defence League reported intervening on behalf of a Jewish woman, named only as 'Madame X' to protect her identity, after reports that she and her dog were being 'persecuted' by neighbours.[105] Indeed, despite changing attitudes to the role and place of animals in the home, some householders continued to keep dogs for security. Leslie King, the first Jamaican migrant to settle in Brixton, was photographed outside his terraced house in 1952 accompanied by a large and impressive Alsatian. Paul Gilroy, the historian who collected and identified the photograph, writes, 'Looking at him sitting outside his house, it is impossible not to wonder what it was about his life there

A Jewish immigrant family from India, 1957.

that made him want the company and protection of the large and alert Alsatian dog with which he has been photographed.'[106]

For some people, though, distaste for keeping dogs indoors never went away. Even when dogs were trained to defecate outdoors, the vagaries of bowel habits and human stupidity meant accidents did happen. Staying with an army acquaintance in Kent, Ackerley recalled Queenie waking him in the night with persistent nudges. Considering that she couldn't possibly need the loo at that hour in the morning, Ackerley ignored her only to hear distinctive 'plop, plop, plop' sounds on the bedroom linoleum. Ackerley spent twenty minutes clearing up with drawer liners and multiple trips to the bathroom. His host never invited them again.[107] Certainly, entertaining people and their dogs could challenge relationships, even when 'home' was rather grand. Recovering from having her sister Pamela – and her dogs – stay at Chatsworth for Christmas in 1960, Deborah, Duchess of Devonshire, declaimed: 'Woman [Pamela], I think, is mad. Her whole life is dedicated to those dogs . . . Their names are fantastic and so is their behaviour.' The dogs went out before breakfast, made a racket, came back muddy and got 'straight on the sofas & she makes no attempt to move them except by speaking very loud to them, which interrupts any other talk that might be going on. But they don't notice.'[108]

While house training had always been key to keeping pets inside, dog specialists now placed a new emphasis on training dogs to be compatible with domestic life. The historian Justyna Wlodarczyk shows that in the USA from the 1930s some dog trainers began to focus on 'obedience training' – training dogs never to bite and making it easier for them to live among humans.[109] In the UK Barbara Woodhouse advanced similar ideas in 1954 in her ground-breaking manual *Dog Training My Way*. The book's fresh approach focused on problem solving and suggested that animal misbehaviour was rooted in the failings of owners. In her first chapter, 'Every Owner a Trainer', Woodhouse outlined the ideal dog–human relationship, before detailing potential misdemeanours. There were many: dogs that constantly jumped on people and furniture; dogs that stole food, illicitly entering kitchens and snapping up the Sunday joint; dogs that refused to relinquish favourite chairs; dogs that settled in the marital beds of their owners and would not get out. According to Woodhouse, such domestic delinquency could be quelled with a firm hand, but she clearly considered such hands in short supply.[110]

While domestic routines and rituals had changed by the mid-twentieth century, the presence of animals was just as disruptive as it had always been. Many homes lost their Victorian clutter. Drawing rooms gave way to sitting rooms, kitchens and food preparation were no longer banished to the basement and daily routines were less rigidly organized and etiquette based. There is little evidence, though, that animals were less unruly. Prep school headmaster and cat devotee Percy Soderberg wrote thirteen books on cat, bird and fish keeping in the 1950s and '60s. In print, Soderberg took a firm line with felines: 'If a cat is kept in the house it should have its own particular bed and be restricted in its use of chairs and settees – no reason why all the furniture should be covered in hairs.'[111] In practice, Soderberg was a less than adequate feline disciplinarian. According to one former pupil, favourite cats ran amok at Soderberg's Caterham prep school, and could settle in the boys' beds. 'Pooey', a large blue Persian, was often found in the dorms.[112]

In *Cats on the Hearth* women were represented as the main carers for pets. Immaculately coiffed and manicured 1950s housewives were shown carefully feeding cats in modern kitchens, investing time and emotional labour in helping pets acclimatize to new homes ('make them feel like they are wanted') and gently chiding children who brushed pets overenthusiastically. The reality was more complex. During the Second World War many women stepped outside conventional gender roles to work in a variety of occupations. At the end of the war, government advocated a return to the previous status quo. However, labour shortages led to an increase in women's participation in the workplace and there was a steady rise in married women working outside the home. Although working-class married women had almost always been obliged to engage in paid work, this attracted much comment and was perceived as a significant social shift.

Some commentators believed that pet ownership would help fill newly empty homes with clatter and companionship. Harold Bridger and Stephanie White, sociologists who produced a report for the Tavistock Institute in the 1960s, argued that with the rise of women in part-time work, the demise of domestic service and more eating out, people spent less time with each other. Pets had the potential to help 'knit' fragmented families together and encourage them to reconnect with home.[113] But there were also concerns about what would happen to pets if people were less present to monitor and engage with them. Woodhouse's critique of failing dog owners was rooted in a perception of the post-war socio-economic world where working husbands and wives created 'absentee' dog ownership. Woodhouse did not mention working women specifically but when it came to explaining why dogs would not come when called, she suggested that some owners did not spend enough time with their animals: 'Many dog owners see their dogs for only a short period each day. They are too busy to do otherwise.' She did not believe that working couples should be 'denied the companionship of a dog when they come home in the evening' but that they should devote leisure time to their dogs.[114] The perception that dogs were increasingly adrift in the post-war working world was also invoked in 1950s discussions about new legislation for dog licences. Dogs were left alone and uncared for, probably chained, while owners of both sexes were away from home during the day or distracted by new technologies. In presenting a new motion for dog licensing in 1959, Lord Ailwynn declared: 'The owner of to-day has a motor car, and likes to take his wife and family for a drive in it. He has a television set and wants to sit with the family hour after hour with eyes glued on the screen. The dog, meanwhile, desperate with longing for human companionship, remains tied up.'[115]

The efforts of Doreen and Charles Tovey with their new kitten Sugieh exemplify some of the problems of trying to balance pet keeping with working life. Doreen and Charles both commuted to day jobs from their Somerset cottage, so the Siamese had to be left alone during the day. The antics of Sugieh and her offspring inspired Tovey to write her first book, *Cats in the Belfry*, published in 1957. Such was the comic potential of the cats, and the extent of the domestic devastation, that Tovey was able to keep the formula going for a further eleven animal-themed memoirs. Some months after the arrival of Sugieh's kittens, Tovey surveyed the battered state of the couple's living room.[116] A side lamp was permanently crooked. Three bureau ornaments – a glass jug, a Breton spinner and a Toby jug – had been smashed in quick succession. Stuffing leaked from clawed chairs. The spare room was permanently out of use as it now housed an earth box for the kittens. The cats completely disrupted the Toveys' world. But they had become essential to it too. In a changing world where men and women spent more time outside the home, animal presence became more difficult to manage. Yet for some owners this made pets more vital to the creation of domestic security and comfort.

In the decades that followed British homes became increasingly diverse, and – although challenged by tension and ongoing problems created by racial discrimination – Britain moved towards becoming a more multicultural society. Different kinds of religious ritual were important in many homes and pet animals could be incorporated into these worlds. In the 1970s Mrs Nenk, a Jewish mother, took over a pet shop in Golders Green. She quickly realized that there was a market for special pet foods that helped Orthodox Jews observe Passover, necessitating the removal of all 'chametz' or leavening from the home. After consultation with bird manufacturers Trill and her rabbi she established that budgies should be fed on plain canary seed and fish should have freeze-dried food during Passover. Rabbanic Judaism classed domestic dogs as impure and many Orthodox families would have chosen not to keep dogs indoors. But, Nenk observed, there were always exceptions – people who bent the rules for their pets. One local Orthodox couple, despite being religiously observant in other ways, kept 'a corgi they adore' at home: 'Obviously your religion is how you want it to be, isn't it?' she remarked.[117]

The new domestic order

If the seemingly anarchic domestic arrangements of George Sims and his pets provoked responses from bemusement to horror in readers at the turn of the twentieth century, free-range pets were much more the norm at the turn of the twenty-first. While toilet training and animals chewing the upholstery remain challenges for modern pet people, standards for domestic behaviour appear to have relaxed overall. New technologies help manage mud and pungent aromas and, as expectations that pets will share indoor (and even intimate) space increase, products that promote pet comfort and style in the interior have become ever more available. There has, however, been an increasing sense that owners are responsible for what their pets do beyond the home. The dangerous dog legislation of the nineteenth century was followed by a new emphasis in the twentieth on the responsibilities and failings of owners, which were increasingly guarded against through regulation. Flat owners were increasingly forbidden from keeping pets. And new legislation made dog licences mandatory in 1959. While dog licences were abolished in 1987, a new law in 1991 made it a criminal offence for an owner to allow a dog to be dangerously out of control in either a public place or a 'place where it is not permitted to be'.

The way people keep pets at home continues to be shaped by socio-economic circumstance. Since 2010 the numbers of rough sleepers and homeless people in the UK has risen exponentially. A sizeable percentage of these people have dogs. As the charity Dogs on the Streets notes, many of these dogs are vital in helping their humans overcome mental health challenges and people will refuse housing that is not dog friendly: 'the bond between these owners and the dogs is inextricable, one is nothing without the other. Their dog is their lifeline.'[118] From the 2000s the rising cost of housing made home ownership increasingly unaffordable for young people in Britain, which led to a big increase in renting. According to the Office of National Statistics, around a fifth of the UK population live in private rented accommodation in 2020 while 2021 saw the highest ever median rents in Britain (£730 per month); they are even higher in London, where renting outstrips other forms of property ownership.[119] For those who can't afford to buy their own homes, or who move into rented or sheltered accommodation later in life, the right to keep pets remains an ongoing battle. According to research carried out by the Dogs Trust in 2008, 78 per cent of pet owners in rental accommodation experienced difficulties finding a property that would allow them to keep pets, 47 per cent of landlords banned pets but gave no reason and 10 per cent of landlords forbade even goldfish.[120] The charity continues to campaign for changes in landlord practice, not least because the majority of dogs in its rehoming centres are there because of changes in the owner's circumstances – often a move into new accommodation prohibiting pets.[121]

Given the difficulties involved, why is it that pets remain so important to our idea and experience of home? When the animator Nick Park launched his *Creature Comforts* series and the first Wallace and Gromit film in 1989, he depicted animals with the capacity for canny manipulation and shrewd insight into human affection and anxiety for them. In Wallace and Gromit, domestic order in the Yorkshire suburban semi shared by man and dog is maintained (or restored) because of Gromit's astute management of his human and his perceptive interaction with other animals and their humans. Part of the humour rests on Wallace's misconception that, as the human in the relationship, he is in charge. Of course, Gromit and the viewers know that domestic harmony depends on the dog. But much of the humour relies on this (supposedly) skewed power dynamic, resonating with viewers who suspect not only that their pets have no regard for human social hierarchies and the niceties of domestic respectability, but that it's the pets that are running the show. Pets aren't just at home in the twenty-first century: for many humans, pets *are* home.

FOUR

We've Taken to You:
Pets in the Family

W hen Gwen Raverat, daughter of an academic household in late Victorian Cambridge, sat down to write the story of her family life, one dog played heavily on her mind: Sancho, an overweight brown water spaniel, with a 'wonderful power of putting people in the wrong. He would sit there staring at you; brown and fat and smelly; slobbering, and sometimes giving a heavy sigh; and however long a walk you had taken him, he made you feel that it ought to have been longer; and however many biscuits he had had, he made you feel that he ought to have had more.'[1] The family had many pets but Sancho was the one she remembered the most. 'We had at different times several more interesting dogs; but, just because I have a weak conscience, Sancho remains in my memory as the principal dog of my childhood.' Sancho is frequently portrayed as gloomy and disapproving, a looming 'Eeyore' presence in family life. Sancho eyed the family's activities askance: 'My mother had the first lady's tricycle in Cambridge. Our dog Sancho was horrified to think that anyone belonging to him should ride such an indecent thing.' He was also, apparently, mortified by the display made by a group of children taking to the Backs on bicycles, remarking, 'Of course they'll all be killed, and then they'll say it was my fault. How unjust people always are.' Writing the animal into the story, and giving Sancho a voice, provided Raverat with a useful moral counterweight, a means of expressing her family's identity and values in the late Victorian age, through the animal's disapproving commentary on their social travesties. But the way in which Raverat wrote the dog into the story also showed just how central pets were to family life.

This chapter focuses on stories people told about their families, and the role that animals played within them. Historians who have written about family life have seldom mentioned pets but memoirs, diaries and letters suggest that people often perceived them as integral to their family lives. Animals could alter the nature of family relationships. The family itself was in flux. From the late nineteenth century, family size fell as some middle-class professional couples began to limit pregnancies. As reproductive knowledge, contraceptive technologies and women's empowerment grew in the twentieth century, working-class family size also fell. By the mid-twentieth century the average family size had fallen to 2.4 children; people were living longer, and they were marrying earlier too. Having children earlier in the lifecycle and the introduction of universal pensions produced new forms of relationships and children were more likely to know their grandparents. The nature of human relationships, and perceptions of authority, were also changing as the First and then the Second World Wars challenged social norms and hierarchies and, in some cases, patriarchal authority within the family. While we can point to change in demographic norms, it's important to acknowledge that households remained diverse. There were notably larger numbers of single women after the Great War, for example. A further important differential was whether a family had animals. As this chapter shows, human–animal families were often very different to their purely human counterparts, as Sancho would no doubt have been keen to point out.

Pets at the Victorian family table

Frederick Cotman's painting *One of the Family* (1880) presents animals as members of the human family. It depicts a farming family at home as grandmother, mother and three cherubic children gather around a table for their noonday meal. Both furniture and food are substantial as adults and children share generous portions of pie. The man of the house has just returned from work but, confined to a dark corner, he is upstaged by a large horse, which, reaching over a half-open door, has joined the family for lunch. A dog presses its nose into the mother's lap in the hope of securing its own portion. Just outside the window, a dovecote is filled with birds. The idealization of family and rural life were common staples of Victorian painting. But it was the presence of animals, and their sentimental and comic potential, that was the main attraction here. The painting was hugely popular and part of a wider cultural trend in late

Frederick George Cotman, *One of the Family*, 1880, oil on canvas.

Victorian Britain in which novels, didactic literature, illustrations and paintings framed animals as part of family life. Meals were an important ritual for middle- and working-class families: it was the moment when fathers returned from work and the family came together to affirm their roles and status. The animal seeking to participate in family meals was not entirely fanciful (horses were known to knock on the door at family teatime to participate in a 'sugar butty')[2] and Cotman's painting, and its popularity, is a telling statement about their presence in family life.

Victorian family dinner tables were often crowded. At all social levels it was the norm to have large numbers of children: Queen Victoria had nine, the labourer poet John Clare had nine (two died) and Charles Dickens had eleven. The family historian and sociologist Leonore Davidoff explains that this led to a completely different kind of family life: houses were fuller, small children were present for a large portion of the adult lifecycle and children saw more of their siblings than their parents.[3] Animals could be a heady addition to the mix. The family home in West London where the author and publisher Leonard Woolf grew up in the 1880s is a case in point. The family had nine children and a large assortment of pets. These animals accompanied the family on their summer holiday:

> Every year in the last week of July or the first of August, the whole Woolf family went away for a summer holiday to the country. It was a large-scale exodus . . . When the day came, six, seven, eight and eventually nine children, servants, dogs,

cats, canaries and at one time two white rats in a birdcage, mountains of luggage were transported in an omnibus to the station and then in a reserved 'saloon' railway carriage to our destination.[4]

Families like this did not keep lone pets but many animals: one led to another. Twenty-first-century sociologists have noted that pet acquisition is often driven by demand from children.[5] In the Victorian era, having larger numbers of children probably encouraged more animal keeping as each child demanded a pet to call their own. Nor were multiple-pet families restricted to the well-to-do. The caretaker of an ironworks in 1890s Barrow-in-Furness was 'father' to four girls, three boys and a multitude of pets. Despite his relatively low (sometimes precarious) income, he was 'very fond' of birds, canaries, a monkey named Lena, squirrels, jackdaws, rabbits, ferrets and dogs.[6] Sidney Day, growing up near Highgate in the early twentieth century, describes the full range of chickens, dogs and birds that were packed into the family's small, terraced house alongside six brothers and sisters.[7]

The granting of the status of family member to pets in homes across the social scale can also be seen visually – in the growing number of family portraits produced by photography that included animals. In the late nineteenth century photography became cheaper and more accessible as technology improved. Even though longer exposure times made photographing animals difficult (some Victorians resorted to posing with stuffed pets in early photos), many families made the effort to include their pets. Animals are increasingly present in surviving photographs. In this portrait of a smartly dressed Edwardian young Black man, the sitter holds two dogs reassuringly (the photo appears on a postcard that describes him as 'Boots' and was posted in Clacton, where he may have been a worker in a local hotel).[8] Although we can't tell exactly what his relationship with the animals was, they clearly knew and trusted him enough to sit still for the photograph. The image is one of the rare visual depictions of human–animal relationships in pre-First World War Britain that include someone from a minority ethnic background. Another image of a working-class family outside their home during the First World War is also unidentified – but a fluffy cat is carefully held at the centre of the large family group. Pet photography expanded still further in the twentieth century, as more people owned cameras and often used them to capture their animal companions. For

Clacton-on-Sea, 1907, photograph.

the more affluent family, professional studio portraits of pets or humans and pets together provided artistic visual testimony to the status of animals in family life. In Liverpool, for instance, Margaret and Edward Chambré Hardman ran a thriving photography studio catering to the city's elite from the 1930s. Pet portraits (cats, dogs, rabbits, hamsters,

Real-photo postcard,
no identifying marks,
c. 1914.

birds and mice) represented a significant income stream and the couple
were sufficiently experienced in managing animal behaviour to have an
arsenal of props and bribes ready to pacify camera-shy pets.[9]

Despite the popularity of Cotman's painting, Victorian advice writers frowned on pets at table. *Cassell's Household Guide* (1869) urged that
dogs 'should be rigorously excluded at mealtimes'.[10] *Bennett's Everyday
Book* (1880) cautioned that parrots should on no account be allowed to
sit down to meals with children.[11] That such advice was deemed necessary implies that plenty of families valued their pets more than social
niceties, much as Thomas and Florence Hardy did in the previous chapter. And for all that wives valued scrubbed tables and pressed tablecloths,
their husbands often had different notions of mealtime propriety. An
1880s Oxfordshire chimney sweep wouldn't dream of sitting down to
lunch or supper without the children or his dog; a 1900s County Durham
tea dealer not only permitted his elderly Yorkshire terrier to sit at the
family tea table, but chewed food before passing it onto the toothless
dog too.[12] If this exasperated his wife, the children saw their father's

indulgence of pets at family mealtimes as testimony to his generosity of spirit. It wasn't just dogs, either. In the home of a South Wales carpenter, the family gathering at teatime included an elderly cat that snuggled on Dad's shoulder.[13] Even some advice writers wavered. Caroline Pridham wondered if it was not 'unkind' to exclude pets from this significant part of the family day.[14] If mealtimes were a key ritual in family life across the social scale, decisions to include or exclude pets were pivotal to the constitution of family relationships.

The inclusion of pets at these key moments could cause discord or, at least, expose the emotional hierarchies of family life. Horace Collins, an architect's son who grew up in a large home in Maida Vale in London, was very familiar with pets at the dinner table. There were eleven children in this late nineteenth-century household, nine boys and two girls.[15] In this busy and noisy family world, their father worked away from home during the day and was a remote figure. This was not helped by his special relationship with his dog. The animal was privileged at the family dinner table, leaving the children out in the cold. 'At meals a pet Pomeranian dog called Punch sat on a chair by the side of my father, who regaled it with special, tender morsels of food. Often he would say quite seriously to my mother, carving the joint: "Punch won't like that bit; give it to Frank or Horace."'[16] Collins's mid-twentieth-century account of his childhood poked fun at the Victorian age and its hierarchy and values. Telling the story about the dog allowed him to criticize his father, the formality of Victorian domestic life and what he had come to see as its hypocrisy. But it also shows the way that animals could intervene in the hierarchy of the family, subverting the assumed norms of father–child relations.

More traumatically, pets could provide teatime fodder, making family meals a source of antagonism. Grace Platt (later Foakes) and her siblings 'adored' the rabbits they kept. They were 'horrified' when Father killed one for food: 'none of us wanted to eat any.' Father killed one every few weeks after that and insisted his children eat the 'hateful meal'.[17] In this memoir, the transformation of pets into family food indicates her father's harsh pragmatism, a characteristic that Foakes grappled with throughout her writing, and that allowed her to demonstrate her father's lack of sympathy with his offspring. Ivy Port, the daughter of a builder who grew up in rural Surrey in the 1900s, tells us in her memoirs that there were firm rules on animal presence at table in her home. Mealtime rituals were an important part of family discipline. The family favoured cats and her father had a special relationship with one tom, Billy Boy, whom he would talk to while laying the fire in the kitchen each morning. But, 'there were two very hard and fast rules with all cats (a) all cats go out at night – should be out hunting (b) no cats to be fed with titbits from the table.' After her father's death, domestic discipline relaxed and animals (and, one suspects, the rest of the family) were allowed more latitude. Chickens also featured heavily in the life of the Port family and after her father's death they acquired a fine cock chick known as Pretty Dick: 'He really was a pet and strutted around anywhere and everywhere, indoors and outdoors spending quite long hours in the kitchen.' Unlike earlier pets, Dick shared the family repast and received 'titbits' from the table.[18]

A large family meal, especially one that involved pets, generated a significant amount of clearing up. In some families, such work fell to wives and daughters, but those with sufficient means employed servants. During the nineteenth century the middle class expanded, creating a demand for domestic service: in urban England in 1851, one in every five women aged between fifteen and thirty was listed as a domestic.[19] In Victorian and Edwardian homes boundaries were drawn between masters and servants. In a typical terraced house, servants slept in attics and worked in kitchen basements, and the home was organized around a rigid timetable that protected the privacy of the family. In the nineteenth century increasing distinctions were made between blood family and waged domestic servants.[20] Servants and animals could have positive relationships – the kitchen cat, cook's pet, asleep before the range was idealized in fiction and popular prints – but all too often the difficulties caused by unruly pets were a frustrating reminder of servants' subordinate status within the household. In one late Victorian Scottish household a maid was tasked with cleaning out the family parrot's cage each week. Knowing the maid was afraid of it, the bird would terrorize her, much to the amusement of human members of the household.[21] Jane Loudon's early pet-advice manual recalled her mother's servant who disliked cats and was aggressive towards a large black cat belonging to the family. The cat waited for its moment and attacked the servant when she was coming down the stairs with her hands full.[22] The middle-class Loudon's sympathies were clearly with the cat, but such mutual antipathy made the hard manual work of a servant more difficult.

When gentleman's daughter Beryl Lee Booker penned her memoir, she also drew on the supposedly comic potential of interactions between servants and pets. Her depiction of nursery days features a long-standing battle between her nanny and the family cat. The servant struggles to protect her personal china collection from the marauding animal. Readers, assumed to be middle class, are invited to enjoy the comedy inherent in the episode. The anecdote allowed Booker to assert her own cultural status by suggesting that the china collection is in dubious taste.[23] Booker's placing of the cat and servant on a similar level clearly displays her own prejudice: both were subordinate in this late Victorian household. But it's hard not to sympathize with the hard-pressed servant here, devoting her life to the care of privileged children for a paltry wage, deriving pleasure from her knickknacks and all the while being forced to contend with a destructive cat. Worse, servants could be blamed for death or injury to pets. When the maid accidentally stood on six-year-old Stevy Bowditch's kitten in a middle-class home in Lewisham in the late 1850s, his father remarked that for days afterwards, the distraught boy told everyone he encountered that the maid had killed his 'poor kitty' and he simply couldn't love her anymore.[24] While the father may have viewed this forthright verdict as humorous, it seems likely that the maid was mortified and anxious about her job.

Animal moralities

As Gwen Raverat's memoir indicated, pets had an important moral function within the Victorian family, particularly where children were concerned. Some animals, notably Newfoundlands, St Bernards and collies, were considered to have intrinsic breed qualities of loyalty, trustworthiness and devotion. The popular late Victorian and Edwardian artist Arthur John Elsley, renowned for his pictures of children and dogs, frequently depicted large canines acting as patient moral guardians to exuberant and mischievous children, teaching them to handle puppies with care, watching over their play or keeping them safe from danger. Provided animals weren't displaced by babies (some parents feared that petted dogs and cats would be jealous), Victorian art, advice literature and fiction also represented children caring for pets as a means of practising virtue and acquiring moral competency. When large breeds weren't acting as nanny to petted children, Elsley liked to paint human infants playing at being grown up, feeding or bathing the puppies or small terriers who stood in as their (unlucky) charges.

In more prescriptive depictions, training children to keep pets was a means of teaching them to become good Christians invested in notions of religion as a salve to discord and conflict. In Olive Patch's storybook *Familiar Friends* (1880) multiple species co-exist peacefully under the calming influence of the morally perfect little girl Linda Harcourt: 'That is her nursery, and as you see, she is lying by old Theo, the Newfoundland, whilst she feeds her pet Bunny. The tortoise-shell Tom is sitting quietly by, although the birds are flying all about the room as if no cat were near.'[25] Juliana Horatia Ewing's *Papa Poodle and Other Pets* (1884), published by the Society for the Promotion of Christian Knowledge, began with Papa Poodle taking 'care of me when I was a baby' but the roles were soon reversed with the shaggy dog 'in disgrace' for prioritizing his food over learning to spell. In 'Little Master to His Big Dog', a pious infant teaches his Newfoundland to 'learn manners' and 'dine like a gentleman sitting at table'.[26]

Advice books from the 1860s were explicit that pet keeping was a means of learning responsibility, acquiring emotional knowledge and demonstrating Christian virtue. Beeton's *Book of Home Pets* (1861) states:

Let parents try to inspire their children – the best of all 'Home Pets' – with a fondness for natural science; whether it be

'Linda's pet', illustration in Olive Patch, *Familiar Friends* (1880).

encouraged by keeping and caring for a dog, a cat, a rabbit, a pigeon, or a song-bird; by rearing flowers; by forming an herbarium, or a collection of moths and butterflies, or by other kindred means, and they will surely be better boys and girls, and make better men and women, better members of society, and above all better Christians.[27]

Pets were particularly valuable because their care required commitment, consistency and kindness. Silkworms, for instance, were highly desirable pets for both boys and girls because 'the most thoughtful and tender care is requisite in everything connected with their treatment and management.'[28] Small animals, such as rabbits, guinea pigs and mice, were seen as particularly suitable for children as they required daily care and commitment – building responsibility, an understanding of hygiene and the capacity to care for other living creatures.

The potential of animal care to teach children domestic responsibility may well have been on the minds of the Port parents when they allowed Ivy and Dorcas to keep pet rabbits in 1906. 'When I was about eight or nine years old my sister and I expressed a wish to keep rabbits. Dorcas had a grey one and mine was black. Father knocked up a nice hutch and everyone was happy, but as usual we were told that we had to get food (hogweed and cold parsley) for them every evening *or else!!* But after a while the pleasure of rabbit keeping began to pall. Hutch cleaning was particularly tiresome, taking up the whole of Saturday morning and involving the tricky transportation of the rabbits (by their ears) to an enclosure in a nearby field. 'Like with most children this was becoming a chore and we were constantly having to be reminded "Don't forget the rabbit's food."' This incremental lack of enthusiasm was clearly noted, as one day the girls returned to the hutch to find it empty. 'Evidently father had noticed the inertia and decided THE TIME HAD COME.' The children were 'not frightfully upset about this but wanted to know where they had gone. The reply was "Never you mind, you didn't want to look after them did you?" The very next day we had a large rabbit pie for lunch and no doubt Mopsy and Smut were in it. I had a sneaky feeling at the time but no questions were asked.'[29] As moral lessons go, this was particularly harsh.

Other children were less forgiving when parents' intended moral lessons backfired. Growing up in Edwardian London, Dorothy Scannell recalled a Christmas dinner when she and her siblings realized they were

'Saturday afternoon', illustration in Caroline Pridham, *Domestic Pets* (1895).

being served their pet rabbit: 'Father had murdered it and none of us would eat it . . . a pet, a friend.' Father's point, it seemed, was to teach children a lesson; he wanted them to understand what it was like to starve. For Scannell, this lesson might have been acceptable had the family been facing hard times but things weren't especially bad. In retrospect, Scannell suspected her father knew he'd made a grave mistake and his foul-tempered response to her siblings' distress sprang from his 'guilty conscience'.[30]

Ideally, then, pets encouraged children to cultivate notions of domestic responsibility and internalize social hierarchies; caring for pets replicated models of parenthood and moral guidance. The artist Charles Burton Barber specialized in painting human–animal domestic scenes and was one of Queen Victoria's favourite painters; he painted human and animal members of the royal family (and Victoria's ghillie John Brown) on multiple occasions. His gift for depicting emotive expressions and the moral conflicts of children's everyday lives made his art popular and many of his paintings were appropriated for advertising commercial goods, notably Pears Soap. In *Time to Wake Up* (1883), Barber showed a pet terrier standing on the covers of a little girl's bed, instructing her to get up. If here the little dog performed the role of mother or nanny to a sleepy truculent child, elsewhere Barber reversed the roles. One of his best-known paintings, *Suspense* (1894), depicts a little girl in bed with a breakfast of boiled egg and toast. As she dutifully clasps her hands to say grace, her pet terrier and kitten are at her side, focused entirely on the breakfast. It is the little girl's careful omission to close her eyes in prayer that lends the painting its title and mischief: we know as much as she does that these opportunistic pets are just waiting for the moment when they can dive into the repast. Here, the little girl acts as watchful moral authority over more prosaic animal appetites, although part of the painting's charm is the viewer's suspicion that any moral order here is precarious.

While advice manuals often portrayed an idealistic image of children caring for pets, others acknowledged that children and animals could form alliances to subvert the hierarchy and orthodoxies of the Victorian family. Again, Charles Burton Barber perfectly captured the loyalty between children and their pets in the face of adult-inflicted injustices. Different versions of *In Disgrace* (1886) show a little girl in the corner of a bourgeois family room, clearly having been reprimanded for some misdeed. The pet terrier leaning into the little girl's legs, sharing her

'"Ratto's" Dessert', illustration in Caroline Pridham, *Domestic Pets* (1895).

shame, amplifies the pathos. *A Special Pleader* (1893) offered a variation on this theme. The same little girl is back in the corner of the room, petulantly turned to the wall and clearly in disgrace again. Here, a tri-colour collie dog is positioned before her, depicted as her loyal defender.

The popularity of Barber's bourgeois childhood fantasies suggests how far his images resonated with popular perceptions of the ties that bound children to pets. Probably, his pictures prompted adults to remember the subversive childhood allegiances they enjoyed with animals. Grace Platt recalled trying to entice the family cat into bed on winter nights. This was for warmth but also the thrill of breaking rules: knowing her hygiene-obsessed mother would be furious, Grace lured the cat into her bedroom on a nightly basis. Allies in subterfuge, cat and child snuggled under the covers: the cat would purr with Grace 'stroking and loving her until we both fell asleep'.[31] In contrast, another little girl growing up in early 1900s Durham could recall her dog sitting patiently for bedtime prayers before she and the dog climbed the stairs to bed with mother's blessing.[32] This story of topsy-turvy hygiene and hierarchy, where it was more common for dogs to be confined to back yards or kitchens, demonstrated that this was a loving family where animals were treated as playmates and companions.

In some cases, subterfuge was more explicit and animals might be used to challenge the authority of the adult world. Percy M. Clark grew up in a large family in Cambridge in the 1870s and '80s and kept rabbits in the loft of his family home. At one point, he had twenty white rats in his bedroom.[33] There was also a tortoise, which, doubtless rather unwillingly, participated in domestic tricks played by Clark and his brothers – at one point the animal was placed in the bed of a visiting clergyman.[34] Here the presence of animals contributed to the creation of an alternative childhood world that deliberately subverted adult rules. Elsewhere, children delighted in animal naughtiness. In the terraced home of a sailor at the turn of the twentieth century, the family parrot afforded the children 'an enormous amount of amusement'. One of the bird's tricks was to steal Granny's thimble when she was sewing and refuse (shouting 'Oh no') to bring it back, much to the older woman's annoyance. What made this disobedience so funny was that the parrot got away with behaviour that the children would never dare attempt. It would also call abuse to drunken men passing in the street. The parrot, described as 'ugly as sin', was a Mr Punch character in household life, providing endless entertainment with his blatant disregard for the authority of adults.[35]

Charles Burton Barber, *A Special Pleader*, 1893, oil on canvas.

For other children, pet animals provided the straightforward loyalty so often found wanting in human relationships. In one early twentieth-century home on the rural outskirts of Bolton, sheepdog Gyp grew up alongside the family children. The patient animal permitted the small children to ride on his back. But he especially 'worshipped' the eldest daughter, escorting her everywhere and waiting in the church porch whenever she went to sing with the choir. He was a model of faithful devotion and embodied all the qualities the children thought 'gentle-manly'.[36] Pets could compensate too for children's disappointments in adults and help build relationships. Oliver Lodge, son of a businessman in the City of London and later an eminent scientist, grew up at a distance from his father but was closer to his mother, who engaged keenly with his boyhood interests. 'Whatever she took up she went into thoroughly. At one time I kept rabbits, and she had a many storied shed and enclosures built for them.'[37] For children, then, the presence of pets was an important part of their emotional worlds but also a way of measuring the adults in their lives. Parents who indulged children's pets clearly earned claims to affection; others, it seems, fell woefully short.

The ability to keep pets was dependent on family stability: keeping animals was difficult in families with little security or who moved on a regular basis. Stanley Lupino, an actor's son, had an unconventional late Victorian and Edwardian childhood as the family travelled in London and elsewhere. For Lupino the potential acquisition of a pet represented a much-longed-for emotional stability. He recalls with pain an incident in which he fought with another boy for possession of a dog, his rival delivering the wounding blow that Lupino was unable to provide a good home for it.[38] For some Victorian children animal presence could help illuminate some of the problems inherent in family life. Grace Platt's family always had a cat but her father drowned its kittens in the kitchen copper each time it gave birth. When the cat had 'grown old and dirty in its habits', father decided he should drown that too. But when the old cat put up a fight and twice escaped, Grace and her mother managed to cajole father into letting it live.[39] Gruesome in its own right, the story nevertheless enables Grace to tell us more about the dynamics in her family. Feline members were clearly at the bottom of her father's pecking order but Grace's emphasis on her mother's sympathy for the geriatric cat establishes her as the *feeling* centre of family life. In contrast, her father was unable to demonstrate emotion although, as in this case, she suspected that he wasn't entirely without empathy; it just had to be dragged out of him.

Three's a crowd?

While pets could be crucial to the experience of growing up, animal presence was also an important facet of married life for some men and women. This wasn't always harmonious, particularly in families where space, food and tempers were stretched. However much a working man might love to return home to 'forty winks' and the demonstrable affections of his loving monkey, his wife – whose domestic labour was significantly increased by the presence of large, hairy pets in the house – was just as likely to 'detest' the poor animal.[40] In Bolton in the late 1890s a sailor bought his sweetheart a parrot as a gift. The pleasure taken in this colourful (in feather and language) companion palled with marriage and children. When the family moved to a new house, the harried woman insisted there was no space for the parrot and told it to 'kick the bucket'. When the parrot duly keeled over and died, there was a 'real family row about it', with the once romantic sailor convinced his wife had poisoned the bird or, at the least, 'broken its heart'. The learned opinion was that it had died of a fatty liver but, even so, the pathetic scene left each spouse in no doubt that the wife's priorities had shifted over time.[41]

Typically, working-class women were ambivalent towards animals in domestic space on account of the additional labour they created. It is notable that most pets in labouring homes belonged to husbands and children. One little girl in late Victorian Nottingham cried bitterly when her harassed mother refused the gift of a terrier puppy. But when her father, a handloom knitter, asked what all the tears and shouting were about, he cajoled his wife into capitulation. The little girl's feet 'never touched the ground' as she raced to collect the puppy before anyone changed their mind. The outcome was inevitable. Mother ended up doing most of the labour but grew to love the dog. Father, enjoying his leisure with the dog sleeping on his lap, loved him 'more than anybody'.[42] Elsewhere, a husband bringing home a wild baby rabbit met hostility from his wife: as she pointed out, she already had ten 'babies' of her own. In the face of collective pleading from children and spouse, she gave way: the rabbit was fed with a doll's bottle and trained to defecate in the privy.[43]

Apocryphal stories abound of working men fonder of pets than wives or children. For one middle-class commentator, the costermonger who kicked his wife while fondling a pet rat to his bosom was expressing his disillusionment in marriage.[44] In a few cases, animals really were privileged over human family members. One stationmaster drank himself out of a job but, as a 'great lover of animals', managed to feed his cats, dogs and hens. His young, widowed daughter and grandson, with whom he lived, had to fend for themselves.[45] In one poor family in 1900, a mother remarked that 'many a time [we] 'ad ter send the children ter bed wi' empty stomachs but Benny [her husband's pet fox] 'as allus 'ad 'is bellyful'. Notably, the fox pre-dated the wife and was like her husband's 'twin', although she could 'not abear the sight of the animal' and insisted after marriage that Benny be caged.[46] One can only imagine how Benny felt about the wife. Elsewhere, a notorious criminal faced a long jail sentence. He requested his wife bring their son and pet owl to court before he got sent down but advised that if she couldn't manage both, to prioritize the bird.[47] While some men (and probably some women too) undoubtedly did care more for their pets than human relations, such stories were often related by earnest social workers apt to take literally the hyperbole and joshing of their interlocutors. As one working man waggishly noted in 1865, it was easy to fall out with relatives but canine affection held fast. As a youth, he had often received 'hard words and harsher treatment' from his 'inexcusable parents' who objected to his preference for howling mongrels over 'sleepless relations'.[48]

Even so, pets could make awkward third parties in marriages, whatever social class their humans belonged to. When Leonard and Virginia Woolf acquired their pedigree cocker spaniel, Sally, in 1935, the plan was that she should make up for her high price by producing pedigree offspring.[49] Great efforts were made to mate Sally (she was 'married' to a fellow cocker from the stud at Ickenham in April 1937).[50] A few months later, Leonard hopefully prepared a lying in bed for her in his study at Monks House.[51] But to no avail: Sally remained stubbornly barren that year and with subsequent attempts at mating. For Virginia at least, the reason for this was clear: 'Our bitch [Sally], mated for the 2nd time 5 weeks ago, again shows no signs of childbirth, like Princess Juliana; and its laid to L's charge. Love for him they say, has turned her barren.'[52] Virginia did not say if the adoration cut both ways but does appear to have viewed it rather archly.

Animals could build, or at least bridge, relationships too. Adopting the voice of a much-loved pet in correspondence enabled writers to be playful and affectionate, and to cement bonds. The Reverend Patrick Brontë acted as amanuensis for 'Old Flossy', a spaniel, when writing to his daughter Charlotte in 1853, a tactic that celebrated her fondness for the dog while allowing Patrick to undermine common acquaintances in a way that would have been unseemly for the respectable clergyman he was.[53] Sometimes, the pet avatar enabled relations – particularly couples – to navigate their interpersonal dynamics. Jane and Thomas Carlyle's marriage could be strained. Jane's dog Nero was a helpful go-between, 'writing' to Thomas with dog (and cat) news when Jane was 'out of the way of writing to you she says' and receiving missives from his mistress (to be read aloud by Thomas) when she was away.[54]

Sometimes, shared love for a pet was what made a relationship bearable. The novelist and poet Thomas Hardy and his first wife, Emma, married in 1874 and lived in Dorset before permanently settling into their house, Max Gate, which Hardy built on the edge of Dorchester. The early years of their marriage were happy, but Hardy's biographers agree that later years were fraught. Emma became increasingly religious, while Hardy's faith was on the wane. There were no children, a matter of regret for Hardy. Divorce and separation were still rare in this period and, like many others, the couple tried to find the best way of living with an unhappy marriage. From 1899 Emma removed herself from the marital bedroom to sleep in the attics, where she had a small private suite of rooms. Hardy, meanwhile, had no qualms about publicly pronouncing the failure of marriage as an institution, in both novels and letters.[55] Yet the couple continued to share some interests, notably a passionate concern for animal wellbeing.[56] Both were devastated when one of their pets, 'a fine and dear cat', suffered a horrible death on the railway line outside the house in 1901: 'Tom used to carry it to the stable every night, as a rule, & just left it out once to enjoy a fine moonlight when lo! He's gone. (Chopin's funeral March!)'.[57] But worse was to follow. In 1903 Snowdove, a beautiful and much prized white cat, was sliced in half on the railway line. Emma wrote, 'You would scarcely perhaps, imagine what a gloom this event has cast upon us – but he was a personality and worthy of lamentation.'[58] Hardy, meanwhile, carved a special stone for Snowdove, which stood in the little pet cemetery at the edge of the Max Gate garden.[59] A year later, the little white cat was still on his mind when he wrote his famous poem 'Last Words to a Dumb Friend': 'pet was never mourned as you, purrer of a spotless hue'.[60]

Melancholic reflections on the passing of cats proved a rich poetic vein for Hardy, and in 1910 he was at work on another poem, 'The Roman Gravemounds', featuring an archaeologist wandering around a graveyard in the evening, surrounded by the remains of the past but completely preoccupied with the burial of a small white cat, 'My little white cat was my only friend.'[61] The poem was criticized by Thomas's secretary, Florence Dugdale, who came upon him writing it in his study. 'That was too much even for my sweet temper, & I ramped around the study exclaiming: "This *is* hideous ingratitude." But the culprit seemed delighted with himself, & said, smilingly, that he was not exactly writing about himself but about some imaginary man in a similar situation.'[62] The secretary, 39 years Hardy's junior, married the poet after Emma's death in 1912. At this point another important player appeared on the scene: a small wire-haired terrier, Wessex, arrived at Max Gate in 1913 in the interim between Emma's death and Florence's installation.

The acquisition of the dog came before the wedding and was an important subject in the letters Hardy wrote to Florence before they married: 'Wessie goes up into the attics to look for you, but secretly believes you are inside your bedroom, the door of which is kept shut.'[63] Hardy's own desires intertwined with the dog's longing: 'missing you, however, every minute', he writes in the same letter. Regardless of such romantic idealism, Wessex (whom we first met when he gate-crashed social gatherings of the great and good in Chapter Three) had his own powerful personality. 'Noisy and boisterous', said Florence, in a letter of 1917.[64] The small animal was frequently combative, biting visitors and postmen, and causing difficulties for servants. According to Florence: 'He is really a good dog – but all of his kind are fighters – more or less.'[65] Although Wessex was often referred to as Florence's dog, Hardy doted on the animal, apparently kissing him each night before he was carried off to bed. Sometimes, indulgence went too far for Florence: 'We had a very quiet Christmas, we two, alone, with Wessie – our only diversion being that T.H. *would* give Wessie goose and plum pudding, & the result was what might have been expected – & he (T.H.) didn't even clean up the result, as he ought.'[66] Hardy, meanwhile, revelled in the animal's disruption of the domestic hierarchy. In 1922 he writes: 'Our Wessex is as ill-behaved as ever, and acts as if he were quite the Master of the house, which indeed he is.'[67]

Both Florence and Thomas were devastated by the dog's death in 1926. Hardy died the following year. Florence writes: 'Of course he was merely a dog, & not a good dog always, but *thousands* (actually thousands) of afternoons and evenings I would have been alone but for him, & I always had him to speak to. But I mustn't write about him, & I hope no one will ask me about him or mention his name.'[68] For all Hardy's devotion to Florence, marriage to a man of literature was in many respects isolated. Alone while Thomas worked on his manuscripts and left to deal with callers and the voluminous 'fan' correspondence, Florence found that the turbulent and boisterous Wessex smoothed the way, making the marriage a little easier.

While the Hardy human–animal family was coming to an end, another literary home was being set up in London by the publisher and writer Michael Joseph and his second wife, Edna Frost, who married in 1926. Historians have argued that marriage after the First World War began to take a new form: war dealt a blow to (some of) the privileges of patriarchal authority and there was greater emphasis on companionship and equality in marriage.[69] Couples had to negotiate to find a balance, and animals were often an important part of these negotiations. This was certainly the case in the Joseph household. When cat-loving Joseph married Edna, she was already attached to her wire-haired terrier Peter. He writes: 'there were times when that dog made me feel as a second husband must feel when his wife describes the virtues of his predecessor.'[70] Edna, for her part, was confronted by a small colony of cats presided over by regal matriarch tabby Minna Minna Mowbray. Peter's arrival saw a battle for dominance that played out through competition for Peter's basket, which Minna quickly claimed for her own. 'The basket war', as Joseph put it, divided the household into two factions: 'the pro-Peterites, led by my wife, and the pro-Minnaites, which was me'.[71] The animals continued to fight over the bed for the next two years, but fortunately the couple adjusted to marital life more quickly – Michael growing more used to the dog, and Edna tolerating the cats. There were still difficult moments, especially when Michael later acquired his favourite Siamese cat, Charles. Edna was particularly annoyed by his encouragement of the animal to sit by his side at the dinner table: 'to this day my wife had not forgiven me'.[72]

For the most part, Joseph's 'cat' books present a modern marriage and family based on human and animal compromise and companionship, consisting of cats, dogs, birds, two rather aggressive rabbits and a small daughter, Shirley.[73] Joseph presents himself as a devoted father: Shirley features heavily, and he makes much of her preference for cats and excitement at the arrival of a new 'tikken'.[74] Joseph's relationship with the Siamese Charles is explored in depth and he used it to present himself as a 'modern man', enjoying what he believed was the peculiarly modern sound of the Siamese miaow, and emphasizing Charles's outsider status ('the little foreigner').[75] But the Joseph family had a side that was not acknowledged in the cat memoirs. The books made no mention of his first wife, the actress Hermione Gingold, or his two sons

'My desk was part of his domain', photograph in Michael Joseph, *Charles: The Story of a Friendship* (1943).

from the marriage, who co-existed uneasily alongside his new household. According to Richard Joseph (Michael's son, born in 1940, and his biographer), the human–animal world of the first marriage had been darker. Both husband and wife were cat enthusiasts, but the marriage failed, in part because of a disagreement over how Hermione's kitten should be trained. Joseph, the self-professed cat lover, had apparently disciplined the animal by rubbing its nose in pepper.[76] The sons, meanwhile, were treated with disdain and eventually ejected from the house. Writing about cats allowed Joseph to tell a light-hearted family story designed for a commercial audience, while ignoring the traumas that lay underneath.

Acquiring an animal in the early days of marriage, and working out how to look after it, could set up marital and family dynamics for decades to come. This was clearly the case for wealthy newlyweds Alan and Morag Withington as they settled down to married life with their new cairn puppy in the early 1930s. Almost as soon as the little dog arrived it became the subject of marital wrangling. Alan was unsure about the animal from the start, but his misgivings were overridden by Morag, who was smitten with the dog. By the interwar period, an affluent husband like Alan could no longer speak with quite the authority of the Victorian patriarch. In this marriage at least, Alan's strong sense of masculine superiority – informed by a public-school education, working role and gender stereotypes of the age – did not completely hold sway. Morag and Alan appear to have been feeling their way towards a 'companionate marriage' in which compromise was the order of the day. The naming of the cairn is a case in point. Alan hoped to give the animal the androgynous, anonymous moniker 'Smith' (it is not clear why). However, references in his diary to Smith were quickly replaced by 'Sally as I suppose I'll have to call her'.[77]

Although Morag won over the name, the couple continued to bicker over dog training. Alan was very much in favour of taking a firm hand, with the odd slap on the rump to mitigate bad behaviour. But, he notes: 'Morag thinks I'm a bit savage with her, & of course it's no use at all being firm at the weekends if she's allowed to develop annoying habits the rest of the time.'[78] Alan established a link here with children and evidently envisaged the dog as a sort of dry run for later parental practices (Morag was pregnant when he wrote this): 'a dog's just like a child, & will go on doing what *it* wants until you make it quite clear that it's not going to be allowed to.'[79] Later in family life, Alan embraced the role of authoritarian father, insisting that the boys be sent away to boarding school and evacuated to America during the Second World War.

Pets are usually evoked in a light-hearted manner in family narratives, often supplying comedy and sometimes pathos, but they could be part of darker, more dysfunctional family lives too. In Victorian homes, dogs were renowned for their fierce loyalty. Lucky was the wife whose faithful dog could keep a drunken spouse out of the house at night or intervene when men turned violent. Unfortunately, dogs that readily bared their teeth against nasty husbands tended to be dispatched to other households.[80] Likewise, in marriages that were already fractious, pets could get caught in the crossfire, with one spouse's rage being taken out on the other spouse's pet as 'revenge'.[81]

An unusually frank exploration of a difficult marriage is in the wartime diaries of Ruth Rose, a married mother of two and nurse from Leeds, begun as part of the Mass-Observation project in 1941. Although her obligations as a mother and nurse meant her entries were sporadic, her candid writings allow us to see her family life across the course of the war. Her life was dominated by a difficult marriage to an abusive and controlling husband. During the war years he was posted away from home, bringing interludes of peace interspersed with his much-dreaded leave. While relationships between spouses in the twentieth century were, in many ways, more companionate, they also remained profoundly unequal. Marital rape was not legally recognized in Britain until the 1990s, although Ruth used this term to characterize her sexual relationship with Bob, her husband: 'When a marriage boils down to duty & rights – it is time it was packed up.'[82]

By 1944 Ruth had acquired a dog, Paddy, who frequently romped with the children. Bob, however, resented the animal. When he hit Paddy in November that year, Ruth wrote that she 'won't stand for it'.[83] December saw further rows about Paddy, who cowered away from Bob when he came near: 'he must hate him as much as I do.'[84] The tensions between husband and wife crystallized in their discussions of the dog. The animal played out their relationship problems through its behaviour. Later that month, Paddy disappeared. Ruth at first suspected Bob, but it transpired the dog had run away. In a bid to prevent further violence against it, Ruth told Bob she had given the dog away because of his treatment of it, but that it returned of its own accord. It is not clear how successful this strategy was. When Paddy got distemper, Bob was insistent that the animal should be euthanized, to the distress of Ruth and her daughters. Ignoring the girls' attachment to the animal, the controlling husband chose to view Ruth's plea for the dog as evidence of her failure as a mother. 'Girls very distressed! Sent them to bed out of the way, appealed to B to keep dog. Went absolutely raving mad! Called me everything one could think of, ending with "You f-ing c-nt, you think more of the dog than the kids."'[85] Bob then became ill, and was unable to do anything further for several days while the dog presumably recovered. Ruth's war diary ends in 1944 and it is not clear how long the marriage continued after that. Certainly, she longed to end it. Paddy, the focus for much of Bob's antagonism, was a source of comfort in a bleak existence.

Me, my pets and I

In the 1950s, psychologists and social scientists began to argue that pets were a powerful and dynamic force in family life. The Tavistock Institute of Human Relations, a research organization devoted to the application of social science founded in 1947, produced a spate of reports on pets in the late 1950s and early '60s. Bridger and White's 'Forces Underlying the Keeping of Pets' survey (1964) developed a complex approach to the social role of the pet. According to them, pets' role in the family was of paramount importance. These studies were part of the burgeoning field of child psychology and responded to John Bowlby's work on child attachment that revolutionized how childhood was understood after the Second World War.[86] They were also a product of the growing pet economy: pet-food manufacturers funded some of the Tavistock Institute's work. According to the social scientists, certain kinds of people were more in need of pet companionship than others. Gendered assumptions about motherhood played into these ideas, for example, and it was routinely assumed that childless women would seek pets as substitute children. 'It is probable that, in certain life phases, and in certain kinds of social connectedness some aspects of "pet need" are paramount e.g. the childless woman and the pet as a substitute child.' People who lived alone were also thought to be in need of the 'company of pets'.[87]

These ideas were informed as much by social prejudice as evidence-based research. Social surveys from the 1950s, although limited in scope, suggested that families with children acquired pets more often than single or child-free people.[88] But the idea that singletons, especially women, had a special relationship with animals was long-standing even if it had not always been viewed positively. An article in *Tait's Edinburgh Magazine* in 1856 claimed that 'spinsters of a certain age – a conventional phrase for thirty years and upwards – and married ladies without encumbrances [children]' spent immoral amounts of money (over £2.5 million annually) on 'very useless' lapdogs and (aristocratic) cats when they could be investing their time, affection and wealth in worthy human causes.[89] Evidently, *Tait's* considered animals far from worthy recipients of such lavish economic attention. But if the relationship between single people and their animals had long been stereotyped, how did individuals really feel about them?

After the huge loss of life in the First World War, there were more women than men, lowering the chances of women getting married and starting a family. Single women, or spinsters, were a source of social anxiety. But this was also a time when women were entering a greater range of working roles. One such single woman was Florence Turtle, in her early twenties at the end of the war. Born and bred in suburban London, she lived with her parents in Putney above her mother's fur shop. Florence was successful: starting out working at her local library, she then moved to W. H. Smith. By the 1930s she was book buyer for John Barker's department store in South Kensington. She was also an animal lover and found time to keep a detailed diary, spanning the years from 1917 until her death in 1981. Florence was much attached to the family's two dogs, Brunnie and Coney. She wrote about them with great affection, more than she granted to her human relations. She criticized her mother frequently, feeling that she failed to manage the family home.[90] Her frustration boiled over when Brunnie fell pregnant: 'I am so furious about it as I am sure it is entirely due to carelessness. With mother and the girl there is absolutely no excuse.'[91] The family got on top of each other in the flat and Florence was soon laying plans to move out. 'Everybody desperately fed up including myself my wretched family when shall I be quit of them!'[92] Aged 34, she finally managed it, moving to a flat in Fulham with her sister Barbara. Weekly visits to the family home continued, and her diaries make clear that the dogs were the best thing about this: 'the dogs as pleased to see us as ever'.[93] Working and living arrangements prevented her from having a pet of her own at this time, but she took continual joy in the pets of family and friends.

It was a huge blow, then, when Brunnie died in 1936. Florence was devastated. She writes:

I have been reflecting that this has been a tragic year and that five people whom I have known including poor Miss Cretchley and George the Fifth have died – some of these deaths have grieved me very much but none have affected me with the sense of personal tragedy and deep loss as that of darling Brunnie or Toddie-Tan-Toes or any of the other silly names I used to call her – misplaced maternal instinct or frustrated sex your Freudian cynics would say – but I don't think so, after all I have only seen her once a week for the last six years.[94]

Florence was trying to make sense of how the death of a favourite animal affected her more than human deaths she witnessed that year. By the 1930s ideas about psychoanalysis and psychiatry had become embedded in British popular culture: people wrote of consciousness, repression and projection and increasingly used these ideas to explain family life and relationships.[95] Strong emotions were linked to human family relationships and women's behaviour in particular was often judged in terms of sexual repression or the desire to mother. Florence wrestled with these social norms. As a single woman, society expected her to feel deep love for an animal as a projection of something else. But, ultimately, she rejected the 'cynicism' of these ideas: her love for Brunnie, her favourite dog, was not a substitute for marriage, sex or children – it was a relationship in its own right.

The choice to remain single or live alone was not always about a lack of available men. Those who lived alone might value their independence. Jean Pratt, single woman and cat enthusiast, lived in Wee Cottage three miles from Beaconsfield in the 1940s. As part of the Mass-Observation project, Pratt kept a detailed diary of her everyday life. We know from this, and the enormous personal private diary she kept from her late teens, that she was often in love and felt the full force of society's expectation that she should get married. But it was not just a case of the right man never turning up. Living alone in the cottage – a life that Pratt relished – was partly her choice: 'But why am I here instead of married with a family, or a successful career woman? That's too long a story but has something to do with the character I inherited from my mother along with her money.'[96] Jean's cats loom large in her diaries. During the ten-year span of Mass-Observation writing, her primary cat, Dinah, produced over forty kittens. Most of these were given away but a fair number were kept and provided lively activity within the cottage. The early years were marked by a war between the dominant Dinah and her daughter, known as the Kittyhawk. In later years more kittens arrived. The year 1946 alone saw the addition of Pot, Kettle, Twinkle, Podge, Pudge, Smudge and Mackie. Pratt was aware that in living by herself in a cottage with numerous cats she fulfilled a certain stereotype. But she relished her independence and enjoyed playing with the idea of herself as a disreputable old woman:

> In certain circumstances I can see myself becoming the most repellent old woman. Having long ceased to bother about public opinion. I shall never clean my nails or bother about scratches, rough skin, torn clothes or mud stains. My cough by then will be a horribly juicy one ... Cats will be everywhere, hundreds of them, all rather thin and mangy and I shall forget to feed them.[97]

Jean spent a lot of time on her cats. When Dinah and Twinkle became ill in 1947 she nursed them with great devotion. Dinah was particularly demanding, and according to Jean was 'almost as much trouble as a child'.[98] There is no question that she was deeply devoted to them. But they weren't the same as a human family. Jean enjoyed casting the cats in family roles but derived pleasure from their independence and distinctly feline rejection of human expectations for familial behaviour. The failed (in human terms) mother–daughter relationship of Dinah and the Kittyhawk, for example, was an ongoing source of amusement:

> The Kittyhawk is Dinah's daughter (one of them) of whom Dinah is quite unreasonably jealous. She is so spiteful to the Kittyhawk I am moved to rename her Spitfire. Out of doors the Kittyhawk holds her own ... Dinah of course Owns the cottage. She rules with an iron paw and an imperious sweep of her black tail and will brook no rivals. She has without doubt given her daughter a complex.[99]

Jean revelled in such feline indifference to human values and relationships. Again, Dinah's relationship with her son Twinkle was dysfunctional in human terms, with occasional affection giving way to aggression in a parody of the human family:

A. L. Rowse with his cat Peter, 1970, photograph by Derek Parker.

> They sit face to face before the fire licking each other's faces, ears & necks. They go at each other vigorously as tho in competition as to who can lick longest and hardest . . . What touching devotion! What family bliss! Then for no reason we can discover Dinah suddenly breaks away, because all fire & fury, spitting & boxing, & Twinkle sits back on his haunches sullenly with his ears flattened.[100]

Jean Pratt took pleasure in the cats in part because they were different to a human family, rather than substitutes for it.

Men who lived alone could be equally devoted to their pets. In the early 1970s the historian and writer A. L. Rowse sat down to write a new biography – but this time the subject was not another great human of history but a small white cat, Peter. The animal had inhabited Rowse's Cornish home with his housekeeper, Beryl, for sixteen years. Five years after the pet's death, it was still difficult to write about: 'I have put off writing about him for as long as possible – for I know it will upset me.'[101] The cat, a gift from a neighbour, arrived in 1951, just under two years old, and became an important member of the household until its death in 1967. The biography expressed profound emotional and physical attachment to the pet. But it also allowed Rowse to construct an alternative version of domesticity, one that eschewed conventional familial and sexual relationships. As an Oxford academic and writer of popular history, Rowse struggled to reconcile his life and interests with his working-class background. His sexual identity remains ambiguous in the book, although he hints at an interest in younger men. Writing about his attachment to Peter allowed Rowse to construct a different kind of family. His criticism of his parents and family home reflects the unease of social mobility. His relationship with his mother – who required nursing and support for what was probably dementia for the last twenty years of her life – was particularly problematic.[102] Writing about his 'animal family' offered a means of comparison and contrast and he claims to have been succoured by the family cats rather than his mother: 'the little cat would put a paw and arm around me and nurse me, with true maternal instinct – which is more than my mother ever did.'[103]

Peter is often cast in the role of child, with Rowse as nurse or bread-winner: 'I had to earn the family living, including his, at Oxford and elsewhere.'[104] When Beryl leaves the house Peter follows her, apparently crying 'Ma-ma' all the way.[105] Yet Peter is far from a child substitute. The representation is tongue-in-cheek. When Beryl notes that the cat is better looked after than some children, Rowse remarks 'But he's *so* much more beautiful. And *much* nicer.'[106] Throughout the book the cat is described with great love – this is an emotional and tactile relation-ship expressed through routine interactions during the daily pattern of the household, at mealtimes, through physical stroking, cuddling, squeezing and kissing and in Peter's presence on Rowse's bed. The cat was not a replacement for a human child because Rowse did not want a conventional human family; his life embraced a different aesthetic. In the book, Rowse repeatedly used the word 'family' to describe his domestic set-up: himself, Peter, Beryl the housekeeper and the gardener, Jack – but Peter was the emotional glue that held this human–animal family together.

Pets and the future family

The Tavistock Institute researchers saw the role of pets in the mid-twentieth-century family as a direct response to how family life had changed in recent years. Noting the growth of pets in contemporary culture – in pet advice, on TV and in RSPCA campaigns – the social scien-tists argued that a new need for pets had been produced by the decline of the 'close-knit' family.[107] Mothering was (apparently) managed in a more sophisticated and sometimes more distant fashion – there was more eating out, less domestic service and more women in part-time work – all of which, they felt, threatened the close and communicative family group that previously existed. What then, they asked, was the role of pets in future society? Pets, they argued, were becoming more necessary to the family:

> One eventuality could be the lessening need for pets but much more likely is the growth of the practice whereby a family incorporates such a special member – a primitive 'ombudsman' who provides relationships, learning opportunities and experiences which were not so necessary when families were more generally 'close-knit'.[108]

While we would argue with the contention that mid-twentieth-century families were less close-knit, the researchers' predictions proved accurate. In the early twenty-first century British family pets are often seen as intrinsic to family life.

What the Tavistock didn't predict, perhaps, was how radically models of family life would change. By the late 1960s and '70s moral panics about divorce, the rise in single-parent families, alleged delinquency in 'latch-key' kids and the decline of so-called Victorian values would give rise to social anxieties that the reproductive family, still perceived as the bedrock of Western society, was breaking down. The social conservatism inherent in such fears was accompanied by a rising swell of voices that sought to speak *for* new or different kinds of families, demonstrating that economic, educational and social imbalances caused the problems, not shifting family models. In 1968 the novelist Barry Hines published *A Kestrel for a Knave*, turned into the film *Kes* a year later by Ken Loach. Part of the 'angry young men' genre of gritty working-class fiction, Hines's novel outlined the inequities that limited the life chances of its protagonist, schoolboy Billy Casper, giving remarkable detail on changing family formations in 1960s Britain in the process. Billy lives with his working mother and older half-brother Jud. His father has left after discovering his wife's extra-marital affair. When Billy is not being bullied by the various men his mother brings home, it is the gambling layabout Jud that makes his life miserable. The one beacon of joy in this lonely boy's life is the kestrel he rears from the nest. For

Billy, the bird offers emotional connection, loyalty and trust – factors glaringly absent from the relationships with his human family. The intense boy–bird relationship, one that would have been so familiar to Victorian writers, also enabled Hines to depict the 'poor' kid as capable of profound devotion but a victim too, who will be crushed by circumstance (again, this would have been familiar to Victorian writers of 'slum' novels). The kestrel offers Billy a glimpse of what relationships can be and throws the inadequacies of humans into sharp relief.[109]

By the start of the twenty-first century families took many forms. Divorce, remarriage and step- and single-parent families have become so familiar that they no longer provoke widespread moral outrage. Donor conception is more available, enabling individuals and same-sex couples to have children, while those without children are increasingly identified as making positive life choices. Since 2000 the number of people living in single-person households has risen significantly. Accompanying these changes has been the steady rise in the number of households with pets. The biggest increase in pet ownership is among the group market researchers call millennials, those born between 1980 and 2000. These people increasingly choose to live alone and are delaying or opting out of having children. Instead, they share their homes and lives with animals, defining pets as constituent members of their chosen 'family' and prioritizing pet needs over those of human relations or friends.[110] Market research from 2019 suggested that 'happiness', 'love', 'affection' and 'companionship' were the main reasons most people kept pets.[111] Pets still shape the relationships we enjoy (or endure) with our human family much as they continue to mediate our family dynamics and personalities. But for some people, pets increasingly represent their preferred, chosen family.

'Shipmates', photograph in Gordon Stables, *Cats: Their Points and Characteristics* (1876).

FIVE

In Sickness and in Health: Caring for Pets

I n 1878 the author Emma Davenport recollected the death of her childhood pet, a 'lion'-coloured terrier called Tawney, some fifty years previously. Supposedly a watchdog, Tawney became the children's 'constant companion' and proved a tremendous playmate, considered another sibling. One sultry summer's day, Tawney began to behave strangely before lapsing into violent fits. Emma's father, Reverend James Webber (later the Dean of Ripon), and the gardener desperately tried to save his life, to no avail. The family suspected that the terrier had been poisoned, possibly even deliberately.[1] When a similar thing happened to another family's cat, Mick, in a village just outside turn-of-the-twentieth century Manchester, things hadn't changed much. Here, it was the mother who tried 'all' she could think of to save the cat's life. Again, the family suspected the cat had been poisoned and were horrified when he died in agony.[2] Despite being socially distant and decades apart, these families responded to pet illness in remarkably similar ways. Parents took charge of trying to resolve the situation, calling on home medicine and lay understanding of animal physiology to try and cure – or at least alleviate – the animals' suffering. In practice, trying 'everything' amounted to not very much: bathing with water or administering castor oil. These deaths became the stuff of family speculation and deep-seated resentment against perceived perpetrators. But what is most striking to our sensibilities is that neither family thought to call a vet. They were not unusual.

Victorian pet owners certainly fretted over sick pets but this was the era before mass veterinary treatment for pet animals. For the most part, anxious owners nursed animals at home, attempted to administer drugs and even performed home surgery. An expanding market of advice literature offered guidance on what to do with sick animals, giving instructions on nursing and detailed prescriptions for homemade medicines. Medicine makers and pet-health publishers were not slow to see the market potential of this. By the end of the century, pet owners were confronted by an array of products claiming to promote animal and bird health. These and the many pages of advice on nursing sick pets are testament to how much the Victorians cared about animal life, and their emotional and financial investment in pets. It was only at the turn of the twentieth century that some vets, especially in towns, began to expand into domestic animal practice. Certainly, by 1900 vets were reporting on possible treatments for pets like Tawney and Mick that fell victim to suspected poisoning.[3]

From the 1920s it became more common to consult a vet. High-end veterinary practices catered for pets from wealthy households, and working-class owners in urban areas were increasingly able to seek help from charity-run animal hospitals around the country. By the late 1930s elite pets were receiving an array of treatments, including routine maintenance of teeth and glands, vaccinations, neutering and spaying, and surgery when required. The move towards reliance on veterinary specialists was an outcome of human emotional investment in companion animals. In turn, it further heightened the emotional experience of pet keeping. Owners now sought professional help to a greater extent, placing new faith in expert knowledge in times of trouble. But finding the right vet wasn't easy: surgeries were as likely to be a scene of pain and conflict as cure. Vets struggled with unruly animals and owners were loath to hand over beloved pets to unsympathetic medical men. The increased reliance on vet medicine created new emotional and economic terrains. Owners who could afford it now faced a choice: how far to go with pet treatment, and when to stop. With the rise of new forms of surgery, owners had more power to shape the biological destinies of pets. The vetted pet, as owners reflected at mid-century, was a different kind of animal to the one that existed fifty years before.

The home medicine chest

In a small village near Petersfield in 1893, a sheepdog named Capel, the pride and joy of retired clerk Arthur Jones, was having some problems with itchy skin. Today, a vet might look at the underlying issues behind the complaint – ticks, scabies, allergies, dry skin, dermatitis, mange and bacterial infections can all make dogs extremely itchy. Arthur took matters into his own hands and treated Capel himself: 'I rubbed him over with linseed oil & black sulphur.'[4] Oily and reeking, the unfortunate animal was kept outside in the yard for three days before finally being washed and allowed to rejoin the family. There is no further comment on Capel's itchiness, so apparently this 'home physicking' was successful. Eccentric as it may seem, Arthur's treatment of Capel was typical of responses to ailing pets in the Victorian era. Minor ailments were subject to home doctoring and owners drew on an increasing range of patent pet medicines and treatments. In this hands-on culture of home treatment, owners might also perform more invasive surgical procedures on their pets themselves.

In the 1850s and '60s authors of domestic advice rarely mentioned vets in relation to sick pets. While veterinary medicine advanced and developed during the Victorian era, its main market was horses. There was some veterinary interest in pedigree dogs, although this did not always reach the mainstream. 'Veterinary surgeons' were a mixed group of practitioners, some officially qualified and some not, who competed with farriers for equine patients.[5] Other animals, such as cattle, were treated, if at all, by their owners. But there is plenty of evidence, from advice literature on pet keeping and domestic advice more generally, that pet health was a widespread concern in the second half of the nineteenth century, and most pet people expected to treat pet injuries and ailments at home.

One of the biggest worries for dog owners was distemper, a dangerous virus that attacked the canine nervous system and often led to death.[6] Some household-advice books focused purely on home treatment for the illness. In 1858 *The Household Encyclopedia* gave details of an emetic powder.[7] Later, *Sylvia's Family Management* (1886) suggested that the best thing was to keep the infected dog in comfortable surroundings.[8] Writers who were more invested in the pedigree dog 'fancy' tended to insist on sending for a vet, largely because pedigree dogs were so financially valuable. Beeton's *Book of Home Pets* (1861) suggested that in cases of distemper, suspected hydrophobia (otherwise known as rabies, the source of considerable legal and medical efforts to restrict the movement of dogs given its threat to human health) and fits, the advice of a 'veterinary surgeon' should be sought.[9] But both books also expected animals to be nursed at home and included lists of remedies and treatments.

Many remedies were designed simply to alleviate pain or discomfort, not least because so much animal physiology was so little understood. In cases of injury or accident, treatments otherwise applied to humans were simply transposed to animals. In October 1859 Jane Carlyle's much-loved dog, Nero, was run over by a butcher's cart. He didn't appear to have any broken bones but when a servant brought him home, he was all 'crumpled' like a 'crushed spider'; when he tried to stand, he keeled over 'stiff and unconscious'. Not daring to show 'all my grief', Jane swung into practical action: she placed the small dog in a warm bath, wrapped him in a blanket, laid him on a pillow and, when he was still breathing the following morning, fed him warm milk. As the day passed, Jane began to lose hope until Nero answered her wails of 'Poor dog! Poor little Nero!' by trying to thump his tail. Over the next ten days, Jane continued her ministrations and, 'by little and little', Nero recovered some health. Jane was emotionally and physically exhausted.[10] Part of the perennial difficulty with sick animals was the barrier in communication, although, as Charles Dickens noted of his sick St Bernard in 1865 (she had canker of the ear), animals could have a very 'human way of expressing being in pain, and entreating sympathy', which was 'moving'. Yet the inability to affect a cure or relieve the animal's suffering was 'very distressing'.[11]

Concern for pet health in domestic manuals was not restricted to dogs: advice was also offered for ailing birds, the most common pet in homes across the social scale. In the 1850s Jane Loudon's advice book discussed parrot disease in detail and how to treat it with diet, bathing and anointing.[12] Over half of Beeton's *Home Pets* was devoted to bird keeping. The book offered advice on illness in all kinds of British and 'foreign' birds, with instructions for home treatment. Parrots were particularly problematic, and subject to foot troubles, diseased eyes, consumption, fits, asthma and loose bowels, all of which could be treated by an attentive owner.[13] By the 1890s a greater range of bird-related health products were available for solicitous owners. *Bett's Breeding Canaries* (1897), a specialist manual for canary breeders, gave an extensive list of the best canary products on the market in the 1890s: Canarydyne for asthma and wheezing; quinella for derangement of the stomach, and essence of quassia for destroying red mite.[14] Non-specialists also recommended these products. The 1890s *Cassell's Book of the Home* trumpeted the virtues of Tibbs' Canarydyne. Older, more homespun treatments were still used too: constipated thrushes and blackbirds were to be fed on mealworms or spiders dipped in olive oil.[15]

There was also growing interest in cat health.[16] In the 1850s a new authority emerged. Lady Mary Anne Cust, a middle-aged aristocratic woman, published *The Cat* in 1856. This small volume proved very influential among cat-care advisors.[17] It is not clear how Cust, the wife of a general, Lady of the Bedchamber to Queen Victoria's mother and heiress to a British Guinea slave plantation, came to have such a keen interest in cats. She claimed the book was written at the behest of 'the wishes of numerous friends who have applied to me, saying – My poor puss is so ill! And I cannot find any work upon Cats. Do tell me what I must do for it!' Cust described cat ailments in energetic detail and included treatments for 'cat distemper' and 'cat pox'. The book was set apart by her hands-on approach. While other advisors tended to list treatment, Cust wrestled with a problem that had long vexed cat owners – how to give medicine to a cat: 'This is a difficult process in imagination; but easy in the performance, when undertaken with firmness, gentleness, and courage, and without noise.' After putting on gloves, the cat should be rolled gently in a large cloth with the head protruding. Then, 'Place upright between the knees of a sitting person, place another cloth under the jaw to keep that clean, and then with a gloved hand open the mouth wide, but gently, at one effort, holding it open and pouring the medicine from a teaspoon down the open throat.'[18]

Twenty years later, another landmark text on cat care appeared. After voyaging around the world, ship's doctor William Gordon Stables settled in 1875 in Twyford, Berkshire, with his new wife Lizzie McCormack. This was the beginning of a prolific literary career. Stables, known for writing boys' adventure fiction, also retained his medical interests and one of his first subjects was cat health. *Cats: Their Points and Characteristics* and *The Domestic Cat* were both published in 1876.[19] Stables drew on his knowledge of human medicine to propose prescriptions for cats. Treatments were offered for chronic inflammation of the stomach, bronchitis, consumption, fits, mange, 'the yellows' (gastroenteritis), dysentery, milk fever and inflammation of the eyes. Drawing on older humoral theories of medicine, Stables's recommendations were often interventionist. Cats with fits, unresponsive to smelling salts or snuff, were to be bled by making an incision on the lower part of the ear.[20] Owners, he believed, should take scalpels into their own hands. 'Cats stand operations of all sorts well,' he remarked. One can only wonder whether Stables actually had any cats (the cat who appears alongside Stables in his portrait for the book is almost certainly stuffed). Minor surgery, he insisted, was straightforward: 'If a cat's leg is broken and lacerated by a trap, cut it off. Don't be afraid.'[21] Vets, Stables argued, were largely ignorant of feline ailments, and owners were better off treating their pets themselves.[22]

Despite the increased market for dedicated pet-care books in the latter decades of the nineteenth century, most authors remained sceptical about the availability – or usefulness – of the veterinary surgeon, even for dogs. Stables's *Our Friend the Dog* (1884) went through numerous editions.[23] Some concessions were made to veterinary expertise, but most ailments – including distemper, inflammation of the bowels, colic and diarrhoea – could be treated at home.[24] Even in cases of broken bones, 'There is no reason why the dog owner himself may not treat a simple fracture.'[25] He remained suspicious of veterinary knowledge: 'I say that it is my firm conviction, and has been for years, that not five veterinary men out of ten possess sufficient knowledge of common pathology, physiology, anatomy, and therapeutics to enable them to cope successfully with the ailments of dogs.'[26]

While most writers shied away from Stables-style home surgery, a degree of hands-on treatment for dogs was widely recommended. In 1898 John Maxtee's popular manual on dog care argued that all owners should have some knowledge and ability to treat the ailments of their pets:

> Without wishing to even hint that every dog-owner should be his own veterinary, I still think that, if everyone who aspires to keep a dog should first make a study of the common ailments, he would not only in the end save himself much anxiety, but by rendering prompt and efficient aid be the means of saving the patient no inconsiderable amount of pain.[27]

From the 1870s, understanding the complexities of dog care, prevention and treatment of disease was made considerably easier by the emergence of a canine fourth estate, encouraged by the massive expansion of the dog fancy across the social scale: a slew of new books on breeds and all aspects of breeding included manifold publications on promoting and maintaining the health of pedigree dogs.[28]

Breed specialists and more generic advice writers' emphasis on home doctoring was reflected in the availability of products dedicated to pet health. By the 1870s the pet medicine chest had become a marketable entity. The opening pages of *Cats: Their Points and Characteristics* included an eye-catching advertisement for a 'Cat Medicine Chest': 'Beautifully fitted up with everything necessary to keep Pussy in Health, or to Cure her When Ill'. The cost of the chest, 'a nicely finished article' and 'highly suitable for a present', was 21 shillings and marketed by Dean & Son of Fleet Street, who also published Stables's book.[29] *Cassell's Book of the Home*, which came out in the 1890s, recommended 'A medicine chest – small ones can be had – should be in every house for the benefit of the dog and cat.' The book laid out products and recipes for treatments for distemper, colic, inflammation of the bowels, constipation, diarrhoea, catarrh, bronchitis, fits, tape and round worm, ear cankers, fleas and lice in dogs and diarrhoea, dysentry, stomach ailments and fits in cats. Castor oil was an almost universal remedy: *Cassell's* recommended this for colic, diarrhoea and catarrh in dogs as well as fits, diarrhoea and stomach ailments in cats. By this point there was also awareness that not all products on the market were effective. *Cassell's* urged that pet medicines should be bought from respectable firms rather than quacks, a reflection of the proliferation of products available on the market by the 1890s.[30]

In a crowded market, promoters sought new strategies to highlight their products, often using endorsements from well-known animal specialists. In 1893 Spratt's brought out a promotional booklet, *The Dog: From Puppyhood to Age*, authored by Stables, by then a renowned authority on animal health. The book was prefaced by a lengthy advert for Spratt's products and a long list of medicines including cooling powders, skin-disease cures, cough pills, chorea pills, diarrhoea mixture, distemper powders, pills, ear-canker lotion, eczema lotion, hair stimulant, jaundice pills, mange lotion, rheumatic pills, worm powders and soap. The medicine chest itself contained various dog medicines in addition to a 'Lancet Seton Needle, Scissors &c.', retailing at 25 shillings per chest.[31] In the final decades of the nineteenth century the advertising industry became more sophisticated and new printing technologies enabled the creation of striking and novel visual effects. Adverts for a wide range of products drew on new understandings of science and expert testimonies to sell their wares. These trends were also apparent in the advertisement of pet foods.

The most basic staple for pet health was sound nutrition. For much of the nineteenth century, birdseed was cheap and readily available in markets, grocers and early pet shops. In most towns and cities in the early nineteenth century, owners of dogs and cats relied on cats' meat traders selling boiled horseflesh sourced from the knacker's yard. The journalist Henry Mayhew estimated that there were around 1,000 cats'

80 MEDALS AWARDED.

USE JEYES' FLUID
In all cases of Distemper, Mange, &c.

Flush out the Kennel with **JEYES' FLUID** diluted with water. After wards sprinkle Jeyes' Sanitary Powder, especially in the corners. **Jeyes' Disinfectant Sawdust** is very absorbent and invaluable in the kennel.
Price Lists, Testimonials, and all Particulars at
64, Cannon Street, London, E.C.

Advertisement for Jeyes' Dog Fluid, in Gordon Stables, *Our Friend the Dog* (1884).

meat traders in early 1860s London.[32] It was sold for both cats *and* dogs, but the term 'cats' meat' reflected the lower status of cats as pets because it was assumed that most dog owners would buy meat from a butcher, reflecting dogs' greater financial and emotional value. From at least the 1870s, a market for specialist manufactured dog foods – canned meats, 'cakes' and biscuits – expanded to cater to the burgeoning investment in high-value breeds. Many of the manufactured dog foods played on owners' anxieties about canine health, tapping into debates about the influence of meat on canine aggression and concerns about maintaining joint health, for instance, while advertisements and brand names highlighted added ingredients such as cod-liver oil and fibre to emphasize the role of diet in promoting good health.[33] Vero Shaw's *How to Choose a Dog* (1897), for example, carried an ad for Benbow's Dog Mixture (which apparently purified blood, destroyed worms, cured distemper and produced a healthy coat), with testimony from kennel owner and Waterloo Cup winner Joseph Wright.[34]

The sheer success of the dog food market was reflected by the exponential growth of Spratt's, who, by the turn of the twentieth century, were sponsoring Kennel Club dog shows and producing branded calendars, pet publications and associated goods. Although primarily noted for its dog foods, Spratt's (who also promoted high-quality bird foods) expanded early into specialist foods for pedigree cats, capitalizing on expert opinion that horsemeat was bad for feline health. Gordon Stables's landmark *Cats: Their Points and Characteristics* (1876) warned owners that cats' meat was often far from fresh and frequently diseased: his book helpfully carried a half-page ad for Spratt's Patent Cat Food.[35]

But the attempt to crack the cat market was slow to succeed. Cat experts weren't always aware of the availability of specialist foods, even recommending dog biscuits for cats in places; others were unconvinced.[36] According to 'Dick Whittington' in *The Cat Manual* (1902), 'There is, in my opinion, only one correct diet for cats and kittens, and that is the natural one – raw meat.' Cats' meat was still the best option on grounds of economy and quality.[37] Even Frances Simpson's advice manual,

SPRATT'S PATENT

CAT FOOD.

TRADE MARK.

It has long been considered that the food given to that useful domestic favourite, the CAT, is the sole cause of all the diseases it suffers from; nearly all Cats in towns are fed on boiled horseflesh, in many cases diseased and conveying disease.

This Food is introduced to entirely supersede the present unwholesome practice; it is made from pure fresh beef and other sound materials, not from horseflesh or other deleterious substances. It will be found the cheapest food to preserve the health and invigorate the constitution, prolong the existence, and extend the usefulness, gentleness, and cleanliness of the Cat.

Sold in 1d. Packets only. Each Packet contains sufficient to feed a Cat for two days. The wrapper of every Packet is the same in colour, and bears the Trade Mark as above, and the name of the Patentee, and no other Packet is genuine.

DIRECTIONS FOR USE.

Mix the food with a little milk or water, making it crumbly moist, not sloppy.

SPRATT'S PATENT MEAT FIBRINE DOG CAKES, 22s. per cwt., Carriage Paid.
SPRATT'S PATENT POULTRY FOOD, 22s. per cwt., Carriage Paid.
SPRATT'S PATENT GRANULATED PRAIRIE MEAT CRISSEL, 28s. per cwt., Carriage Paid.

Address—SPRATT'S PATENT,

HENRY STREET, BERMONDSEY STREET, TOOLEY STREET, S.E.

Advertisement for Spratt's Patent Cat Food, in Gordon Stables,
Cats: Their Points and Characteristics (1876).

intended for the well-heeled ladies and men who bred pedigree cats, thought butcher's meat too costly, warning that owners 'possessed of a number of queens, two or three stud cats, and several litters of growing kittens' would find 'the butcher's bill' a 'serious consideration'.[38] Simpson was aware of the problems involved with horseflesh, describing 'fanciers' as 'averse' to it, but believed it was acceptable if carefully monitored.

As with most pet-health products and services, manufactured foods remained the preserve of the affluent well into the mid-twentieth century. Registrations of cats' meat traders actually increased in street directories in London and the provinces from 1900 to the outbreak of the Second World War, selling largely to working-class districts where ownership of dogs and cats had increased but few families could afford the luxury of manufactured pet foods. Stan Jasper, who grew up in Hoxton, worked as an assistant to the local cats' meat man, who had 'an enormous round' in the area.[39] 'He had a small cart full of meat and a big basket for deliveries; he stayed by the cart, cutting up the meat in small pieces and stuck them on bits of wood, which I delivered from the basket. If people were out I shoved them through the letter-boxes.'[40] At the other end of the

'Miss Frances Simpson and her Silver Male "Cambyses"', photograph in Frances Simpson, *Cats and All about Them* (1902).

A cat's meat man, *c.* 1900, photograph.

scale, some people compromised their pets' health by overfeeding, often with completely inappropriate foods. As one vet complained in 1894, the phrase 'a dog's life' was often taken to infer hardship but some of the dogs he attended had more 'luxurious' diets than humans he knew: mutton chops, sweets, pastries, ices and even whisky.[41] Part of the problem was that people tried to express their affection for pets through food, a tendency that had severe consequences for the health of animals. Tricki Woo, a much-loved Peke in interwar Yorkshire, was 'like a bloated sausage', listless and vomiting, when the young vet, James Herriot, seized him from his mistress for two weeks of restorative plain food and active play. As Herriot notes, 'Tricki's only fault was greed,' and with a mistress who 'can't bear to refuse him', his diet of cream cakes, chocolate, fudge and rich trifles was slowly killing him.[42]

Vets for pets

According to the 1860s edition of *Cassell's Household Guide*, 'most large towns' had 'a dog practitioner of some high repute' but, 'in the absence of such, it may be needful to consult a veterinary surgeon, huntsman or gamekeeper; but these latter are only to be trusted in the case of large, hardy dogs, such as they are chiefly accustomed to, and the former are very often totally ignorant of the dog's nature.'[43] There is some evidence, though, that early veterinary surgeons did tend dogs. In the archives of the Royal College of Veterinary Surgeons a few intriguing account books from early vets survive that track visits paid, animals helped and medicines dispensed. We know from the accounts of Walter Burt, a vet based in Sussex in the early 1800s, that his practice consisted mainly of farm animals. But he did see a couple of dogs a month, dispensing medicine and performing surgery including spaying bitches and neutering dogs.[44] Around forty years later the accounts of Henry Raynham, based in Biggleswade in Bedfordshire, followed a similar pattern: he dealt primarily with horses but treated one or two dogs a month, mainly performing surgery or applying dressings.[45]

By the latter half of the nineteenth century it was standard to recommend a veterinary surgeon for the treatment of valuable pedigree dogs, although the market for this was restricted to affluent people. The growth of the elite pet-doctoring market is evident in another late nineteenth-century trend: exclusive vets for cats. Although not as prestigious as the Kennel Club, the National Cat Club was established in the late nineteenth century and there were cat shows at Crystal Palace from 1871. Pedigree cats could be valuable and necessitate veterinary care.[46] Some canny practitioners covered both markets. The 1884 Kennel Club Show Catalogue boasted a full-page advert for 'The London Royal Canine & Feline Surgery', 'Under the Patronage of Her Majesty the Queen' at the exclusive address of 55 South Molton Street, Bond Street, London. Here, the ad stated, 'Mr Rotherham, Professor of Canine Pathology, may be consulted daily upon Canine and Feline Diseases.'[47] The advert featured a long list of international royalty who had apparently all consulted Rotherham. Frances Simpson's *Cats for Pleasure and Profit* (1905) named useful veterinary suppliers for cats, but suggested that vets in general remained aloof from feline practice: 'Mr Ward may rightly be considered the wizard of the north, for he was the pioneer of "practical pussology" apart from the regular qualified veterinary who may look with a pitying eye on cats' ailments and infirmities, but yet is just a little superior to the treatment of these often despised animals.'[48]

By the late 1890s professional veterinary treatment for cats and dogs increasingly came within the reach of middle-class pet owners in provincial towns, and some vets were actively increasing their canine practice as a self-conscious business strategy amid concerns that the profession might be becoming overcrowded, diminishing individual practitioners' prospects.[49] As the surgeon H. Leeney noted in 1897, the motorcar would deprive vets of horse business, so it was worth considering expansion into treatment of the 'beautiful pets of the drawing room and ladies' boudoir', for these animals had a 'monetary as well as sentimental value'. Leeney recommended vets pursue cats as a new avenue for enterprise, reassuring practitioners that they were easy to handle provided their vanity (the only constant feline characteristic) was flattered.[50] Some vets were also patenting instruments to render the administration of pills to cats and dogs much easier, something Lady Cust's readers would have found helpful.[51]

Owners could also call on the expertise of other or, in some cases, lesser professionals.[52] Sometimes, doctors for humans were involved. When Jane Carlyle could no longer bear to witness the suffering of her dog Nero in the winter of 1860 (he never completely recovered from being run over), she pleaded with a medical practitioner to end his life in the kindest way possible – with pills.[53] Less traumatically, Arthur Jones acquired pills that were usually given to humans to successfully treat his dog Capel.[54] In 1900 a periodical reported that a sailor had arrived at his local hospital carrying a scalding victim in a blanket and pleading with the practitioner to 'charge wot yer will' but 'save the poor crittur'. Shocked to discover that the bundle contained a gazelle rather than a human infant, the doctor did what he could in a 'good natured' way.[55] But, as an expanding profession, some veterinary surgeons resented both the higher social status of medics and interference on their territory, taking perverse pleasure in relating tales of disasters such as the doctor who 'treated' a patient's bird by setting its broken leg back to front.[56]

In the absence of professional veterinary services, druggists were also a common port of call. When Badger, a 'thorough mongrel' belonging to the night watchman of a coalyard, broke his leg in 1860s Manchester, his owner – much attached to the dog – bathed and bandaged the leg, doing 'everything he could' to 'relieve' the dog's pain. As soon as morning came, the man carried Badger to the druggist and 'wailed' outside until the man opened up and dressed the leg 'properly'.[57] But while chemists could be helpful in stocking supplies for the home medicine chest and performing rudimentary tasks, by the 1890s vets increasingly railed against 'quack' remedies and chemists, claiming to set 'petty' professional jealousies aside in the interests of advancing 'sound knowledge'.[58] Working people often had access to 'practitioners' experienced in the treatment of animals, although these individuals lacked any veterinary training or qualification. The Veterinary Surgeons Act of 1881 prohibited unqualified individuals from representing themselves as veterinary practitioners but, as a court case in August 1894 showed, this turned on the use of the word 'veterinary'. It did not necessarily include chemists who sold remedies for pets or people that advertised as the cat or dog's 'friend', a lay person that claimed long experience with pet diseases and the ability to 'skilfully treat' any ailments they might have.[59]

There remained little question of involving medical professionals in the treatment of smaller animals, however. While the professional journal *Veterinary Record* regularly reported on treatments, drugs, equipment (such as forceps and operating tables) and surgeries for dogs *and* cats from the early 1890s, they rarely mentioned birds or small animals such as rabbits or guinea pigs. For the owners of fancy birds, specialists and societies remained the recommended source of advice. According to William Betts, Honorary Treasurer of the Cage Bird Club, the best course of action if a bird could not be cured at home was to write to the Hon. Sec. of the Cage Bird Club, Inns of Court Hotel, High Holborn, WC, or get a copy of *Bazaar, Poultry, Fur and Feather, The Feathered World* or *The Stock Keeper*, which gave instructions for enquiring after bird ailments and on post-mortems.[60]

Ivy Port had no memory of her family using vets at all. In the Port family home, sick animals just disappeared:

> We didn't have vets in those days, too expensive I expect, and we had no transport for transporting sick animals to Cranleigh. I remember when I was young there was always some mystery about their sudden absence . . . I asked many questions but they were met with an evasive reply and I tried not to think about it but sometimes I did see a bucket in the wood shed that was not normally there. Still I accepted the things that happened in the strange adult world.[61]

But sick animals were not always consigned to an early death. In rural families like the Ports a level of familiarity with animal physiology persisted that allowed them to treat pets in ways that appeared effective. Port recounts the story of a favourite hen, 'Henny Penny', who was found lying on her side one day, choking to death. Port's resourceful brother-in-law seized the ailing bird and, using a pocket knife to make an incision in her neck, removed the object and sewed Henny Penny back together again. This rudimentary surgery was reputedly a great success and the hen survived to cluck another day.

All creatures great and small

In February 1947 Jean Pratt was confined to her cottage in Beaconsfield nursing Dinah and Twinkle, who were struggling with sneezing and catarrh. After consulting the local cats' home, Jean bathed their nostrils with diluted TCP, rubbed on Vaseline and put Vicks VapoRub on the bridge of their noses.[62] The 'cat doctor' was called in, and she acquired a small tube of inhalant that she attempted to put up Dinah's nose two to three times a day.[63] Despite these pharmaceutical aids, the basic challenges of cat care had not changed. Getting Dinah to swallow cough pills was particularly difficult. As Jean noted, 'Nursing them has been a test of my patience.'[64] In early March this mixture of home nursing and modern veterinary innovation appeared to have paid off: Dinah was better and Twinkle appeared to be 'on the mend'.[65] But three days later the situation changed: 'Much worried about Twinkle . . . chest and throat like the wrath of God.' Overnight, Twinkle took a turn for the worse and died in the morning. Jean agonized over whether she should have sought medical help sooner. 'Twinkle was obviously (now it seems so, but I never give up hope with animals) dying last night and in great pain & I didn't know what to do. Felt if only I could keep him alive til I got him to the clinic all would be well (that blind, primitive faith in witch doctors & magicians).'[66] By the mid-twentieth century it had become normal for owners to turn to vets for help with sick pets. There was growing faith in medical care provided by experts rather than the homespun and marketed remedies that the Victorians had relied on. Jean's story reveals the new emotional importance of veterinary care: in times of crisis pet owners turned to these new authority figures for help.

By the 1920s veterinary treatment for pets began to expand. Vet-turned-historical-researcher Andrew Gardiner has recently shown that small-animal practice was increasingly part of the vet trade in this era. Caring for small animals was still seen as second rate by a profession that presented itself as primarily concerned with horses.[67] Nonetheless, there is evidence of growing interest in veterinary practice for small animals from the start of the century. Professor Frederick Hobday refined and popularized an operating table specifically for cat and dog surgery in 1898 (he claimed to have treated some 3,000 cats and dogs on the table in four years), followed by publication of his pioneering student textbook *Canine and Feline Surgery* in 1900 (it went through many editions and was still popular in the 1950s).[68] The first veterinary text exclusively on cats, written by Hamilton Kirk, was published in 1925.[69]

Using records kept by vets, Gardiner suggests that from the late 1930s there was a move towards increased small-animal practice, as the horse market declined in towns and rural practices became cattle- and canine-focused.[70] This is supported in memoirs of the period. The owner of a veterinary practice in the Yorkshire market town of 'Darrowby' (a pseudonym for Thirsk), Siegfried Farnon, instructed the newly qualified James Herriot that, although the surgery didn't have much small-animal work, he was 'trying to encourage it'. Acknowledging that 'a lot of the old hands won't look at a dog or a cat,' Farnon felt the 'profession has got to change its ideas' and 'do the job right': the 'old castor oil and prussic acid doctrine', the staple of *Cassell's* home guides from fifty years previous, was 'no good at all'.[71] There were also breakthroughs in pet treatment. In the early twentieth century there was a public campaign, led by landed kennel owners, to fund research into producing a distemper vaccine. The vaccine became available on the commercial market in the early 1930s.[72]

The treatment received by the pets of the wealthy is revealed in the records of a high-end practice located at Staines in Surrey. The Willett practice, founded at the beginning of the Victorian period, opened a special branch of its surgery to deal with companion animals in 1948. Even before that, dogs and cats formed a substantial part of its business. The ledger book for the practice – accounts recording the treatments given to individual animals – survives in the archives of the Royal College of Veterinary Surgeons.[73] The practice's proximity to Windsor meant that animals belonging to the Royal Family – the queen's corgis and Princess Margaret's Sealyhams – were on the books from 1937. The first named pet in the royal record is Dookie – Elizabeth's first corgi – who received regular treatment, including worming, nail clipping and teeth cleaning.[74] The records go up to the early 1960s, with Margaret's Sealyhams regularly trimmed and stripped and supplied with ointment and tablets. Leafing through the pages of the account book, it becomes clear just how extensive treatment could be for privileged pets. The accounts for Mrs D. of Sunningdale are a case in point.[75] Kept from 1929 until 1943, the accounts show that pets in the household were receiving frequent and intensive treatment. The main recipients were two Pekes – Que Que and Qui Qui – who received dressing of anal glands, supplies of worming meds and the scaling and cleaning of teeth alongside occasional more serious and invasive treatment.

For well-heeled dog owners, veterinary treatment for minor ailments and maintenance had become relatively normal by the 1930s. The children's author Alison Uttley may have been happy to treat her Scottie dog Hamish's blisters at home but she dutifully 'dragg[ed] the little dog along' to the vet to have his coat trimmed in summer.[76] When Alan and Morag Withington acquired their cairn terrier Sally, the first place they turned for help was the vet. In November 1934 the dog began to vomit. This was enough to trigger a trip to the vet, where she was kept overnight and given treatment.[77] Like the Pekes, Sal received treatment for a range of minor conditions that would previously have been dealt with at home: 'Sally's been to the vet today to have her scratching habit seen to. Internal treatment's been prescribed.'[78] Other kinds of dog care were also part of the remit – Sally was left with the vet when she came on heat, received 'beauty' treatments, and was clipped and stripped when she first arrived in the household.[79] Sometimes serious intervention was required. In November 1938 Sal was diagnosed with an infection of the uterus. This required an invasive operation. Alan described it in his usual brisk, jocular language: 'immediate operation . . . no danger. It sounds like the sort of thing I had done to my antrum & I imagine they'll clear out all the rubbish, cushions, bits of lemon peel, Bonio, paper etc.'[80]

Vets also treated small animals from working-class homes. James Herriot recalled that dogs, cats and rabbits were brought to the surgery from six to seven every evening.[81] Herriot presents such work as a business practice but he also believed that vets had a moral duty to animals and their owners. His depiction of treating animals belonging to the poor conveys that idea (although sometimes a feeling of futility too). In *It Shouldn't Happen to a Vet*, Herriot recalls regular visits to a Miss Stubbs, an impoverished and bed-bound older woman. Here he takes responsibility for nursing Irish setter Prince, Sealyham Ben, cocker spaniel Sally and two cats, Arthur and Susie. The animals were all over ten years old and keeping them going was a challenge, but Herriot viewed the work as an emotional and moral responsibility: 'The one thing that brought some light into the life of this brave old woman was the transparent devotion of this shaggy bunch whose eyes were never far from her face.'[82]

While veterinary medicine remained a luxury for much of the early twentieth century, poorer pet owners in urban centres did have an expanding range of options for healthcare and treatment. The best-known scheme for providing healthcare for pets of the poor, the People's Dispensary for Sick Animals, began in London in 1917 before expanding into the provinces. By 1924 the PDSA operated seventeen clinics across the UK and in 1934 could claim to treat 1 million pets for free each year.[83] Much to the horror of some professional vets, the PDSA reflected the popular model of animal healthcare, relying on lay practitioners or 'technicians' with PDSA in-house training in caring for cats, dogs and small animals rather than qualified vets, until a rapprochement was reached with the Royal College of Veterinary Surgeons in 1939 and the two organizations agreed to work in mutual support.[84]

But there were other options too. From 1879 the Royal College of Veterinary Surgeons in London ran a free clinic for the animals of the poor. The *Veterinary Record* related the occasional story of injured dogs

Vet William McAuliffe and a veterinary nurse bandaging the leg of a cat on an examination table, undated, photograph.

Clients waiting outside early Walworth clinic, undated, photograph.

that either made their way to the clinic independently or, after being discharged, returned to the clinic as a seemingly preferential 'home'.[85] From the late 1890s the animal-welfare charity Our Dumb Friends' League (established 1895 and later renamed the Blue Cross) worked to promote the care and protection of a range of animals. From 1900 they made grants available to owners to take their sick animals to the London Animal Sanatory Institute (also known as the Brown Animal Sanatory), although the institute's association with vivisection made this unpopular. From 1901 they began to raise money to establish a fund for a 'National Animal Hospital', which finally opened in the metropolis in 1907. Initially intended for horses and donkeys, pivotal to many working-class livelihoods, the schemes nevertheless included pets.[86] By 1921 the Animal Hospital employed three dedicated veterinary surgeons for cats, dogs and smaller animals and treated an estimated 10,000 pets a year.[87] In 1925 the Canine Defence League (established 1891; later renamed the Dogs Trust) began to open a series of 'Canine Clinics' to treat the dogs of the poor, the first at Bethnal Green, London, with plans to open another clinic with inpatient facilities in Middlesex. They also issued 'Veterinary tickets' to 'poor people', enabling them to seek professional treatment for pets while the charity covered the bill. By 1928 Defence League clinics were treating over 30,000 dogs, cats and 'other' animals (mostly rabbits and poultry) a year, a figure that increased to over 40,000 by 1929. Despite the supposed low value placed on cats as pets, they treated feline and canine patients in almost equal numbers.[88]

Liverpool was the first provincial city to open a dedicated animal clinic for working-class people. From the 1900s the Liverpool RSPCA provided veterinary tickets to poorer people, enabling them to seek professional treatment for working animals. In 1911 they launched an animal ambulance, again for working animals. By 1917, however, they had opened the first provincial animal hospital in the Everton district of the city, catering for working animals but also dogs, cats and much smaller animals such as rabbits and birds. The most common ailments were skin diseases, wounds, fractures, lameness, teeth problems, canker of the ear and gastritis. Staffed by qualified vets with the support of unqualified assistants, the hospital treated 550 dogs and 411 cats along-side 32 rabbits and 40 birds in 1919. By 1920 the hospital was so successful that it moved to larger premises and was renamed the Animal Memorial Hospital in reference to animals sacrificed in the Great War. By 1928 a second site opened to the south of the city near Toxteth. In 1930 as the society prepared to open a third clinic at Birkenhead on the Wirral, the two Liverpool sites were managing over 3,000 attendances each year. Keen to reassure private practitioners that the hospital was not a threat to business, the society repeatedly advertised that its services were for those pet owners who would never be able to afford veterinary fees.[89] In 1935 the Everton site was demolished and a brand-new 'modern Animal Clinic with up-to-date equipment and accommodation' opened in its place with Sir Frederick Hobday, the pioneer veterinary surgeon for small animals, in attendance. That year, the overall number of attendances across the three clinics passed the 10,000 mark, mostly cats and dogs, canaries and rabbits with an occasional tortoise, owl, ferret and monkey for good measure.[90] The hospitals had an educative function too, pro-moting 'prompt' treatment by qualified veterinarians rather than animals being 'subjected to all manner of quack remedies' (no doubt a dig at PDSA clinics, a rival for charitable donations).[91]

By 1949 the RSPCA hosted eighty animal clinics nationally and issued a voucher scheme that enabled poorer pet owners to seek professional medical treatment for their companion animals; the Canine Defence League operated three hospitals and clinics, two in the southeast and one in York; Our Dumb Friends' League had two hospitals in London and numerous clinics across England and Wales; and the PDSA operated five hospitals nationwide, 25 dispensaries in London, 43 in the provinces and 11 dispensary-caravans that covered an average of 75,000 miles annually. That the principle of delivering professional treatment to companion animals of all classes had arrived was reflected in veterinary schools establishing purpose-designed animal hospitals that catered for pets. The University of Liverpool built an animal hospital in 1932, followed by the Royal College of Veterinary Surgeons' animal hospital at Beaumont in 1934. Both these hospitals boasted modern facilities for equine and farm animals but also hosted wards and surgeries for dogs, cats and other small animals.[92]

Searching for a high priestess

In 1950s London, at the end of the working day, a middle-aged woman sat in a taxi clutching a cat basket and crying. Inside the basket, wrapped in a blanket, was Victoria, a severely injured kitten. Victoria had been found under a bed – dazed and barely conscious – and bleeding from the head. For her owner, Mrs Bell, 'there was no doubt that there was something very serious the matter with her and the only thing was to take her at once to the vet.' As surgeries were closing towards the end of the day, Mrs Bell had rushed to the nearest one. But when she arrived, she was devastated to find not the vet, but a veterinary assistant. Victoria had previously had an operation at the surgery, where the same assistant had neglected her recovery, leaving her on a bed of bloody rags. Under no circumstances would Mrs Bell hand over the little cat. 'She walked out of the surgery and stood on the pavement, holding the cat-basket, and wondering desperately what to do. She had kept the taxi waiting, in case the vet should be out. But where should she tell him to drive her? Was there a branch of the RSPCA anywhere near, and if so where? And would they have a resident vet on the premises?'[93] Mrs Bell's story – which comes from Antonia White's semi-autobiographical novel about the life of a widow and her two Siamese cats – would have resonated with mid-twentieth-century pet owners. Finding a trusted vet was far from straightforward.

The challenges of finding a vet are expressed nowhere more clearly than in Joseph Ackerley's pet memoir. Queenie was a large and beautiful Alsatian who did not take kindly to vets. Ackerley recounts a series of unsuccessful visits to three separate surgeries. The first ended as soon as it began, as Ackerley and Queenie were ordered out after he was unable to quieten her vociferous barking. A few weeks later, when Queenie sustained a cut to her pad, he was again forced to seek medical help, this time from an ex-army vet. This too, ended badly: 'Having failed, as I had failed, to humour her or shout her down, the Major suddenly lost his temper, and exclaiming, "These Alsatians! They're all the same!" he swooped upon her and beat her about the body with his bare hands.'[94] Unsurprisingly, Queenie cowered under the table, and would not allow inspection of the injury. But worse was to come. Queenie's distemper vaccine was administered by a third vet, this time under restraint: 'he abruptly noosed her nose, with what was plainly the dexterity of long practice, drew her jaws tightly and roughly together, turned the ends of the tape round her throat and knotted them behind her ears.' Ackerley was much stricken at the sight of Queenie 'foaming at the mouth with terror'. And yet: 'I was, indeed, in no position, or even mind, to question whatever methods this busy and helpful man might think fit to employ to exercise over my animal the control I lacked.' Afterwards he noted grimly: 'my ambition was to keep Queenie in such a state of health that she need never visit a vet again.'[95]

Increasingly, though, help was at hand. The story of Mrs Bell had a happy ending. The taxi driver, it turned out, had recently taken a customer to a female vet and Mrs Bell was delivered to the surgery of 'Miss English', 'a rather severe looking woman in a tweed suit'. 'Gruff as her manner was she handled Victoria very gently and Mrs Bell felt complete confidence in her.'[96] Ackerley's quest also ended in the discovery of a female saviour. Tweed-clad and bespectacled, these female vets were shining figures for anxiety-wrung owners. Ackerley's moment of grace came when he met Miss Canvey for the first time in her surgery at Parsons Green: 'Miss Canvey was a short, thickset, young woman with bobbed hair, spectacles, and a homely peasant's face. She wore a white overall, not intimidatingly clean, and as she advanced across the large, bare room towards me, I took an impression of calmness and competence.' While Queenie reacted to the surgery in her usual way, Miss Canvey calmly took control of the situation – removing the dog to another room, and suggesting to Ackerley that it was his presence (and anxiety) that was causing the problem. Ten minutes later a calm and treated dog emerged from the surgery. For Ackerley this was nothing short of a 'miracle'. 'I was already her slave and gazed at her with a veneration with which we behold a saint.' Miss Canvey was 'a high priestess' – the handing over of Queenie 'an act of faith'.[97]

The entry of women into the veterinary profession was hard won. Back in the 1890s when women began to agitate for access, the professional mouthpiece *Veterinary Record* opined that if practice consisted only of 'making a round of visits among lap dogs, or drawing room pets' to diagnose conditions and give advice on diet and hygiene, women would probably manage. But this constituted such a modest part of the vet's work that it was impractical for women to think they could earn a living in this way. More to the point, no 'lady' had the nerve for surgery and certainly would not countenance examining animal reproductive organs.[98] Other vets thought women made perfect 'sleeping partners' in practice: feeding sick animals and caressing those that were distraught. Such tasks required aptitude rather than skill and a keen domestic servant who loved animals was more than adequate for this work.[99]

The historian Julie Hipperson has researched the lives of Britain's first female vets and shown that they were encouraged into the profession in the 1920s and '30s by senior figures in the veterinary world. But they were expected to perform lower-status activities such as research (which was perceived as mundane and repetitive), administrative support or caring for small animals. The latter was strongly associated with perceptions of women as natural carers. As Hipperson shows, early female vets did not always want to fit into this mould. Connie Ford, for example, who qualified aged 21, had hoped to go into cattle treatment, but as a woman was unable to get a position as a veterinary assistant treating farm animals. She made the best of it and opened her own practice caring for smaller animals but it was harder to turn a profit (small animals brought in less income) and she wasn't particularly keen on dogs or their wealthy owners. Early female vets were often astute businesswomen and fully aware that when it came to treating pets the emotional relationship with owners was often as important as the medical treatment of the animals. Hipperson points to female vet Kathleen Hermanen-Johnson who in 1934 gave a conference talk on the 'psychology of client management'. Establishing a relationship with the owners – and inspiring faith and trust on first meeting them – was all important. So too was getting the bill in 'while the tear was in the eye'.[100]

Vet economics

In 1955 Florence Turtle was 58 and living in a house in Southfields in southwest London with her brothers Bernard and Brian, Toesie the cat and Dinah, an Alsatian dog. She was working full time as a buyer, and running the household, looking after the pets and the two men. At the beginning of the year she wrote in her diary: 'I do not particularly want to give up business but as I run a home with two brothers a cat & a dog find it a bit of a strain.'[101] While life was not perfect, Dinah was the centre of Florence's world.[102] In August she wrote: 'Dinah or Bella as I like to call her is in wonderful condition and looks a picture' and 'she gives us all so much pleasure' although 'she costs as much as a child to feed and keep'.[103] In 1957, however, Dinah began to have difficulty moving her hind legs. A worried Florence consulted a specialist Alsatian vet and Dinah was dispatched to the Royal College of Veterinary Surgeons for an x-ray.[104] The vet produced some pills to help with the condition. Treatment, however, came at a price. Florence writes: 'Enough tablets for one weeks treatment cost £3 it shook me.'[105] There was no immediate improvement and later that week Florence remained distressed: 'The poor darlings legs seem no better & she is not herself – very sad she seems.'[106] The vets recommended continued treatment – pills and a change in diet. Handing over £6 for a further two weeks' worth of pills, Florence reflected that she 'would not spend that on myself' but was more than willing to find the money for Dinah.[107]

The increasing use of veterinary medicine to treat pets fundamentally altered the economic and emotional relationship owners formed with them. Even basic treatment for animals was far from cheap. In 1960, for example, the Willett practice books show us that Miss G. of Virginia Water spent around £10 on veterinary treatment for her cats: costs

Florence and Dinah, 1952.

included spaying, examination, meds and 'keep and treat'.[108] In the 1960s this was no negligible sum – and would certainly have been beyond the means of many working households.

There was also a general suspicion that vets exploited people's emotional investment in their pets. As professional canine practice was expanding in the late 1890s, a judge had found in favour of an owner who complained he had been overcharged by a cynical vet for the treatment of his dog (the vet had refused to surrender the dog until the extortionate bill was paid).[109] Certainly, some pet owners spent inordinate sums on veterinary care for their animal companions. One of James Herriot's most pleasing clients was an extravagantly rich elderly widow, Mrs Pumphrey and her Pekinese dog, Tricki Woo. Although careful never to exploit Mrs Pumphrey, Herriot was mindful of the 'advantages' to playing 'uncle' to a dog whose mistress not only paid for every kind of (often unnecessary) medical attention but rewarded Tricki's personal physician with excellent sherry, Fortnum & Mason's hampers and personal gifts. Little wonder Herriot was 'genuinely attached' to the little dog.[110] But effusive pet love combined with deep pockets could make pet owners vulnerable to unscrupulous practitioners. Even vets assumed that town pet people were vulnerable to economic exploitation. Rural Suffolk vet Tim Swift commented in 1967 that town pets were members of the family: 'lovers, partners – anything you like'. Owners would pay 'fantastic sums' on pet healthcare and treatment. In the country, you could only treat a pet 'up to the economic level' and, even then, this applied mostly to dogs because 'cats don't rate as high in the country as in the town.'[111]

While pet keeping had long been about balancing emotional investment with the availability of economic resources, the growth of extensive vet treatment brought a new level of calculation into the process. For Florence Turtle, a successful professional woman with a relatively large disposable income, as well as a strong emotional attachment to her dog Dinah, this calculation was relatively straightforward. When the Withingtons' Sal had surgery in 1938 there was no real question of it not going ahead. The couple were well off and devoted to the dog (although Alan struggled to admit it). He writes in the diary: 'It'll set us back about 4 guineas – but Mum's upholstery bill would have topped that by the end of the week anyway.'[112]

But for many owners, a sudden bill of £9 for pills would have been out of the question. Socio-economic difference was a fundamental factor in determining the degree to which pets were treated by vets. Many less wealthy owners used the vet in a different way – repeat, routine maintenance was too expensive but vet costs might be viable in absolute extremis. Doreen Budd, born twelve years after Florence Turtle, also kept a daily diary from the 1930s.[113] Her life was very different. The daughter of a carter, Doreen worked as a domestic servant before marrying Howard, an agricultural labourer, in 1934. They lived in rural North Hampshire and Doreen often took on cleaning for the families Howard worked for. In February 1939 Howard brought home a spaniel puppy whom they named Peter.[114] While Doreen rarely wrote about her feelings, frequent references to Peter in her diary and his constant presence on walks suggest emotional investment in the animal. She was clearly anxious about his health too, weighing him weekly and noting the result.[115] Peter was sometimes ill or injured but these afflictions did not warrant a visit to the vet.[116] There was one occasion, though, when their tight household budget stretched to accommodate medical assistance for their pet. This was in February 1948 when Peter had a stroke.[117] The bill for this was 7/6, a substantial sum for the small household.[118] For couples like the Budds, veterinary treatment was still very much a last resort.

For owners with some means, but perhaps not quite enough, the increasing availability of medical treatment for pets could pose a difficult conundrum. Hard decisions had to be made. In 1959 Jennie Gauntlett Hill was living at home with her mother, Ellen, after her father's death. Jennie was 53 years old and working in a local bakery, although she gave up the job that year to support her mother, who at 89 could no longer be left by herself.[119] Jennie's new life as a full-time carer was challenging and it was increasingly difficult to care for Ellen in her physically debilitated state. Mother and daughter never had an easy relationship, and sometimes things were difficult between them. Despite the challenge, Jennie's diary tells how she built a new domestic life for herself and her mother with two cats – ginger Teddy and tabby Tibs, known as 'the boys' – at its heart. The cats had persistent health problems and veterinary intervention was often required. Teddy suffered from sinus problems and an eye infection and needed ointment.[120] Tibs, an older cat, had digestive problems. On 20 December 1959 Jennie grimly records emptying seven pans of diarrhoea.[121] In early 1960 Tibs was diagnosed with fibrosis of the liver – a permanent condition.[122] The necessary veterinary treatment strained the finances of the small household – Jennie had given up her job and they were now living on a modest private income. The tipping point came in 1961. Tibs had a kidney infection – requiring repeat vet visits and injections. Jennie rarely wrote about her feelings but on 21 January she recorded an argument with Ellen – about the cats. Ellen, near the end of her life, was worrying about the level of resources required to maintain Tibs and how Jennie would manage financially after she had gone. The subject was a source of considerable tension. Jennie writes 'M & I had a row over Tibs being put to sleep at her death. I was made to agree to this, but it grieves me.'[123]

Pets transformed

In the twentieth century veterinary intervention was increasingly used, not just to preserve animal life, but to shape it too. Fertility was increasingly controlled. According to many commentators, this was a matter of public health and animal welfare. The late nineteenth and early twentieth centuries witnessed a proliferation of animal 'shelters' dedicated to 'destroying' stray cats and dogs, seen as vectors of disease. That most were run by animal-welfare charities with financial support from borough councils highlights the perceived threat of stray animals to human health. All the major animal charities, from the RSPCA to Battersea Dogs Home, Canine Defence League and Our Dumb Friends' League, colluded in euthanizing populations of strays, the rate of cats destroyed far outstripping that for dogs – a reflection, some thought, of the low value placed on cat life. Urging financial donations to support cat shelters in 1921, Our Dumb Friends' League argued that those who loved cats should donate because euthanasia ended the stray cat's misery; those who hated cats should donate to help rid towns and cities of a pest problem.[124] A minority of charities, such as the Mayhew Home for Stray Cats and Dogs, prioritized rehoming but they were generally frowned upon and, according to some observers, utterly overrun by 'disreputable' cats.[125] From the 1910s RSPCA cat shelters in Liverpool received or collected thousands of cats every year from across poorer and 'comfortable' neighbourhoods. By 1925 the city centre shelters alone destroyed upwards of 25,000 cats a year.[126]

The problem, most charities agreed, was unchecked fertility. The value attached to pedigree breeds evidently generated health problems for dogs from repeated inbreeding but it did encourage notions of planned reproduction. Dogs left to their own devices would breed 'mongrels', often described as weak, despised and 'worthless'.[127] These were the dogs that were most likely to be collected as strays. A Canine

Defence League information leaflet issued in the late 1920s advised owners to drown mongrel pups immediately.[128] But if stray dogs continued to present a menace, the population of stray cats was phenomenal. According to the zoologist Colin Mathieson in 1939, the urban dog population at any time was approximately 5 per cent that of the human. In contrast, the cat population represented a staggering 13 per cent of human numbers and most of them were strays.[129] RSPCA promotions advised destroying kittens at birth, preferably in a humane way: the charity was willing to collect newborns from homes to carry out the work but such wholesale destruction was expensive and depressing.[130]

Neutering male cats was common from the nineteenth century although there was an increased expectation that this would be done under anaesthetic by a vet.[131] In 1925, according to top cat vet Hamilton Kirk, 'in a busy feline surgery the number of male castrations a surgeon is called upon to perform is really remarkable.' Kirk also spayed female cats – to prevent pregnancy – but this happened less often, and there were many possible complications. Kirk himself had a 90 per cent success rate for the operation but not all vets could claim the same.[132] While neutering male cats was widely recommended in the 1930s, spaying females was slower to catch on.[133] The first reference to cat spaying in the Willett practice records comes in 1941 when the practice charged £1.1.0 for spaying a cat by the name of Ginger (this was probably a rare ginger female cat).[134] But by the 1950s many middle-class cat owners were writing about their choice to have female cats spayed.[135] When the Tavistock Institute surveyed 773 cat-owning housewives in 1965, they found that 62 per cent of pet cats had been neutered: there were still fewer spayed females than neutered males, but wealthier social groups saw it as normal.[136]

For some owners the decision to spay was fraught with anxiety. For John and Frances Smyth, keeping their female Siamese Pooni in a flat meant that kittens were out of the question, 'but when the horrid day came we were demented. Friends had told us terrible tales of cats who died, cats who were never the same again and so on, and although we had every confidence in our vet, we loved Pooni so much by now that we felt sure that the worst would happen – just to teach us not to be so silly about an animal.'[137] Antonia White's Mrs Bell also worried over spaying Minka, her Siamese: 'though spaying a queen when done by a competent vet was now reputed to be no more risky than the much simpler operation on a tom, Mrs Bell could not help being nervous.'[138]

Seasoned animal-owner Doreen Tovey found the choice much more straightforward. Tovey's books make much of her and husband Charles's failings as novice cat carers but her matter-of-fact tone speaks of acquired expertise (later, she went on to be president of the Siamese Cat Club). Knowing her books would be read by panicking cat owners, she adopted a level-headed approach. Her first Siamese, the beloved Sugieh, died on the operating table during spaying, but she played up the unlikeliness of this event and did not hesitate to put her second Siamese queen, Sheba, through the same operation.[139]

Ultimately owners chose spaying because controlling female fertility made cats better pets. Successive litters of kittens might be difficult to rehome or required other (more gruesome) means of disposal. Tovey allowed Sugieh to have one litter but they found selling on the Siamese kittens difficult. Tovey had no qualms about ending Sugeih's motherhood: at the end of the day Doreen and Charles wanted a pet, not a mother. 'We had bought Sugeih primarily as a pet, and that since having kittens she had grown so preoccupied with them she had undoubtedly grown away from us. She had become very thin and nervous too. We didn't want her to be like that all her life.'[140] Others expressed more anxiety about altering the 'natural' qualities of their pets. After all, cats in the nineteenth century had often been praised for their mothering abilities. Mrs Bell was 'half tempted to let her have one litter of kittens by a Siamese mate before being operated on, but she decided against it'. She worried, though, about the consequences of not finding a 'husband' for the cat: 'when a female Siamese is in season and remains unmated, she becomes almost hysterical with frustration.'[141] When Pooni was spayed, John Smyth also felt uneasy as the op had, he believed, caused his pet to 'develop an absolute scanner against men'.[142] There was some personal guilt here about subjecting the animal to the operation, and a sense of discomfort with altering what was perceived as the natural order.

Cat owners were more comfortable with neutering male cats. This was a less intrusive procedure and well established. The castration of a tom tended to be dealt with by owners in brisk terms emphasizing that the fundamental maleness of the animals remained unchanged. Smyth had no qualms over the neutering of his male Siamese, Tomkin, who had the operation at three months and 'took it in his stride and, apart from being minus certain reproductive organs, he has remained a very male cat'.[143] White adopted a similar tone in her depiction of the procedure for Mrs Bell's Curdy: 'He remained as essentially masculine in temperament as Minka remained feminine.'[144] The Toveys had their male cat, Solomon, neutered on the grounds that 'even our best friends wouldn't have lasted long in a house with an unneutered Siamese.' The decision was helped by the individual qualities of the cat, who appeared to be temperamentally unsuited to breeding: 'We could as soon imagine Solomon a stud tom as pretending to be a lion at a zoo.'[145]

The vetted pet

What HAVE we done to deserve this?! Here's Marsden home after an 11hr. run, with an 8 weeks old Cairn bitch, a present for my birthday! I do hope I wasn't too uneffusive with my thanks! Because it is a pedigree animal & must have cost him quite a number of Scottish roubles. But I'm really thoroughly the reverse of enthusiastic, let's face it. And, well, let's face it – we've got a dog again.[146]

It was 6 June 1961 and the Withingtons had acquired a new dog. Alan, now retired, potentially had more time to devote to dog care, but the new pet was as much a burden as it was a blessing. After the arrival of Dame Flora, Withington's wife Morag was swiftly despatched to the local vet to inquire about injections. This was the beginning of a long and involved relationship, as their new pet turned out to be hosting a rich variety of parasites. Ointment and pills for scratching and worms were duly supplied. In the first few months they were in and out on a regular basis, for these issues and a series of injections. After the distemper injection, Withington remarked on the difference between current veterinary practice and his 'young days' when, he believed, all dogs had distemper and many died: 'Now it seems to be just give 'em a prick & think no more about it.'[147] For well-off owners veterinary intervention brought a wealth of solutions to irritating minor ailments and pet problems. It brought emotional security too, removing the previously pervasive threat of dog distemper. A trusted vet, though, supplied more than just medical support. On 7 November Alan wrote: 'Took Flora to Mrs. Evans this morning; primarily for the second half of her Epivax injection, but I used the opportunity to have a chat about this wretched barking up the garden & general uncontrollability. And, to some extent, I was comforted.'[148] Vitamins were recommended and there were some reassuring words: 'Anyway Cairns were stubborn little animals & often

Morag Withington and Flora, 1961, photograph.

didn't really reach their best until 18 months. So it looks as if we must be patient & not be downcast because early promise is being slow to develop.' For the Withingtons, the vet was a source of guidance on dog behaviour and psychology as well as an emotional prop. By the mid-twentieth century vets had become a new form of authority, intervening and shaping pet–owner relationships in new ways.

But the massive expansion of veterinary technology and medicine since the Second World War raised ethical issues too. The possibilities of veterinary technologies raise queries about whether *all* veterinary treatments are in the interests of animals or for the benefit of owners who cannot bear to part with their pets. People's choices about pet healthcare continue to be shaped by 'vet economics' and there is, undoubtedly, a tiered system of access to treatment and healthcare that depends very much on owners' ability, and willingness, to pay. In his 2016 biography of Nigel, a golden retriever, the popular author and gardener Monty Don recalled the devastating moment when Nigel broke his back. The local vet initially refused to attend the emergency and veterinary nurses only collected Nigel because Don refused to go away. The prognosis was gloomy: Nigel would need one leg amputated but he also appeared to be incontinent and semi-paralysed. Fortunately for Nigel, Monty Don had 'friends in high places' and gained access to celebrity 'supervet' Noel Fitzpatrick, widely acknowledged to be 'the very best'. Fitzpatrick's practice was 'an extraordinary place, fitted with the latest and most modern technology'. Fitzpatrick was also renowned for his willingness to perform 'extreme surgery' in order to save an animal's life. Within a week of being an inpatient, Nigel was pretty much restored to his dynamic, fully functioning self. As Don points out, a 'good and trusted' local vet had not held out much hope; Fitzpatrick's ready access to expensive technology and willingness to take risks produced a recovery 'little short of miraculous'. What pet owner wouldn't want such healthcare for their companion? As Fitzpatrick says: 'the only things that matter are love and health. That's it! There is nothing else!'[149] Sure. Unfortunately, the deep pockets of love do not always stretch to the financial costs of health.

Since the late 1940s UK pet owners have been able to take out insurance policies to cover the costs of veterinary care, pet theft and death.[150] As veterinary treatment for pets became more sophisticated (and expensive) in the latter half of the twentieth century, pet insurance policies became far more widespread. Some of the most successful pet insurance providers in the early 2000s were established, or began to offer pet insurance schemes, in the 1980s. By 2016 gross written insurance premiums for pets in the UK totalled over £1 billion, 97 per cent of them for cats and dogs.[151] The logic of pet insurance is that it covers the costs of exploratory tests, surgery and treatments that would otherwise be inaccessible to the majority of pet owners. But for many people, pet insurance premiums are a luxury too: the average annual cost for a lifetime policy in 2020 was over £400 for a dog and £350 for a cat. In these circumstances, it shouldn't surprise us that the PDSA – and other animal charities – continue to provide much-needed veterinary assistance to households who would otherwise struggle to gain access to diagnoses, medicine and treatment. In 2020 the PDSA ran 48 animal hospitals across the UK and multiple clinics. The possibilities for pet health have come a long way since Victorian advice writers advocated castor oil as a cure-all but access to healthcare for pets remains unequal.

SIX

In Loving Memory: Mourning for Pets

I n December 1886 the twenty-year-old Beatrix Potter reflected on her year. Of particular note was the death on 18 October of 'Poor Miss Mouse'. Potter was 'very much distressed' at this death, partly because it was unexpected: Miss Mouse had been 'so sensible in taking her medicine' that Potter thought 'she would get through'. But, assailed by asthma, the little mouse had 'laid herself out in my hand and died'. Two months later, Potter still lamented the 'poor little thing'. Despite Miss Mouse's 'great age', her white eyebrows and loss of sight, her demise seemed hard to believe: 'at one time' Potter reflected, 'I thought she would last as long as myself.' She was an especially well-connected mouse, counting the Liberal parliamentarian John Bright, artist John Everett Millais and explorer Benjamin Leigh Smith among her acquaintances (they all 'admired and stroked her'). The mouse had been 'affection-ate and apparently happy' to the end and 'in many respects', Potter wrote, was 'the sweetest little animal I ever knew'.[1] Potter had many pets throughout girlhood and expressed dismay each time one died, although, as with Miss Mouse, some affected her more than others. Living with difficult parents and mixing with few people her own age, Potter forged keen bonds with the animals she spent hours drawing and training to perform tricks. Elsewhere in her journal she described burying deceased pets in the family garden and exclaimed that the Manchester authorities annually collected 'seven tonnes' of dead dogs and thirteen of cats from the city's streets: 'They are boiled down and the oil is said to be worth a good deal to make *Olio Margarine* and other alternative butters!'[2]

Potter's diary reflects the spectrum of pet death and bereavement at the end of the nineteenth century. People forged strong emotional ties to animals they cared for. Pet death was a wrench, even when the animal was a 'poor little mouse'. But, as Potter indicated, mourning for pets was an uneven experience throughout society, despite increasing recognition of the emotional dimensions of animal companionship across the social scale. From the 1880s, following a trend for burial of dogs in a small corner of London's Hyde Park, commercial pet cemeteries began to emerge across Britain but most of their early clientele were the rich and celebrities. As Potter's retelling of the 'dead dogs make margarine' urban myth makes clear, disposal of a dead pet presented a problem for people without access to gardens or the resources to pay for burial. While the twentieth century witnessed the expansion of accessible cemetery and crematoria facilities, attitudes towards pet grief were slower to change. For much of this period, pet grief was overwhelmingly associated with the sentimental and silly. Put another way, while cultural depictions of pets as family members became increasingly common throughout the Victorian period and afterwards, pet mourning was often considered frivolous, the preserve of women (especially the unmarried) or just immature, the privilege of children learning to comprehend what death meant.

A break in the family

In 1906 the *Illustrated London News* ran a double-page image, the kind that could be pulled out and framed to decorate a sitting-room wall. Titled 'A Break in the Family: Tears for a Lost Pet in London's Dog Cemetery' it showed a young mother and her children watching the interment of 'Carlo', a dog 'faithful unto the death'. A plain white wreath lay beside the tiny grave and one of the little girls clutched a floral posy. An older boy stood at the back of the group, sombre and slightly detached, while his younger brother, dressed in a sailor suit, gazed on with curiosity. The absence of a father confirmed this as a nursery scene rather than a family funeral. As the caption noted, the scene was typical of the 'many little tragedies' and 'broken hearts' played out in the pet cemetery.[3]

Continuing a tradition from at least the eighteenth century, images and stories of pet life and death were often didactic, teaching children moral values but also about death itself. Until the 1870s human mortality rates remained stubbornly high and most children across the social scale would experience the death of a close relative before they

H. H. Flère, 'A Break in the Family: Tears for a Lost Pet in London's Dog-Cemetery',
Illustrated London News, 8 September 1906.

reached the age of ten. Children's storybooks and magazines were
unabashed in relaying graphic accounts of deathbed scenes, especially
of other children. This wasn't simply the Victorians being gruesome
(though, of course, they could be); the logic was to teach children about
death, ideally before they experienced it in family life. Pet deaths were
another way of introducing children to the mysteries and sadness of
death, both in real time and in fiction.

Children who kept pets with typically short lifespans, such as goldfish, guinea pigs or hamsters, were almost guaranteed to encounter death
within a year or so. Birds were notoriously fragile, with many surviving
just hours or days in domestic cages. The demise of these animals could
teach children harsh lessons about nature and responsibility. Children's
author Emma Davenport did not shy away from death in her book
Little Toys (1878), a collection of personal anecdotes about pets in childhood: a terrier was poisoned by strychnine, a kitten run over by a train
and pet pigeons shot by neighbouring farmers. This litany of death
warned children that pet lives were fragile and raised awareness of human
obligations to animals. An extended anecdote about a pet jackdaw ended
with his violent demise in the jaws of a weasel. The fault lay with the
children for 'not having safely fastened him in a cage in the house'. Once
they found the remains of 'our poor pet', there was nothing they could
do 'but bury the body of poor Jacky'. And, of course, learn their lesson.[4]
When children formed special bonds with pets, the bewilderment of
loss could make a lasting impression. Davenport discriminated between

the deaths of animals that might be considered less companionate and those with whom children were expected to forge strong affective connections. When Tawney, her terrier, died suddenly from poisoning, she and her siblings regretted 'heartily' the 'loss of our dear play fellow'. Compared to her apparent ambivalence towards the other dead 'pets', Davenport noted that 'We had not another dog for a very long time, and never shall love one so well as Tawney.'[5]

The value of such experiences in learning about personal responsibility and the finality of death was not limited to the Victorians. Pets often featured in moralizing literature for children from the eighteenth century.[6] What distinguished the Victorian period and afterwards was the expansion of pet keeping across the social scale and the number of sources that document it, especially those composed by children themselves. As schoolboy Michael wrote to children's author Alison Uttley in the mid-twentieth century, his pet tortoise had died 'for ever and ever'.[7] Arguably, pets that were less tactile provoked less anguish than those that children imagined as playmates. Oliver Henry Lloyd kept multiple pets in the Victorian villa he shared with his solicitor father, two older brothers and governess. His diary entries from 1869 record silkworms, an aquarium, kittens and mice. On the death of his eel in 1870, nine-year-old Oliver simply noted that the eel was 'found dead' having been chased from the aquarium by minnows. Oliver composed an 'Ode' commemorating the life of the 'sweet waterworm', believed to be twelve years old, but this was more an exercise in rhyme and recounting the eel's habits than a mournful epitaph. The final verse struck a grimly humorous note: 'The greatest possible mess for you/ Is when you shall get in stew.'[8]

As Emma Davenport noted, children could be clumsy and thoughtless. In 1872 Oliver Lloyd's older brother Bob killed one of their 'pretty' white mice by kneeling on it (in the ensuing chaos, another mouse took the opportunity to escape). The boys subsequently got boxes for the mice to live in.[9] Girls, socialized to care and nurture, perhaps felt more responsibility for pet deaths. Suspended between girl and womanhood, seventeen-year-old Beatrix Potter lamented the death of an entire family of snails as 'an awful tragedy'. Potter had named the snails and noted their 'different character[s]' but she felt responsible for their deaths as she ruminated on whether she should have kept their winter habitat moist.[10]

Some pets' demise taught children about injustice too. According to his father, a clerk in the General Register Office, the first words uttered by Stevy (born in 1851) were 'Bow Wow'. When the maid accidentally killed his kitten after he had gone to bed, Stevy, then aged six, was woken by the commotion. On being told the cause of the noise, the little boy 'burst out into such a torrent of grief as I have ever seen him in, crying ceaselessly while the tears stream down his face for "his kitty his Dear Kitty Oh! They'd killed his dear kitty" nothing would pacify him; we knew not what to do with him'. After 'cuddles' from his parents for 'a long time', he finally exhausted himself and went back to sleep.[11] At the end of the century, another boy 'broke my heart' when his father, a hard-headed farm labourer, got rid of his pet rabbit claiming he didn't have space to accommodate her offspring (she'd just had six babies). Decades later, his bafflement and grief remained raw: 'Oh I cried mind. I thought a lot of the old Dutch rabbit. Yes.'[12] Sometimes a pet's unexpected or violent death generated feelings of rage. When his cat was run over by the horse-drawn night-mail van on its route from Oxford to Reading, one outraged boy waited for the van the following night declaring his intention to 'kill' the driver responsible.[13]

Many children would have been familiar with the nursery rhyme 'The Death and Funeral of Cock Robin', a story of birds organizing a funeral for a murdered robin (spoiler alert: Sparrow was the villain).[14] There were more saccharine variations that depicted children organizing funerals for birds, such as Juliana Ewing's 'The Burial of the Linnet' (1884), which tells the story of children burying the dead bird 'softly' and 'nobly' in a garden alongside other deceased pets.[15] Pet funerals were instructive for children, teaching the ritual practices that accompanied bereavement and generating experience of their supposedly cathartic purpose. Encountering the graves of pets, meanwhile, could prompt reflection on the character of life and death. In a Cornwall village at the turn of the twentieth century, the 'big' house was a venue for local fetes. Of recurring fascination for one child who attended was the 'little' cemetery with 'little headstones' for the family's pets: it was 'lovely' to 'look around', pausing for a moment of quiet contemplation at an otherwise exuberant event.[16]

Most children with gardens or access to public land enacted some ritual for disposing of their dead pets. Pets could be placed into a makeshift coffin, such as the cat Trilby (the lone pet in a family of twelve children), whose youthful mourners repurposed a box for burying him.[17] Oliver Lloyd buried his white mice in a homemade 'tomb' in the family garden.[18] Parents could provide guidance on ritual and validate children's

Bury him softly - white wool around him.
Kiss his poor feathers - the first kiss and last.
Tell his poor widow kind friends have found him:
Plant his poor grave with whatever grows fast.

R. André, 'The Burial of the Linnet', illustration in Juliana Horatia Ewing, *Papa Poodle and Other Pets* (c. 1884).

grief. One post-office clerk in 1910s Llantrisant assisted his children in conducting a funeral 'with great ceremony' for their canary.[19] In the summer of 1905 a thirteen-year-old ginger-and-white cat, Mick, died at his village home just outside Manchester. When Hilda Winstanley, nine, and her seven-year-old sister Lily learned the news they 'cried loudly' and asked their mother if they could wear black hair ribbons: they had known Mick all their lives. Here, adults not only validated the children's grief, but shared it. Mother struggled to keep her composure, her 'face working' while she 'dramatically' exclaimed 'He's gone! He knowed everything, our Mick did.' He was 'one of us' and deserved 'a proper burying' in a 'proper tidy grave and us'll all be there'. Grandmother, who was 'allus one for Mick', participated in the funeral, as did Hilda's older brothers, aged fifteen and seventeen. The father, a farm labourer, dug the grave 'heavily' and the entire family stood 'miserably around'. With 'tears rolling down', Mother laid Mick in the grave. Everyone placed white and purple asters on top of the small body and 'solemnly' scattered soil. The women dressed for the occasion: Mother in a clean white apron, Grandma in her Sunday bonnet and black beaded cape and the girls in their best white muslin frocks. For weeks afterwards, Hilda and Lily put a jam jar of flowers on the tiny grave before installing a 'little wooden cross' declaring 'In Loving Memory of Mick', his date of death and age, and the familiar words 'REST IN PEACE'. Telling this story in middle age, the author Margaret Penn (Hilda in the book) emphasized that *family* love cut across blood and species ties. This really mattered because Penn, an adopted child, had no blood ties to the Winstanleys.[20]

For working-class children without access to green space, pet loss could be amplified by witnessing rather more prosaic animal disposal. According to some commentators, waste ground or water were typical destinations for the dead pets of poorer people.[21] In 1930s Liverpool, the Ladies Committee of the RSPCA noted the number of cat remains found in the city's streets or deposited in lime pits on building sites.[22] This reflected the limited options for the disposal of dead pets in urban centres when families could not afford pet burial. It also reflected a phrase in common use since the nineteenth century when being 'buried like a dog' was taken to be a slur on the rudimentary burial of paupers whose remains were treated like trash.

But for the children of families with gardens, pet graves could mimic the human graveyard. In April 1890 a young Lawrence Pilkington (the following year he and his brother would establish the hugely successful Pilkington's Tile and Pottery Co.) wrote to his fiancée Mollie Gavin Stevenson that he had 'very suddenly' taken a house for them on a seven-year lease. It was, he thought, the most perfect abode. There was one curiosity in the garden though: a tiny pets' graveyard consisting of two headstones with 'regular' stonemason inscriptions to the 'faithful' pets of the current tenant's children.[23] If Pilkington was touched by the dogs' graves (describing it to Mollie gave him a rush of love for her as he imagined her sympathetic response), the 'regular' features of the headstones were replicated in gardens across Britain and, increasingly, public pet cemeteries.

Pet cemeteries

The first commercial pet cemetery nestled in a small corner of royal Hyde Park. What began as a special favour to a family whose children were fond of playing in the park set a trend as others – a high-ranking priest in the Catholic Church, distinguished members of the British army, a well-known 'burlesque actress' – clamoured to inter their beloved pets there too.[24] By 1901 the small cemetery was declared full. As the *Illustrated London News*'s sketch 'A Break in the Family' demonstrated, Hyde Park Pet Cemetery generated considerable public interest. Multiple newspapers reported on the novelty of rows of tiny headstones recording the sentimental and sporting characteristics of animals buried there. It also touched a nerve: small commercial pet cemeteries opened in the provinces from the 1880s to reflect the growth in other services and products – from grooming parlours to specialist foodstuffs to diamond collars – for pets in the latter half of the nineteenth century. Nor was the trend confined to Britain. Public pet cemeteries opened in Stockholm and Helsinki in 1872.[25] The Paris Dog Cemetery, an elaborate, purpose-built affair, opened in 1899 while in America, a 'national cemetery' for pets opened in Hudson Valley, New York, the same year. It boasted over 110 acres of 'picturesquely situated and artificially-beautified land' and provided full embalming services, mourning paraphernalia and a 'tasteful' chapel of rest alongside a crematorium.[26]

Molesworth Pet Cemetery, Cambridge, was the closest Britain got to the American and Parisian examples. Opening in 1903, it comprised several acres of land, the layout clearly inspired by cemeteries for humans. Owned by John Grey and his wife, formerly of Hyde Park Gate, they instituted differential prices for graves based on location and size, insisted on the installation of headstones and operated sliding scales of cost for size, material, lettering and kerbstones. Molesworth provided a full 'funeral' service for pets, performed by Mr Grey in a velvet coat and hat, wheeling small coffins in a barrow reserved for the purpose.[27] Early cemeteries like Molesworth were frequently called dog cemeteries, a reflection of their overwhelmingly canine residents and the higher status accorded to dogs as prized pets. A cat cemetery was established in 1880s Essex and cat burials increased as the status of cats rose and public pet cemeteries expanded during the twentieth century.

Elaborate funerals for pets could seem like a caricature of human burial but, as any heartbroken child could have testified, the rites attached to funerals were cathartic and symbolized affection for the animal. Many mourners placed floral tributes on their pets' graves. At Hyde Park in 1897, one new grave was covered in a 'magnificent mountain of wreaths'. They contained the Victorian flora of grief and remembrance: maiden-hair ferns, lilies and stephanotis.[28] At the Paris Dog Cemetery, grave owners regularly laid wreaths on their plots, especially on All Souls day, much to the consternation of the Catholic Church who resisted practices that suggested animals had souls.[29]

Pet cemeteries at this period were undoubtedly the preserve of the urban elite. Commentators from the 1890s were explicit in noting that burial in Hyde Park was for dogs with the 'good fortune' to have wealthy friends.[30] The *Daily Mirror* marvelled at the expenditure and novelty of Molesworth.[31] The tone persisted into the 1920s and '30s. As the *Daily Express* noted in 1928, pet cemeteries were for 'aristocratic dogs'.[32] Ten years later, the *Daily Mirror* commented that 'handsome' memorials, much like those to 'some dear parent or loved child', 'cost a pretty penny'.[33] People with access to gardens or common land tended to bury pets closer to home. Jane Carlyle requested her dog Nero be buried at the top of her garden and commissioned a headstone when he died in 1860.[34] In 1880s Italy, the artist and lyricist Edward Lear placed his much-loved cat Foss in a box and buried him 'deep' beneath the fig trees at the end of the orange walk. The following day, a stone with an inscription to the memory of Foss was installed above the tiny grave.[35] Bachelor Arthur Jones mentioned Capel almost daily in his diary until the dog died unexpectedly one spring morning in 1895, moving Arthur to record that the dog had been his 'faithful companion for over thirteen years'. The following day, Capel was interred at the top of the kitchen garden walk. Although he moved to a new house not long after, Jones had 'photographed [Capel] as he was lying by [the] side of his grave' as a memento.[36] When a second dog, Boffin, died in 1909, Jones made his grave under the apple tree in the garden.[37] Leonard and Virginia Woolf buried their dog Pinka in the orchard of their garden.[38]

Garden graves were cheaper and, arguably, more intimate than commercial cemeteries, which, even by the interwar period, were mostly located on the outskirts of large urban areas and continued to cater primarily to those with significant disposable income. But private pet graves were also vulnerable to changes in human life cycles, a harsh fact realized by the little girls who sought Lawrence Pilkington's reassurance that he and Mollie would not disturb the pet graves when they took over the lease of their house.[39] When the family dog, Brunnie, was buried in her mother's garden on Putney Bridge Road in 1936, Florence Turtle 'felt depressed' to think of her 'lovely silky body and bright eyes' rotting in a garden that, when her mother died, would be sold with the house. She wished the dog had been interred instead on her own 'grass plot'.[40]

One way to feel closer to a deceased pet was to memorialize within the home, a mode of mourning that cut across classes as locks of hair, visual depictions of a pet or pet possessions could be turned into commemorative artefacts. Rather more extravagantly, writer and dramatist George R. Sims, a well-known animal lover, had an inkstand made from the hoof of his favourite mare. A widower for extended periods, Sims merged classic modes of sporting manhood with dandyism and his relationship with animals epitomized a playful reimagining of the bourgeois, heterosexual family. He held a 'christening' ceremony for his dog Barney Barnato in December 1895 and boasted that he regularly enjoyed sharing the dinner table with his pets.[41] The most striking objects in Sims's study were two large French immortelles hanging over the mantel. Both wreaths bore inscriptions: 'In memory of Dinkie, for 15 years the faithful friend and dog of George R Sims' and, more tongue-in-cheek, 'In Memory of Pickle who for 14 years was devoted to the very best master a dog ever knew.'[42]

Few owners fused commemoration with such irreverence, but pet graves indicate the importance of practices borrowed from human mourning ritual to express the significance of pets in individual lives. Many inscriptions in Hyde Park and Molesworth indicated relationships

Grave for Judy, Jesmond collie.

between human and animal, using words like 'friend', 'companion', 'pal' and 'pet'. Bobbie, for example, was the 'choicest pet' and 'truest friend'; 'Rex' was 'For nine years the devoted companion of Lady Bancroft'; 'Dear Fitz' had been a 'most faithful companion' for almost seventeen years to 'Captain and Mrs Shirley'. Sometimes the friendships commemorated were between animals, so Jimmie was the 'Beloved and Loving Companion of Jum and Kitty'. Some headstones recorded the name and age of the deceased but the majority carried some kind of emotive or qualitative indicator. At Molesworth, the most common inscriptions mimicked those of graves for humans, beginning with 'In Loving Memory'. 'Faithful', 'devoted' and 'loving' were common adjectives. Many epitaphs used the word 'little' between adjective and noun: 'Dear Little Jinkie', 'Poor Little Prince', 'Faithful Little Companion' – and the anguished memorial to 'Faithful Little Viper – If I thought we'd meet again, it would lessen half the pain'.

Inseparable companions

The word 'little' on headstones indicates animal dependency on humans and similarities to the bonds between parent and child. Some Molesworth inscriptions explicitly referenced motherhood: 'In Memory of My Beloved Baby' or mourned by 'Mummy'. The trend wasn't restricted to the Victorians and Edwardians: a headline in the *Northampton Mercury and Herald* in 1939 about women visiting graves at Molesworth drew attention to an inscription to 'Goggles, My Baby'.[43] It isn't surprising that women were especially associated with animal love or that single women, widows or women without children were particularly aligned with pet grief. Cultural depictions of women as the nurturing sex were endemic in this period. Certainly, headstone inscriptions in pet cemeteries indicate a heavy preponderance of women. As earlier chapters outlined, single or widowed people and those without children were most likely to emotionally invest in animals. But of all these categories, women were especially associated with pet grief.

As historians Philip Howell and, more recently, Diana Donald have noted, it was mostly women who lobbied for animal welfare and the inclusion of pets into conceptions of the afterlife, a position made plain by the number of women who included reference to spiritual reunions with dead pets on headstones in Hyde Park. As Howell points out, some women's desire to include animals in the afterlife represented the close intertwining of their feminist and animal-welfare politics.[44] Howell is at pains to take seriously the graves and inscriptions in Hyde Park. But the earnest sympathy betrays the orthodoxy that pet love has at best been treated with amused indulgence and at worst with contempt.

Bereaved pet people, especially women without children, who expressed pet grief often felt the need to apologize for or at least explain their melancholy. Reflecting on the death of Flossy, her sister Anne's spaniel, in 1854, Charlotte Brontë noted that 'the loss even of a dog is very saddening'.[45] Writing to a female friend in spring 1850, Jane Carlyle shared her delight in having acquired a 'little dog' (Nero) that 'I make more fuss about than beseems a sensible woman.'[46] When Nero died ten years later, Jane was distraught. Writing to thank the doctor who attended Nero at his end, she challenged: 'Oh don't think me absurd, you, for caring so much about a dog? Nobody but myself can have any idea what that little creature has been in my life.' Even so, Jane attempted to explain it: 'My inseparable companion during eleven years, ever doing his little best to keep me from feeling sad and lonely.' The defiance is a little defensive, an insight into Jane's painful awareness that others were unlikely to grasp the gravity of her grief for the dog. Jane wrote because she thought the kind doctor might call but 'wished not to treat you to more tears; of which you had had too much [yesterday]' while she 'wouldn't be at home for [other] visitors to criticize my swollen eyes, and smile at grief "about a dog"'.[47]

In correspondence and exchanges with friends, freshly bereaved writers tended to feel some account for deep distress was owed. Writing to Margaret 'Betty' Black (later married to the third Lord Aberdare) in spring 1908, Alison Cunningham related that her 'dear doggie' had died unexpectedly a couple of days previously. She was 'quite breaking my heart'; 'he had been my constant companion for 11 years so I miss him'. The house felt so different 'without my dear loving faithful devoted doggie'. Alison signed off apologizing for 'saying so much about him' but hoped Betty would understand: 'I know your tender heart and also that you too love our dumb friends.' She hoped she would meet her dog again in 'the silent land'.[48]

As women increasingly forged independent lives following the First World War, pets were companions in otherwise solitary lives. Aged thirty in January 1936, single and living at home with her parents, Jennie Gauntlett Hill acquired a 'perfectly sweet' kitten she named Trixie. While Jennie didn't have to work, she was not always happy at home and

Photograph inscribed by
Jennie Gauntlett Hill as
'Trixie and Self 1937'.

struggled to assert her independence, periodically working as a mechanic
in a local garage until her disapproving mother made her give up the job.
The cat was an important emotional investment. But at just two years
old, Trixie developed kidney trouble and, following a month's illness,
was euthanized by the vet just before Christmas. His death 'struck' her
'to the heart': 'no one will ever know what I went through . . . My little
Trix, my little pal I loved you so. Grief and loneliness it is for me.' Jennie
continued about her daily duties and social obligations, pouring her
feelings into her diary. The day after Trix's death she felt 'quite ill, it is
such grief to me. Everywhere reminds me of him and his dear, funny
little ways.' Embarrassed about sharing her grief, Jennie 'could scarcely
tell' someone who inquired if all was well. Jennie seemed unsure how
she *should* respond or whether her feelings were rational. The day after
the cat's demise, she exclaimed that she 'can't get over the loss. Oh, I
miss him so. Poor little fellow. I suppose I loved him too much, but he
twisted me round his little claw.' Trix had been intrinsic to her everyday
routines so that 'it was awful to go and get supper and no Trix to feed';
to sit with 'no little fellow on my lap'.

In the first week of her loss, Jennie wrote constantly about her grief.
Her diary suggests it was not just the loss of 'such a beautiful little sweetheart' but loneliness too: 'no little friend to greet me'; the sadness of a
silent home and empty lap; the absence of someone to 'love and make
a fuss of, to think and care for'. As Jennie observed, Trix 'filled my heart'.
The household atmosphere worsened when, on 29 December the same

year, the vet told her 'heartbroken' mother she had to have her dog Tim euthanized.[49] The festive period probably accentuated the loneliness. The gardener turfed Trixie's grave so it 'doesn't look so stark and naked now' and Jennie spent New Year's Eve making a wreath for what would have been his third birthday. Jennie carefully photographed the grave and pasted its image into her family album, alongside a photo of the grave of her brother Sonnie.

When Florence Turtle lost her family dog Brunnie in 1936 she wrote about her profound and deep loss in her diaries, relating it to her feelings about her human family. But she also reflected how difficult it was to deal with a loss that meant so much but was not taken seriously by those around her. After Brunnie's death, Florence kept a social arrangement with a friend but when she arrived she 'felt very "weepy", went home and literally howled in the bathroom'. In her diary Florence reflected the tension between public obligations and the private confusion over pet loss, writing about her pleasure in that day's working lunch and choir practice (before Brunnie died) while noting that, throughout, she had been thinking 'on and off' about 'darling Brunnie and what a character she was' in the knowledge that the dog was 'sinking'. Ensconced in the

Page from Jennie's album showing Trixie's grave, 1938, and Sonnie's grave, 1931, as well as a photograph of Tim.

privacy of home that night, Florence's awareness of her sleeping flatmates made her feel self-conscious about crying but she was unable to stop. Having gone to bed, Florence woke at three and 'kept thinking of all the happy times I have had with "my Brun"'.

Over the next few days, Florence returned in her diary to her loss, tears springing to her eyes as she wrote. She worried that it was 'very silly' and 'only a dog people would say'. Her friend Barbara understood, noting that her idea of heaven would be for 'one's favourite dog' to run and 'meet one on the other side'. Florence agreed although both women were saddened by theologies asserting that dogs had no souls. Although hesitant, Florence did tell people at work of her loss, presumably seeking to explain her subdued demeanour. As it turned out, even male work colleagues were sympathetic, one observing that 'of all the dogs' he kept, 'one special one stood out above all the others', another confiding that he 'trembles to think of' when his eight-year-old chow would be 'gone'. Another friend sent a message of sympathy that prompted Florence to reflect that there would be 'tragedy' when 'anything happens to [the friend's pet] Judy'. Still, Florence sought to understand and rationalize her 'sense of personal tragedy and deep loss' for 'darling Brunnie'. Her mother confided that she had missed the dog more than when her own husband went into hospital. Florence's initial response, 'what a thing to say', was tempered on reflection: it was 'no doubt true!'[50]

Florence wasn't unique. Jean Pratt moved into her dream home, Wee Cottage, in July 1939, declaring in her diary later that year that she 'cannot be lonely' with the companionship of her 'little' cat Dinah, 'one of the dearest animals I have ever known'.[51] Mostly unhappy in love affairs, Jean used love for her cats and cottage as a benchmark for measuring the men she became involved with. Writing in her diary in 1943, 34-year-old Jean was losing hope of marriage and knew that she talked of her cats 'foolishly' and was 'foolishly fond of them': after all, she wrote, 'I adore them.' But when a friend 'suddenly' said that the cats 'gave her the pip' and Jean must 'not forget that they were only animals', she was 'hurt and surprised', raging against the woman's 'damnable cruelty' and her 'little, hard, rigid streak'. After all, the friend had 'all she needs as a woman to lavish her affection on (and a baby on the way) and she does not have to find substitutes'. Jean expected 'more sympathy, more tolerance' from female friends and felt she had been 'despised' and 'reproved' for loving 'extravagantly' an 'unworthy' subject.[52]

Over the next decades, Jean experienced many forms of pet loss, from selling or rehoming the many (many!) kittens that her unneutered cats produced through to unexpected or unexplained deaths. Each parting affected her differently and most of them deeply. In March 1947 she reflected on Twinkle's illness: 'Why does it matter so much?' Twinkle was 'only a cat, one of many'. But he was, she thought, 'as much a person in his way as any of my friends' and this explained why his dying will 'rend me to pieces so that I weep as much as I would for a loved human', 'more perhaps'. Every cat she loved and lost was 'a separate, individual friend' with a 'distinct, loveable personality, a miracle of independent life to watch and love'; every time a cat died, or left, 'something in me goes too'. And although animals were replaced in one sense, they were 'never exactly the same'.

After Twinkle died, Jean wrote that she wanted to 'howl my heart out' when a bank clerk inquired about the contents of her (empty) cat basket. Once she got home, she couldn't stop crying and turned to her diary to pour out her anguish. Of course, she had 'so many cats' but 'My heart breaks every time.' Twinkle's suffering exacerbated her despair at death's 'cold, remorseless' victory: 'There are no compensations, none.' His death brought back memories of her parents' deaths too, for they both died in pain. Jean wished that there was 'something more' for Twinkle after the 'pool of life' and trusted that the 'little bit of me that loved you' would go with him. Returning to her diary later that day, she went 'over and over' Twinkle's end and mused with horror at the inevitable prospect of Dinah, her first cat at Wee Cottage, dying. As Jean closed her entry that day, she 'couldn't feel more grief, more loneliness at the loss of a human friend'. But, she pondered, this proved that she needed human companionship too. Meanwhile, her cats 'help fill a gap and to satisfy some of the emotion that must be satisfied'.[53]

Alison Uttley, a successful children's author by the 1940s, was widowed relatively young (her husband took his own life). When her only child, John, left home, she experienced acute loneliness. Her chief companion was a Scottie dog, Hamish. When he became unwell in April 1944, sixty-year-old Uttley was 'very anxious'. She hated to see her 'little friend in such pain' and, as she lay in front of the fire with the sick dog, began to recount their shared life: 'I feel very very sad, I adore him little chap. All the things we have done! I remember how he came to me and licked my hand once when I wept.' Hamish had been her core companion at the lowest moments: 'How he brightens up life always.'

His friendship, 'patience' and 'faithfulness' were 'more than human'. Uttley lay with Hamish as he died. Afterwards, she stayed and 'stroke[d] him a long time as he lay on the blanket before the fire'. Placing a sprig of rosemary for remembrance on his small body, Uttley expressed her despair to her diary: 'Never have I loved a dog as I loved Hamish. I've said a prayer to God to be with him. Say goodnight little Hamish . . . I feel so lost & lonely & sad. Dear God take care of him.'[54]

All the following week, Uttley found it difficult to work, slept fitfully and felt sick. She was wracked with self-recrimination, wondering if she should have called the vet sooner. The more she thought about Hamish, the 'more and more unhappy, lonely' she felt. She kept looking at his lifeless body 'so beautiful, curled up so charmingly with his little paws crossed. I kissed him, talked to him.' As she reflected the day after he died: 'I have really felt unhinged, quite crazy with sorrow, grief.' She kept 'weeping bitterly in sorrow'. Hamish was so ingrained in everyday life: 'Everything I do is mixed with his life. I miss him more than I can say.' In the following week, her grief for Hamish was almost all Uttley recorded in her diary: 'my heart is heavy for Hamish darling' and 'Oh, my heart aches for him all the time.' Hamish was the buffer that made living alone bearable. Without him, life was 'so sad and lonely'.[55]

Loving pals

It wasn't that men didn't grieve for dead pets. But if public expressions of pet grief were embarrassing for women who, according to contemporary perceptions of femininity, were expected to be emotionally incontinent, it was much more difficult for men, supposedly models of emotional rectitude, to express a profound sense of loss in this context. When Nero died, Jane Carlyle did not want visitors to see her visible distress. In his reminiscences after Jane's death in 1866, her husband Thomas conceded that he was 'still surprised' at the 'degree of pitying sorrow' Nero's demise provoked, 'even from me'. Carlyle's grudging admission of 'memorable, sad and miserable' sorrow, hedged by caveats of disavowal, suggested embarrassment and awkwardness but also a degree of honesty in owning that 'even' intellectual men could be moved by the death of a dog.[56] Some 75 years later, another literary couple (again without children), Virginia and Leonard Woolf, would lose their dog Pinka. Virginia, typically disdainful of excessive emotion, reflected in her diary 'how odd' it was to experience such 'intensity of the sense of death – even for a dog'. She suspected that there was something 'pathetic' or 'grotesque' in the 'depression' of spirits the couple felt and, of course, a 'fear of sentimentality and so on'. The following day, she recorded that Leonard was still 'very depressed too'. Perhaps because they both had low spirits, it helped to rationalize them: '8 years of a dog certainly mean something', a 'part of our life' that had gone.[57]

If girls were encouraged towards emotional attachments to animals, the socialization of boys tended to focus on learning to contain feelings. These polarities hardened in the Victorian period as cultural ideals amplified supposed differences between the sexes. Thomas Inman, lecturer at Liverpool's Royal Infirmary School of Medicine in the 1860s, wrote regularly to his son Teddy who was at boarding school. The letters were full of family news, funny anecdotes and firm but affectionate advice on studying hard. Writing in September 1864, Inman broke the news that the family dog had died suddenly. The letter was not without emotion, but this focused on the dog's newly born pups (what would they do without her?), a measure that acknowledged sadness without rendering it a personal tragedy. Inman followed the sad news with more upbeat chatter about the pony who was getting fat on apples 'lest he should fret at your absence too greatly', a tacit concession that the schoolboy had relationships with the family pets.[58] In Lewisham in the 1850s, even six-year-old Stevy Bowditch's indulgent father was horrified at his son's unstoppable tears for his dead kitten. He 'promised him another' in a futile bid to curtail the crying. Stevy refused, perhaps teaching his father a lesson or two about the irreplaceability of loved companions.[59]

Nevertheless, some adult men were profoundly attached to their pets and inevitably experienced devastating grief when they died. As Lady Cust pointed out in 1856, those who 'laughed' at cat love and associated it with simpering women were woefully ignorant of the feline's long association with 'celebrated' men who were never 'ashamed' to own their affection for the creatures.[60] She might have predicted the deep affection Edward Lear held for his cat, Foss. Perpetual ill health meant Lear eschewed human relationships in favour of isolation with his cat Foss and long-standing manservant.[61] Foss died in November 1887 at the age of seventeen although Lear, aged 76 and confused about how long they'd been together, claimed in letters that he was thirty. Writing to an old friend, the former Liberal MP Lord Aberdare (Henry Austin Bruce), from his home in San Remo, Italy, Lear noted that he was 'little able' to write 'nowadays', even though he had much correspondence to attend to. 'For, whoever has known me for thirty years', he explained, will know that 'my cat Foss has been part of my solitary life'. Lear took small comfort in knowing that the cat 'did not suffer at all' but, in ink that looked suspiciously smudged with tears, reiterated that 'all those friends who have known my life will know that I grieve over this life.' Of course, he concluded to Aberdare, in a few days 'all will be as before, except for the memory of my poor friend Foss.'[62] Lear died just weeks later.

There was public acknowledgement that some men missed animals when they died but this tended to take a more 'masculine' form in commemorations of dogs as pals and sportsmen rather than loves, a trend reflected in the inscriptions on pet headstones installed by male owners. Indulging in mourning paraphernalia at home for his dogs, George R. Sims placed a notice in his weekly *Referee* magazine column in 1907 when his favourite pony, a 'good and gallant little fellow', a 'good friend and faithful servant' for over twenty years, died. *Horses Illustrated* reproduced the notice, offering Sims the 'sympathy of all horsemen'.[63]

One of the greatest twentieth-century testimonies to human–animal love was J. R. Ackerley's *My Dog Tulip*, first published in 1956. As Ackerley noted elsewhere, the years spent with Queenie (Tulip's name in real life) were 'the happiest of my life'.[64] But for a memoir with such minute detail about a life shared and from a queer writer who hardly fitted a sporting masculine norm, Ackerley's silence on Queenie's inevitable death is deafening. Instead, the book concludes with them walking in a birch wood and Ackerley's musings: a young man committed suicide over there, this tree here is diseased, seasons change . . . Queenie explores, leaving only a dissolving 'fume of breath': 'She has been, she has gone, nothing now remains. Soon it will be over. Soon it will be too late . . .'[65] When the book was reissued in 1965, a new appendix raged at people who put dogs 'to sleep' without care while noting that Queenie lived to the great age (especially for Alsatians) of sixteen and a half.[66] In a memoir stuffed full of dog bodily functions, canine sex and so much human–dog love, musing explicitly on the impending end of Queenie's life (or, in the additional appendix, his decision to end her life) proved an intimate detail too far, even for Ackerley. Then again, what could he have said? As so many writers seeking to express devastating grief – for animals or humans – have found, words simply don't cut it.

Profound male grief at pet loss was not the preserve of a queer cultural elite. Labouring men also experienced emotional anguish on the death of a pet. Yorkshire vet James Herriot recalled visiting an aged dog in the impoverished home (Herriot thought it unfit for habitation) of an elderly widower, Mr Dean. The fourteen-year-old dog, Bob, a Labrador cross, clearly meant the world to the man but had inoperable cancer and was visibly in pain, despite thumping his tail at the sound of his master's voice. Although he 'always aimed at a brisk, matter-of-fact approach', Herriot dreaded having to navigate the need to end Bob's life: 'This wasn't going to be easy.' The elderly man looked 'bewildered and his lips trembled' while Herriot 'swallowed hard', knowing the 'old clichés' ('he's had a good long innings') had 'an empty ring'. Understanding that nothing could be done for Bob, Dean painfully lowered himself to his knees and caressed the dog for 'a long time' before 'huskily' giving Herriot permission to euthanize the dog. He could not meet the vet's eye. As Bob's life ebbed away, the elderly man clasped and unclasped his hands before gathering himself to ask what he owed for Herriot's services. Affected by the man's poverty and evident devastation, Herriot did not charge for his visit.[67] Despite the clichés and apparent stoicism, the emotional stakes here are unmistakable.

Herriot's recollection of his awkwardness demonstrates men's self-consciousness regarding sentiment. Alan Withington wrote in his diary regularly, usually adopting an irreverent tone. But when his dog Sally died, unexpectedly and after a short illness, around the age of seven, Withington made an unusually long entry while decrying being 'senti-mental about such things'. Rather, Withington deflected sadness onto his wife: she had a closer bond with the dog and it was so much easier to relate feminine feelings. He conceded that he would have liked to 'have seen [Sally] again myself of course' but brushed this off with the note that 'Morag was the one she always loved . . . Poor Sal!' Withington veered towards reflection – he admitted to feeling 'more than tempted' to write 'an essay for her epitaph but must resist' – pulling back to keep the tone light-hearted. He hoped Sally got 'full value out of life' and, putting all the naughtiness of puppydom aside, concluded that there 'couldn't be a nicer little dog to have'. But he finished in a more serious tone, noting that the dog's death was particularly hard for his wife: 'Everything's wrong these days, poor Morag. And on her birthday too.'[68] Pet love – and death – was not just about human feelings for animals but often reflected relationships between humans too.

Sir William Beach Thomas was a journalist. After making his mark as a war correspondent in the First World War, he became well known for his publications on country life. He was a keen sportsman too. In the late 1920s he published 'A Letter to My Dog' as an essay for the journal *Atlantic Monthly*; it was subsequently published as a pamphlet in 1931. The letter reflected on Thomas's feelings when his 'best' dog, Whuff, was run over. Despite it being billed as a letter *to* his dog, Thomas began by expressing distaste for anthropomorphism; it smacked of 'patronage and a sense of [human] superiority' whereas dog and man were 'different'. Thomas thought men and women's relationships with dogs were different too: men enjoyed friendship and country sports whereas women had a tendency to coddle and 'spoil' dogs.[69] So far, so manly.

Much of the letter recounted things Whuff and Thomas had done together, eliciting notes on breed traits alongside anecdotes about hunting, walking and playing. The stories enabled Thomas to identify Whuff's individuality as a dog and his emotional universe: delight, fear, loyalty, affection and disappointment, his likes and dislikes. Towards the end of his letter, Thomas briefly recounted Whuff's road accident and death three days later. A final section, just one paragraph, ruminated on the different kinds of human friendships with a range of animals, concluding that relations with dogs came first. Although some people believed dogs had souls, Thomas settled for accepting that he and Whuff had the pleasure and pain of 'finite hearts that yearn'. In life, Whuff looked to Thomas with 'appeal' that 'no sentiment could exaggerate': 'if you were less than human, you were more than beast.' Thomas's feelings for Whuff were not the same as for his human friends and Whuff was not even his 'greatest friend'. But he had been Whuff's and it was this responsibility, being at the centre of the dog's emotional world, that filled Thomas with sadness and made his grief rational – and masculine.[70]

The pain of parting

For some people, pet loss was so traumatic that they swore never to put themselves through it again. A young woman on the cusp of leaving her 1900s Yorkshire mill-town home wept bitter tears with her mother and sister when Prince, the family dog, died: they 'never' forgot the dog and agreed to 'never have [a dog] no more'.[71] Adjusting to married life in interwar Britain, another woman resolved never to have another dog after the Pomeranian who went 'everywhere I went' was run over.[72] It wasn't just dogs either. Reflecting on the bereavement of cats in childhood (it 'break[s] your heart . . . when you lose them'), some people simply couldn't face the loss again as adults.[73] For those that did brave the heartache a second (third, fourth) time, there was some comfort in knowing, as one of Leonard Woolf's associates put it, that the 'hell' and 'agony' of pet bereavement would ease with time.[74]

Minimizing animal suffering at the end of life, especially in a Victorian context where access to veterinary assistance was minimal, was beneficial to animals and helped assuage grief. Charlotte Brontë was grateful that Flossy 'died quietly in the night without pain'; her belief that 'no dog ever had a happier life or an easier death' was a balm to the rawness of loss.[75] Edward Lear's cat Foss died soon after suffering a stroke. Lear took small comfort in knowing that the cat 'did not suffer at all'.[76] Arthur Jones was 'thankful' his dog Capel 'passed away so quietly and did not suffer long'.[77] As Chapter Five made clear, veterinary treatment for domestic pets was limited in the nineteenth century and for much of this period, pet owners seeking to release an animal from suffering had to rely on rudimentary modes of euthanasia, notably shooting or poisoning an animal. They either had to perform this act themselves or find someone willing to assist. After Jane Carlyle's dog Nero was run over in October 1859, he lingered for another four months. When it became clear that he was in constant pain ('to such a pass had things come'), Jane's personal medical practitioner agreed to administer strychnine to the dog. Jane knew she was lucky to be able to call on the physician's 'kindness' to execute the euthanasia.[78]

By the late century, as animal charities sought to address large numbers of stray cats and dogs in towns and cities, they developed the 'lethal chamber' that released gas to euthanize multiple animals at once (the chamber at Battersea Dogs Home could euthanize a hundred dogs of terrier size at a time).[79] Gruesome though these technologies were, animal charity records from the 1910s suggest that pet owners also made use of the chambers to access a 'merciful end to [pet] sufferings'. Those that could made donations to cover the costs but 'animals of the poor' were euthanized 'free of charge'.[80] Other technologies involved electrocution in a 'lethal box', a quick and efficient mode of euthanasia (the General Electric Company manufactured such boxes). For those that could afford it, the veterinary surgeon could administer drugs to end the pet's life. A cheaper but less satisfactory option was to purchase poison and seek advice on dosing from a chemist (it was risky getting the dosage right and many found it too painful to administer poison themselves).

By the 1920s the Canine Defence League was distributing leaflets on the cruelty of *not* euthanizing pets that were suffering and advising on the best modes to accomplish painless death.[81] The phrase 'put to sleep' was increasingly in common parlance, replacing the somewhat more literal and certainly more heartrending 'destroyed'.[82] The first purpose-built small animal hospitals from the interwar period had 'lethal chambers' as well as mortuaries.[83]

The availability of euthanasia technologies enabled owners to be proactive: there was some comfort, in theory at least, for humans in curtailing periods of distress and discomfort for the animal. In the 1930s, when Florence Turtle's Brunnie died, the death lasted several days. Three years later, the other family dog, Coney, was 'put to sleep', the 'poor old dear'. Aged sixteen, in pain and with paralysed legs, it was 'useless to patch her up'.[84] The administration of barbiturates was a simple, humane response to ending her life. But even when humans thought ending suffering in an animal's best interests, the capacity for guilt remained, either from a sense of betraying an animal's trust (how to explain to the animal that the human decision to end its life was in its best interests?) or, equally, when owners believed they had been too slow to spot an animal's suffering. When siblings Florence, Bernard and Brian Turtle's 'lion-hearted little cat' was put to sleep in June 1956, Florence was 'very sad all day and cried when on my own'. While she was relieved the cat no longer suffered, Florence regretted being 'impatient with him when he mewed so constantly', realizing belatedly that he had probably been ill for some time.[85]

Worse was the guilt of killing a pet from economic necessity. At one terraced home in Edwardian Limehouse, the father of the family, a horse-and-cart driver, turned the backyard into a small paradise: climbing plants and creepers prettified the space while two pet rabbits in home-made hutches lent a rustic flavour. The man took on extra jobs to buy rabbit food and 'idolized' his pets, especially Billy, a large white rabbit. But when the family hit hard times and there was 'no money' for food, he 'had to kill' his rabbits to feed his children. Decades later, his daughter recalled her father being 'near to tears' eating Billy: it 'Broke his heart. But there. No money you see'.[86] Such hard-headed pragmatism was far from unusual and pets in labouring homes were always vulnerable: cats and dogs might be surrendered or abandoned as purse strings tightened (or when dog licences were due for renewal) while the status of rabbits and chickens, typical foodstuff in hard times, was especially shaky.[87]

Less obvious, perhaps, were the tough economic decisions of the middle classes. When Ellen Hill died in 1964, her daughter Jennie had to face up to the difficult promise she had made when their cat, Tibs, had been repeatedly unwell. Ostensibly the cost of the cat's medication lay behind the dying Ellen's insistence that Tibs be euthanized after her death and she hadn't let it rest until Jennie agreed. But it is hard not to read Ellen's demand in the context of tensions in the mother–daughter relationship in which Ellen could be domineering. In her diary, Jennie related her anguish at making the promise – but also writes that after her mother insisted that Tibs be put down, it was she, Jennie, who declared that the life of her favourite, Teddy, should also be ended. Jennie was angry with her mother. The uneasy power dynamic between the two women forced them into an emotional standoff, with the two cats caught up as emotional pawns. It is possible to see how Jennie's fury at her mother's demand for a senseless death (Tibs) extended into a feeling of hopeless fatalism that caught Teddy up as collateral.

Jennie prevaricated over the deaths, putting off the moment after her mother died while tormented that she had made the promise. In the end, she attempted to be pragmatic, arranging for the cats to be euthanized the day before leaving for a holiday to Scotland. In theory, this would give her a sense of closure and enable a period of recovery. The trip, meanwhile, would symbolize the start of a new – independent – chapter in her life. There was logic in this. But for all her practicality, Jennie struggled to accept that she was killing her much-loved cats for no reason other than a pledge made to her dying mother.

The period between the older woman's death and the euthanasia was characterized by anguish and despair in Jennie's diary as she mused on 'the pure agony of knowing how little time there is left for us together'. Her love for 'darling faithful Teddy' was particularly strong and she knew 'life will be desolate without him'. Jennie recorded her mother's death with stoicism but her anticipatory grief for the cats was devastating: 'Have felt heartbroken all day. Have never felt so desolate & alone . . . Usual cooking, also for the last time. I feel as though I was slowly dying of grief, parting from these darling pets.' Over the next three days, Jennie repeatedly confided to her diary that she was 'Heartbroken. Wept my heart out.' She felt ill at the thought of killing them and 'couldn't eat'.

Jennie's grief was undoubtedly exacerbated by guilt and recrimination. Awaiting the vet's arrival was 'A *dreadful* morning of tension and grief' [her emphasis]. The vet was 'kind and thoughtful' and helped Jennie bury the cats, and she placed two remembrance crosses over their grave. But she felt 'numb, weak and lifeless' and couldn't eat. Over the following six weeks, she returned again and again in her diary to record her grief and guilt: 'How could I have had my darling Teddy killed' and 'I cannot believe I've had him done in. How could I do it?' Musing on grief for 'the boys' and Teddy in particular, Jennie never once openly expressed resentment towards her mother, turning her recrimination inwards instead. But her diary does note the reassurance she received from other relatives that she had done the 'right thing', suggesting she shared her guilt and grief with others. Most of all, she turned to God, writing that only 'He knows what it means' and placing her faith in 'Him to care about me'. A month after the deaths, she still felt assailed by 'the dreadful desolate feeling of loneliness' and could not 'help weeping with overwhelming sorrow', especially when returning to the empty house.[88] Jennie's painful experience reminds us that not all pet deaths occurred from decision-making about an animal's best interests and highlights the precarity of pets' status as members of family.

Most pet deaths resulted, however, from decisions made on account of illness or old age. But even when owners believed this was the right action, initiating or agreeing to euthanasia was difficult. Jean Pratt long dreaded the death of Dinah, 'the light of my life here at Wee from the very beginning'. By autumn 1950 Jean believed Dinah was dying. She wondered 'where my little one will go when she goes at last' but 'cannot bear' to think of her being 'anywhere unhappy'. The likelihood that life with Dinah was nearly 'at an end' 'haunt[ed]' her, and brought 'pain', a 'sense of losing things, of some sort of doom descending'.[89] After months of Dinah growing weaker, Jean determined in January 1951 that she should not suffer any longer. She called the cat clinic to request their ambulance because she could not face the 'drawn out agony' of taking the cat to the clinic herself. But this attempt to mitigate her own distress (Dinah would be confused by the trip whatever happened) only transferred the trauma into their home. When the ambulance arrived the following day, Jean found parting wretched: 'I kissed the top of her little black head quickly and turned to my handbag. I could not see the lid being closed.' All that remained were tears, and 'more tears'. Jean's entry for that day recorded 'It is finished. Little light of my life is gone from me.' Unusually inarticulate, she resolved to write more later when she could think 'without tears'. She mused that those who had never known the 'strange, joyous, mystic communion' that was possible with a 'loved' animal would never understand her loss. Several days later, Jean turned to her diary again to record that she had wept every day since Dinah's parting, not least from guilt and remorse at letting the ambulance take Dinah away: 'that frightened, reproachful little face'.[90] Animals knew humans and Dinah knew that something was amiss. Even when humans acted as responsible guardians of animal life (and death), the scope for self-recrimination at how – and when – that life ended was enormous.

The death of Dinah appeared to affect Jean more than any other feline loss – she never wrote quite so much or with such anguished despair in response to a cat death again, although she did continue to record guilt and grief whenever cats died throughout the rest of her life. In 1952, just a year after Dinah's death, her cats contracted enteritis, several kittens dying one after the other. She turned to her diary to 'spill my grief' and 'release the knot that is tightening in my heart' as she buried four cats in turn underneath the blackberries at the bottom of the garden.[91] On 2 March 1963 another cat died in a scalding accident that generated an appalling sense of 'betrayal' in Jean. As she reflected, 'The cats are my great love and through them must come the great griefs.'[92]

For single people especially, pets could be the most important emotional connection in a life. Making a proactive decision to end that animal's suffering was a profound act of love but it could feel like a terrible betrayal of trust and an unbearable emotional blow. During summer 1956 it was becoming clear that Florence Turtle's Alsatian dog, also named Dinah, was struggling with chronic arthritis in her hips. By January 1957 Florence 'fear[ed] we shall have to make a terrible decision before long'. Come April, Florence's brother Brian was raising the prospect of 'having her put to sleep', possibly out of compassion for the dog but also, potentially, because Florence was increasingly asking him for help in managing Dinah's wellbeing, especially her toilet needs. Dinah was almost ten years old, generally considered a good age for such a big dog. But, as Florence agonized, it could be difficult to know when best to act. Dinah had been unwell in 1955 when the vet suggested her case 'was hopeless and putting her to sleep!' Florence had 'refused to accept to defeat' and was so 'glad': Dinah had survived and Florence believed she had a reasonable quality of life.[93] In 1957, though, that quality of life was becoming less clear, yet Florence dreaded having to end the dog's life: the idea of it 'hangs over me like a Sword of Damacles [sic]'. In many respects, Dinah was well and had she been human, she could 'simply . . .

get a wheelchair': to 'put her to sleep' felt like 'plain murder'. Making the decision to end Dinah's life 'breaks my heart'. For six to eight months, Florence had 'prayed for her either to be cured or taken', whichever 'the Almighty thought best'. The silence – 'I have had *no answer*' – made Florence wonder whether she lived in a 'pointless inhuman vortex' without any God. Not especially religious in any other context, Florence felt a sense of abandonment here that stands for a more generic loneliness in making such decisions.

In late May that year, a 'heavy cloud' hung over the house as it became clear that Dinah could not go on: 'we all feel terrible every time we look at her and yet poor darling . . .'. Dinah, dragging herself along by her forelegs, had little discernible quality of life. Florence could not bear to be at home to witness Dinah's death although recording the mechanics of it later that day possibly gave her a rational framework in which to place an emotional end: Dinah was 'peaceful and relaxed' before the vet administered the drugs to 'put her to sleep for ever'. The following day, Florence returned to her diary to chastise God for his singular failure to 'hear my prayer' in either curing or 'taking her painlessly'. So much of Florence's grief for Dinah related to actively ending her life. The 'only slightly consoling thought' was that, had she not acted, Dinah might have had a seizure and died in pain. Still, Florence 'cannot help feeling bitter'. For a whole month, she regularly wrote about 'darling Dinah' in her diary and in her December review of the year concluded it was 'a bad year for me' with 'The Death of Dinah' topping the list of awful events.[94] Pet euthanasia, even with improved technologies and the rational conviction that it was a kindness, was hard to endure.

Everlasting friends

In July 1937, the *Daily Mail* received an 'avalanche' of correspondence after printing a letter from a reader who asked 'what is happening to the sanity of our race that dog worship is tolerated and encouraged to such absurd lengths?' While some wrote to applaud the letter's sentiments, the 'great mass' of letters expressed 'amazement' at the correspondent's failure to grasp the significance of human–animal companionship: 'Dog worship is not a sentiment to decry or to be ashamed of'; a dog was an 'everlasting pal'; anyone with a dog 'could not be lonely for a second'; to those who lived without human companionship, a dog was a 'great comfort'; and, 'money could not buy my dog any more than it could buy my son'.[95] Notably, the *Mail's* comment on this outpouring of correspondence pointed to a coroner's court hearing the previous week on an elderly man that 'killed himself and his mongrel pet because of his dread at parting with it'. As the journalist F. G. Prince-White noted, the history of strong affection between humans and canines was long and 'death itself could not end it.' For those 'men and women who have known human loneliness or lacked human affection' the love of a pet was a 'very precious thing', often the 'sole assurance of goodness in life'. Even for those who enjoyed the full flush of human love, there was something incomparably joyous in the 'uncalculating' love of a pet. The worst of such love was that dogs didn't live long enough: 'When a loved dog dies the depth of the emotion stirred in us is itself proof of the worthiness of the affection we have received and reciprocated.'[96]

By the middle decades of the twentieth century, it wasn't just dogs that generated such heartfelt public grief. Pet cemeteries increasingly catered for multiple species, with cats the second most common pet burial by the 1950s, although still representing only a third of the number of dog burials in most cemeteries. More to the point, by the 1950s pet cemeteries were increasingly accessible to a broader section of the population. From the 1920s animal charities began opening pet cemeteries that operated on a minimum donation basis, reflecting increasing recognition of the emotional investment humans across the social scale placed in companion animals and the desire to express loss in publicly recognized ways. The first was Liverpool Pet Cemetery, operated by the RSPCA on a donation basis (the minimum donation was 2 shillings but grave owners had a year to pay) in 1922. It was located within the grounds of the 'Horses' Rest' in Halewood on the outskirts of the city. Within fifteen years, the allocated space was full.[97] By the mid-1920s there was a pet cemetery next to the PDSA hospital in Ilford, Essex, alongside the longer established Blue Cross Pet Cemetery for military animals in London. Charity-run cemeteries typically invited donations in memory of pets instead of charging fixed prices for graves, while allowing wooden as well as stone or marble memorials. The RSPCA cemetery in Liverpool banned the use of coffins for pets, largely to enable them to maximize space, but because simplified burial practices were cheaper and more accessible too.[98]

Dedicated pet crematoria for public use had been in operation in America since the late nineteenth century. It was slower to catch on in the UK (as, indeed, was cremation of humans), but by the middle decades

Liverpool RSPCA Pet Cemetery, 1948, photograph by Adolf Morath.

of the twentieth century, a growing number of commercial pet cemeteries began to offer cremation as a cheaper alternative to burial, a service that was already used by veterinary practices for the bulk disposal of dead pets. From the late 1970s purpose-built pet crematoria began to outstrip pet cemeteries, especially as vets partnered with crematoria to provide streamlined services. In 2017 there were over fifty pet crematoria and cemeteries in Britain, most offering full pet funeral services. According to a Mintel report that year, commercial companies provided over 10,000 pet funerals a year.[99] While the interment of ashes is popular, providing a fixed space for commemoration, animal ashes can also be transformed into diamonds, incorporated into garden ornaments or tattooed into human skin.

The growing availability of commercial services for pet death is reflected by an increased recognition that pet bereavement can generate a profound sense of grief. In 1994 the animal charity Blue Cross founded a dedicated bereavement support service for pet owners. In the past twenty years its services have expanded dramatically as more humans live alone. Even so, Blue Cross remains one of the few employers to permit compassionate leave on the death of a pet. We may be more willing to validate the profound loss incurred by pet death through commercial services but, as Blue Cross's campaigning indicates, social mores remain a long way from treating grief about a pet with the seriousness of human bereavement. Crucially, there remains a large population of non-pet owners (and, indeed, some pet owners) who cannot comprehend why some people experience searing loss at the death of an animal.

But for some of us, past and present, the death of a pet is a life-defining event. In 2016 the naturalist Chris Packham published his autobiography, *Fingers in the Sparkle Jar.* It recounts his childhood and teen years in the 1960s and '70s and, specifically, his relationship with a kestrel he reared from the nest. Packham's memoir is also an account of living with Asperger's Syndrome, and it is important to understand that the kestrel was this boy's absolute passion, his life's focus and joy. He had a unique connection with the bird that completely evaded him where humans were concerned. When the kestrel died in the mid-1970s, the boy was utterly devastated: 'I knew he was dead, but at the same time he couldn't be . . . Nothing that perfect, nothing that loved could be dead. That wouldn't work. It was impossible.' For almost two weeks, Packham could not speak and for a long time afterwards he lived with a 'clogged, flattened, crushed, smothering feeling you get in heavy snow. Deadened.' For twelve years, Packham visited the kestrel's grave on the anniversary of his death. Still, in middle age, he 'can't talk about it without crying, or wanting to and having to stop myself'. But what really baffled the adult Packham was the complete silence of those around him: 'No one said anything at all, as if he . . . everything, just hadn't existed. No one – said – anything. Ever.' In retrospect, the death of his kestrel represented a point in life when 'too many things broke', things 'that couldn't ever be mended'.[100] Many of us, with or without the qualities of autism, will recognize – and share – Packham's sense of staggering loss. Loving pets will always break our hearts.

Pets and the Way We Live Now

Among the many newspaper and social media obituaries for human lives lost during 2020, there was an obituary to a cat that had 'touched millions of lives' and 'changed the world'.[1] Bob, a stray cat, was the loyal companion of (human) James Bowen for thirteen years. Struggling with drug addiction when they met, Bowen credited Bob with saving his life. Their story, made into a book and film, showed just how powerful human–animal companionship could be.[2] As Bowen declared, 'pets are capable of influencing our lives in so many positive ways. They can save us from loneliness and soothe our mental health. They can give us hope when all else seems lost.' Bowen and Bob worked together selling *The Big Issue*, a not-for-profit magazine aimed at helping homeless vendors make a living. Bowen was grateful to the animal-welfare charities that helped him care for Bob's health and wellbeing during the difficult economic period of his life. When Blue Cross launched 'Link in the Chain' (2019) – a report on the importance of pets in managing human isolation, loneliness and mental health, and the economic barriers to animal companionship – Bowen wrote a personal message for its preface. He believed that this important relationship 'should be available to all, not just the wealthy'.[3]

Bob's death, at the height of a global pandemic when so many humans were experiencing acute social isolation, exemplified the poignancy of losing a much-loved animal companion. In 2020 British households with pets became the majority for the first time since keeping track of such trends began, a pattern overwhelmingly triggered by householders inviting animals into their homes in response to the restrictions and anxieties of COVID-19.[4] But Bowen's loss ('I feel like a light has gone out in my life') in a context where so many humans were dying also highlights the entangled hierarchies between humans and animals. During 2020 Blue Cross's pet bereavement-support service experienced a surge in requests for help as socially isolated humans struggled to cope with pet death, feeling unable to express the depth of their loss in a context where so many humans were dying, or whose grief was amplified by the animal's status as a link with other deceased friends and family.

Our book has shown that Bowen's unique relationship with Bob, the resonance of their story with strangers and the importance of animals during the pandemic was rooted in two hundred years of changing relations between humans and animals. While human emotional investment in animals is longstanding, people began to frame their relationships with their pets in new ways in this period and companion animals were increasingly seen as part of human families. As the way we live has changed, so too has the way in which we keep pets. Which animals we choose to domesticate, where they come from, who gets to have pets, how we acquire, care and grieve for them, and the agencies that support our relationships all have a history. During the nineteenth century pets were increasingly commodified; their economic and social value increased as well as their cultural representation. Pet keeping became increasingly acceptable across a range of social groups. There was a 'pet revolution'. We contend that understanding what has changed and why it mattered is essential to understanding why pets have the status they currently do.

In some respects, today's animals fare much better than their early nineteenth-century counterparts. Now, there are legal barriers to humans snatching birds and animals from the wild and some species that the Victorians tamed (like red squirrels) have additional protection. Since the 1976 Endangered Species Act certain animals have been removed from the pet trade in Britain and the importation of animals from overseas has changed in response to shifting geopolitics. A greater appreciation of environmental concerns and wildlife means that pets are now bred specifically for domestic companionship, although problems with the health and welfare of pedigree dogs remains an ongoing concern.[5] Legislation to regulate the sale of pets continues to develop. In spring 2020, just as demand for pets rocketed, 'Lucy's Law' came into operation to prohibit third-party sales of puppies and kittens. In 2019 the RSPCA rehomed almost 40,000 cats and dogs and carried out almost 220,000 procedures (neutering, microchipping and veterinary treatments). They investigated more than 93,000 complaints of alleged cruelty and secured

1,425 convictions for animal cruelty by private prosecution. Of those successful convictions, the vast majority (1,093) related to animals considered pet species: dogs (810), cats (196) and small animals (87). Although the depressingly high numbers for prosecution indicate that a minority of humans continue to abuse animals, this is a remarkable shift when we remember that cats, dogs and other small animals were not systematically protected until the late nineteenth century.

The Harris Poll of British People and their Pets, carried out in 1970, found that 87 per cent of participants declared themselves 'dog lovers'.[6] In the twenty-first century the English continue to cast themselves as a 'nation of dog/pet/animal lovers' across a range of new media, but this narrative of exceptionalism does not necessarily hold true.[7] According to a global survey conducted by the German market intelligence firm GfK, in the mid-2010s the highest percentages of pet owners were in Mexico, Argentina and Brazil.[8] Pet keeping also varies across the British Isles – the Scots have consistently kept fewer pets than the English.[9] But as we have shown in this book, pet culture in Britain does have a long history that developed early and often passionately. Animal-protection campaigns that developed in Britain first were influential elsewhere. The Society for the Prevention of Cruelty to Animals (later RSPCA) was founded in Britain in 1824, the French Société Protectrice des Animaux in 1845 and their German, Swiss, American and Swedish counterparts soon afterwards.[10] The British RSPCA also inspired the efforts of campaigners beyond Europe – the Istanbul Society for Protection of Animals, established in 1912, was modelled on the British society, with whom its founders were in close correspondence.[11] The culture of pet keeping developed quickly in industrial Britain, but other Western nations kept pace.[12] In 1963 a *Reader's Digest* Survey found that while the British apparently kept more pets than other Western European countries, France, Belgium and Italy had almost the same numbers.[13] In a 2019 survey of pet keeping in the European Union it was Romania that had the largest share of households with at least one dog.[14] In the twenty-first century pet keeping is a truly global phenomenon. A history of global pet keeping has yet to be written but, clearly, this was a culture that stretched much further than the British Isles.

Pet keeping continues to be associated with certain gendered stereotypes – Victorian 'old maids' have morphed into 'crazy cat ladies' but the stereotype persists.[15] As this book has shown, however, pet keeping was a widely shared activity that took place at all social levels and could be equally important to people of different backgrounds, genders and sexual orientations. Historically, the growth of pet-keeping culture has sometimes been seen as driven by the rise of a civilizing bourgeoisie that used 'kindness to animals' as a means of self-valorization.[16] But while it is true that pet keeping was actively promoted in middle-class Christian cultures from the nineteenth century, we have demonstrated that it was hugely important to working people who cultivated pets for reasons of their own. The culture of bird keeping was particularly strong in working-class homes – and this persisted well into the twentieth century.[17] Of course, levels of wealth and resource continue to shape pet keeping at a fundamental level, as do religious and cultural contexts – some Muslim families, for example, avoid dogs on religious grounds,[18] and some Gypsy families prefer animals with contrasting colours in their coats because they bring good fortune.[19] But as recent surveys have shown, gender doesn't always make that much difference to the choice of pet (men are apparently slightly more likely to keep fish).[20] Large numbers of people (around half of the population during this period) don't keep pets at all – and it may be that those who do forge human–animal families have a distinct form of identity.

The phenomenal expansion of the pet market in the nineteenth century has had knock-on effects on technology, medicine and the economy. Large-scale shifts in demographics (fewer children and more single-person households) and developing domestic technologies mean that it is much easier for humans and animals to share homes. Guidance and support for pet keeping has come a long way since Jane Loudon published her landmark pet manual in 1851: pet keepers can turn to a plethora of virtual, textual, visual and in-person training for help in understanding their pet and promoting mutual wellbeing. This is supported by a vast array of products and services dedicated to the health, hygiene and welfare of companion animals. If veterinary practitioners once sneered at small-animal medicine, most practices now rely on the pet market, with livestock and equine medicine important but secondary avenues of practice. Crucially, the pet care industries contribute billions of pounds annually to the British economy. In 2020 the pet-food market was valued at £2.9 billion and veterinary practice at £2.1 billion; even pet accessories (collars, beds and so on) accounted for £900 million with grooming a close second at £300 million.[21] The largest pet retailer, Pets at Home, reported record-breaking sales worth £1 billion with a 35 per cent rise in pre-tax profit to £116.4 million in the year to March 2021.[22]

If a cat named Bob saved James Bowen's life, most people would agree that pet keeping brings them happiness: a survey in 2020 reported that 93 per cent of pet keepers agreed that their pet made them 'happy'.[23] Bowen was adamant that pet keeping should not just be for the wealthy. Numerous charities dedicated to supporting pets and people without access to housing (particularly housing that permits pets) would agree. And yet the very existence of a pet market, where products, services and, crucially, animals themselves are for sale, highlights the thorny relationship between animal companionship, capitalism and consumption. For as much as humans might think of their pet as a person, pets are commodities too. And while for many households, pets are 'family', animal membership of that family is often conditional on variables, some of which are beyond the control of the human keeper – such as job loss, housing crisis or profound illness. This is embedded within the market (given that most animals are bred for purchase as domestic companions), and in the very nomenclature of that companionship: the vast majority of humans, practitioners and service providers continue to refer to pet 'owners' and 'ownership'. These terms are so ingrained in public use that they are taken for granted and, arguably, entirely accurate: most people do own their pet, as both a product with a personality and as a much-valued – emotionally if not always financially – possession (and can seek legal redress if that pet is stolen). But the commodification of pets, in language and practice, reflects and perpetuates the inequities between humans and animals, and the inequities between the people who would – and do – keep pets. It also underpins many of the challenges we continue to meet in doing the best thing for our pets.

For all the improvements in pet welfare over the past two hundred years, there are still obstacles to overcome. More than ever before, we know that our future is inextricable from our guardianship of the environment and all the species that inhabit it. While we no longer extract animals as pets from 'natural' environments, we have come to recognize that our homes, outdoor spaces and gardens are part of a larger shared environment – the animals we keep within our houses and the relationships we forge with those who live close by have an important role to play in humanity's ongoing relationship with a larger ecology. Giving our companion animals their history is part of recognizing that human history is incomplete without them. In acknowledging their importance as actors in our shared past, we also stake a claim for their status as sentient persons whose lives and futures are tied to ours.

REFERENCES

Introduction

1 'Share of Households Owning a Pet in the UK from 2011 to 2021', www.statista.com, 18 August 2021.

2 'Households Buy 3.2 Million Pets in Lockdown', www.bbc.co.uk, 12 March 2021.

3 Ibid.

4 Dearbail Jordan, 'Pets at Home Says Pets Have Been "a Lifesaver" During Lockdown', www.bbc.co.uk, 24 November 2020.

5 For animals and consumer culture see Sarah Amato, *Beastly Possessions: Animals in Victorian Consumer Culture* (Toronto, 2015).

6 John Bradshaw, *In Defence of Dogs* (London, 2012), p. 32.

7 See for instance, Erica Fudge, *Quick Cattle and Dying Wishes: People and Their Animals in Early Modern England* (Ithaca, NY, 2018); Sarah Cockram and Andrew Wells, eds, *Interspecies Interactions: Animals and Humans Between the Middle Ages and Modernity* (London, 2017).

8 Kathleen Walker-Meikle, *Medieval Pets* (Woodbridge, 2012).

9 Ingrid Tague, *Animal Companions: Pets and Social Change in Eighteenth Century Britain* (Philadelphia, PA, 2015).

10 Ibid., p. 2.

11 Erica Fudge, *Pets* (London, 2008). Exceptions to the rule relate to France and America. See Kathleen Kete, *The Beast in the Boudoir: Pet Keeping in Nineteenth Century Paris* (Berkeley, CA, and London, 1994) and Kathleen Grier, *Pets in America: A History* (Chapel Hill, NC, 2006).

12 Tague, *Animal Companions*, p. 3.

13 Walker-Meikle, *Medieval Pets*, p. 1.

14 For more discussion of the term 'pet' see especially Fudge, *Pets*; Tague, *Animal Companions*; Kete, *The Beast in the Boudoir*; Grier, *Pets in America*; Hilda Kean, *The Great Cat and Dog Massacre: The Real Story of World War Two's Unknown Tragedy* (Chicago, IL, 2017); and Chris Pearson, *Dogopolis: How Dogs and Humans Made Modern New York, London and Paris* (Chicago, IL, 2021).

15 For accounts of animal cruelty see Hilda Kean's landmark, *Animal Rights: Political and Social Change in Britain since 1800* (London, 1998) and, more

recently, Diana Donald, *Women Against Cruelty: Protection of Animals in Nineteenth-Century Britain* (Manchester, 2019) and Helen Louise Cowie, *Victims of Fashion: Animal Commodities in Victorian Britain* (Cambridge, 2021).

16 Keith Thomas, *Man and the Natural World: Changing Attitudes in England, 1500–1800* (London, 1983).

17 Philip Howell, *At Home and Astray: The Domestic Dog in Victorian Britain* (Charlottesville, VA, 2015); Michael Worboys, Julie-Marie Strange and Neil Pemberton, *The Invention of the Modern Dog: Breed and Blood in Victorian Britain* (Baltimore, MD, 2018).

18 Charlie Parker, 'How Much Is that Doggy in the Lockdown? Up to £10,000', *The Times*, www.thetimes.co.uk, 13 June 2020; Ben Barry, 'Former Hexham Animal Shelter Boss Given Suspended Sentence', *Hexham Courant*, www.hexham-courant.co.uk, 8 October 2021; 'Dog Theft on the Rise as Charity Reveals Shock Figures on Pets Taken from Their Home', www.bluecross.org.uk, 28 January 2021.

19 May Eustace, *A Hundred Years of Siamese Cats* (London, 1978); Kean, *The Great Cat and Dog Massacre*.

20 The Archive of Market and Social Research (AMSR), R362, *Reader's Digest*, 'Products and People: A Digest of the Marketing Survey of the European Common Market in 1963', Table 28: 'Domestic Animals'.

21 Ann B. Shteir, 'Jane Loudon, 1807–1858', *Oxford Dictionary of National Biography*, www.oxforddnb.com, 23 September 2004.

1 Capture and Taming: Pet Keeping in a Changing World

1 Eliza Brightwen, *Wild Nature Won with Kindness* (London, 1893), p. 27.

2 Barbara T. Gates, 'Eliza Brightwen', *Oxford Dictonary of National Biography*, www.oxforddnb.com, 23 September 2004.

3 Harriet Ritvo, *The Animal Estate: The English and Other Creatures in the Victorian Age* (Cambridge, MA, 1987), pp. 226–42.

4 Helen Cowie, *Exhibiting Animals in Nineteenth-Century Britain: Empathy, Education and Entertainment* (Basingstoke, 2014), p. 2.

5 'Database of Animal Sales in *Exchange and Mart*, 1868–1940', AHRC Pets and Family Life Project (2019).

6 Ritvo, *The Animal Estate*, pp. 235–40.

7 Brightwen, *Wild Nature Won with Kindness*, p. 198.

8 John Simons, *Rossetti's Wombat: Pre-Raphaelites and Australian Animals in Victorian Britain* (London, 2008), pp. 76–9, pp. 114–15.

9 Henry Treffry Dunn, *Recollections of Dante Gabriel Rossetti and His Circle or Cheyne Walk Life*, ed. Rosalie Mander (Westerham, 1984), p. 25.

10 *The Book of Home Pets* (London, 1861), p. iii. The book was reprinted in 1862.

11 Sumner Birchley, *British Birds for Cages, Aviaries and Exhibition* (London, 1909), p. 2.

12 Diana Donald, *Women Against Cruelty: Protection of Animals Against Cruelty in Nineteenth-Century Britain* (Manchester, 2020).

13 Ritvo, *The Animal Estate*, p. 254.

14 Kelly Boyd, *Manliness and the 'Boys' Story' Paper, 1855–1940* (Basingstoke, 2002).

15 A. V. Christie, *Brass Tacks and a Fiddle* (Kilmarnock, 1943), p. 58.

16 John M. Mackenzie, *The Empire of Nature: Hunting, Conservation and British Imperialism* (Manchester, 2017), p. 22. Tom Williamson, *An Environmental History of Wildlife in England, 1650–1950* (London, 2013), pp. 122–6.

17 Wandsworth Heritage Service, letter from Willie to mother Nancy Wooster, January 1882. D211/15/2.

18 Alfred Elliott, *Within-Doors: A Book of Games and Pastimes for the Drawing-Room. With a Chapter on Feathered Pets* (London, 1872), p. 180.

19 Henry Mayhew, *London Labour and the London Poor: The Condition and Earnings of Those That Will Work, Cannot Work, and Will Not Work* (London, 1864–5), vol. II.

20 John G. Wood, *Every Boy's Book: A Complete Encyclopaedia of Sports and Amusements* [1856] (London, 1860), p. 214.

21 Ibid., pp. 225–47.

22 *The Book of Home Pets*, p. 258 and p. 263.

23 *Cassell's Book of the Household: A Work of Reference on Domestic Economy* (London, 1893–4), p. 117, p. 231.

24 *The Book of Home Pets*, p. 263.

25 *Cassell's Book of the Household*, p. 343.

26 Ibid., p. 343; Henrietta Wilson, *Chronicles of a Garden: Its Pets and Its Pleasures* (Edinburgh, 1864), pp. 145–7.

27 'J. B.', *The Pet Lamb, in Rhythm, Intended as an Innocent Exercise for the Memory of Children. To Which are Added, the Ladder of Learning and the Robin* (London, 1824), pp. 34–7.

28 John Cotton, *The Song Birds of Great Britain; Containing Delineations of Thirty-Three Birds, of the Natural Size . . . Coloured Principally from Living Specimens, with Some Account of their Habits, and Occasional Directions for their Treatment in Confinement* (London, 1836), Preface.

29 Wood, *Every Boy's Book*, pp. 225–7.

30 Jane Loudon, *Domestic Pets: Their Habits and Management* (London, 1851), p. 111.

31 Wood, *Every Boy's Book*, pp. 227–31.

32 John G. Wood, *Our Domestic Pets* (London, 1870), p. 103.

33 Donald, *Women Against Cruelty*, pp. 236–56.

34 *Cassell's Book of the Household*, p. 343.

35 Paul Thompson and Trevor Lummis, 'Family Life and Work Experience Before 1918: The Edwardians' (Oral History Collection), 7th edn, UK Data Service (SN, 2000) (hereafter, 'The Edwardians'). Mr Breakspear, 042, b. 1893.

36 Ibid., Mr Morgan, 089, b. c. 1905.

37 Ibid., Mr Bushnell, 302, b. 1900.

38 Ibid., Mr Saunders, 255, b. 1895.

39 John G. Wood, *Every Little Boy's Book: A Complete Cyclopædia of In and Outdoor Games With and Without Toys, Domestic Pets, Conjuring, Shows, Riddles, etc.* (London, 1860), pp. 209–11 and p. 267.

40 Wood, *Every Boy's Book*, p. 310.

41 Wood, *Every Little Boy's Book*, pp. 267–71.

42 Caroline Pridham, *Domestic Pets: Their Habits and Treatment, Anecdotal and Descriptive* (London, 1893), p. 99.

43 Judy Taylor, ed., *Beatrix Potter's Letters* (London, 1989), p. 139.

44 Emma Davenport, *Little Toys; or, Anecdotes of Our Four Legged and Other Pets* (London, 1862), p. 62.

45 Lambeth Archives, IV/138/5. Diary of Arthur Jones, April 1874.

46 Mrs R. Valentine, ed., *The Home Book of Pleasure and Instruction* (London, 1867), pp. 499–505.

47 George Bourne, *Change in the Village* [1912] (London, 1966), p. 177.

48 Thompson and Lummis, 'The Edwardians', Mr Breakspear, 042, b. 1893.

49 William Plomer, ed., *Kilvert's Diary, 1870–79: Selections from the Diary of the Rev. Francis Kilvert* (London, 2013), 11 March 1872, p. 165.

50 Wood, *Every Boy's Book*, pp. 228–30.

51 *Cassell's Book of the Home*, p. 343.

52 Wood, *Every Boy's Book*, pp. 227–53. See also Valentine, *The Home Book of Pleasure*, p. 507.

53 Elliott, *Within Doors*, pp. 195–6.

54 Madeline House and Graham Storey, eds, *The British Academy/ Pilgrim Edition of the Letters of Charles Dickens*, vol. II: *1840–41* (Oxford, 1969). See entries for 13 February 1840, 31 January 1841, 27 October 1841, 2 December 1841 and 20 December 1841.

55 Ibid., vol. IV: *1844–46*, 23 July 1845.

56 Plomer, *Kilvert's Diary*, 8 February 1870, p. 7.

57 Wood, *Every Little Boy's Book*, pp. 267–71.

58 Ibid., pp. 209–11.

59 Ibid., pp. 272–3; Valentine, *The Home Book of Pleasure*, pp. 502–3.

60 Brightwen, *Wild Nature Won by Kindness*, p. 23.

61 Ibid., p. 77.

62 Valentine, *The Home Book of Pleasure*, pp. 503–4.

63 Mabel May, *The Picture Book of Mabel May, Her Friends, Her Pets, etc.* (London, 1868), pp. 26–7.

64 Henrietta Wilson, *The Chronicles of a Garden; Its Pets and Its Pleasures. With a Brief Memoir by J. Hamilton* (London and Edinburgh, 1864), p. 136.

65 Ibid., pp. 142–3.

66 David Elliston Allen, *The Naturalist in Britain: A Social History* (London, 1976), pp. 232–3.

67 W. H. Hudson, *Birds in London* (London, 1898), p. 15.

68 Henry Scherren, 'Bird-Land and Pet-Land in London', in *Living London*, ed. George R. Sims (London, 1902–3), vol. II, p. 326.

69 Davenport, *Little Toys*, pp. 58–62.

70 Wilson, *The Chronicles of a Garden*, p. 160.

71 Plomer, *Kilvert's Diary*, 23 July 1870, p. 58.

72 Thompson and Lummis, 'The Edwardians', Mrs Deacon, 346, b. 1898.

73 *The Field*, 4 January 1902, p. 34.

74 Ibid.

75 *The Field*, 11 January 1902, pp. 69–70, Taylor, *Beatrix Potter's Letters*, p. 58, and Glen Cavaliero, ed., *Beatrix Potter's Journal* (London, 1986), p. 212.

76 Brightwen, *Wild Nature Won by Kindness*, p. 12.

77 W. H. Hudson, *Birds and Man* (London, 1915), p. 249.

78 Dennis Shrubsall, 'William Henry Hudson', *Oxford Dictionary of National Biography*, www.oxforddnb.com, 23 September 2004.

79 Williamson, *Environmental History*, p. 156.

80 David Evans, *A History of Nature Conservation in Britain* (London and New York, 1992), p. 43, and Allen, *The Naturalist in Britain*, p. 235.

81 Donald, *Women Against Cruelty*, p. 255.

82 Hudson, *Birds and Man*, p. 238.

83 'Database of Animal Sales in *Exchange and Mart*'.

84 E. M. Nicholson, *Birds in England: An Account of the State of Our Bird-Life and a Criticism of Bird Protection* (London, 1926), p. 90.

85 Arthur W. Moss, *Valiant Crusade: The History of the RSPCA* (London, 1961), p. 54.

86 Harry Norman, *Aviaries, Bird Rooms and Cages* (London, 1919), p. 41.

87 Harry Norman, *Breeding British Birds, in Aviaries and Cages* (London, 1934), p. 1, and Evans, *A History of Nature Conservation*, pp. 51–2 and p. 103.

88 Robert Stephenson Smyth Baden-Powell, Baron Baden-Powell of Gilwell, *Scouting for Boys: A Handbook for Instruction in Good Citizenship* (London, 1908), p. 126.

89 Successive editions of the 1908 edition of Baden-Powell's book did not update the section on birds.

90 Frank Townend Barton, *Pets for Boys and Girls* (London, 1914), p. 210.

91 Frank Finn, *Boy's Own Book of Pets and Hobbies* (London, 1922), p. 20 and p. 29.

92 Albert James Metcalf, *Pets for Boys and Girls* (London, 1923), p. 15 and p. 56.

93 Birchley, *British Birds for Cages*, p. 2.

94 John Robson, *Popular Cage Birds* (London, 1924), p. 1.

95 William Erroll Glanville Watmough, *The Cult of the Budgerigar* (London, 1948), p. 14.

96 'Database of Animal Sales in *Exchange and Mart*'.

97 Henry Charles Humphries, *Budgerigars for the Beginner, etc.* (London, 1932), p. 16 and p. 19.

98 Watmough, *The Cult of the Budgerigar*, pp. 3–5.

99 'Database of Animal Sales in *Exchange and Mart*'.

100 Anon., *Your Pet Budgie: A Comprehensive Guide to the Care of a Pet Budgerigar, Including Teaching to Talk and Minor Ailments* (London, 1955), p. 3.

101 Eric Leyland, *Pet Birds for Boys and Girls* (London, 1954), p. 15.

102 Watmough, *The Cult of the Budgerigar*, p. 250.

103 Andrew Wilson, *Talking Budgerigars and How to Train Them* (London, 1936), p. 10 and p. 25.

104 Watmough, *The Cult of the Budgerigar*, p. 1.

105 Jennie Gauntlett Hill Diary, 26 March 1937, Hampshire Record Office, 130M82/19.

106 Ibid., 27 March 1937.

107 Wilson, *Talking Budgerigars*, pp. 9–10.

108 Ibid.
109 Katharine Tottenham, *The Pan Book of Home Pets* (London, 1963), p. 108.
110 Gilbert Dempster Fisher, *The Hut Man's Book* (London and Edinburgh, 1938), pp. 11–13.
111 Ibid., p. 160.
112 Ibid., pp. 88–92.
113 Evans, *A History of Nature Conservation*, p. 46; Tim Sands, *Wildlife in Trust: A Hundred Years of Nature Conservation* (London, 2012), pp. 1–18.
114 Sands, *Wildlife in Trust*, pp. 20–21.
115 Williamson, *An Environmental History*, p. 170.
116 E. M. Nicholson, *Birds and Men: The Bird Life of British Towns, Villages, Gardens and Farmland* [1951] (London, 1990), p. 102.
117 Metcalf, *Pets for Boys and Girls*, p. 19.
118 Joan Wheeler, ed., *The New Home Encyclopedia* (London, 1932), p. 753.
119 Edward Grey, *The Charm of Birds* (London, 1927) and Claire Leighton, *Four Hedges: A Gardener's Chronicle* (London, 1935).
120 Nigel Nicolson, ed., *Leave the Letters till We're Dead: The Letters of Virginia Woolf*, vol. VI: *1936–1941* (London, 1980), p. 133. To Lydia Keynes, 5 June 1937.
121 Anne Olivier Bell, *The Diary of Virginia Woolf*, vol. V: *1936–1941* (London, 1984), p. 306.
122 A fictionalized name has been given. Day Survey, Mass-Observation, N DS 99.
123 'Keeping Hedgehogs as a Pet', *Ideal Home*, May 1937, p. 451.
124 Finn, *Boy's Own Book of Pets*, pp. 15–17.
125 Thomas Sidney Denham, *Let's Keep a Pet* (London, 1955), p. 179.
126 Richard Bertram Ogle, *Pets and Their Care* (London, 1955), p. 9.
127 Charlotte Mosley, ed., *The Mitfords: Letters Between Six Sisters* (London, 2007), pp. 499–500 and pp. 508–9.
128 Doreen Tovey, *Cats in May* (London, 1959), pp. 40–58.
129 Doreen Tovey, *Cats in the Belfry* [1957] (London, 2005), p. 10.
130 Tottenham, *The Pan Book of Home Pets*, p. 108.
131 Ibid., pp. 11–21.
132 Ibid., p. 202.
133 Ibid., p. 189.
134 Peter Marren, *Rainbow Dust: Three Centuries of Delight in British Butterflies* (London, 2015), p. 20.
135 Chris Packham, 'Like Owen Patterson, I Had Pet Badgers: But Their Real Place Is in the Wild', *The Guardian*, www.theguardian.com, 27 August 2013.
136 Except in certain circumstances under licence.
137 'Animal Daft Mum of Two Keeps Hand Reared Fox as Pet', *The Scotsman*, www.scotsman.com, 11 December 2017.
138 'Why You Shouldn't Get a Fox as a Pet', *Grazia*, www.graziadaily.co.uk, 3 November 2016.

2 Building Trust and Buying Love: Shopping for Pets

1 Frances Simpson, 'Cat and Dog London', in *Living London*,
    ed. George R. Sims (London, 1901), vol. I, section II, pp. 254–60.

2 Henry Mayhew, *London Labour and the London Poor* (London, 1862),
    vol. II, pp. 47–80.

3 Charles Manby Smith, *The Little World of London* (London, 1857), pp. 105–6.

4 Michael Worboys, Julie-Marie Strange and Neil Pemberton, *The Invention
    of the Modern Dog* (Baltimore, MD, 2018), p. 212.

5 Sarah Cheung, 'Women, Pets and Imperialism: The Pekingese Dog and
    Nostalgia for Old China', *Journal of British Studies*, 45 (2006), pp. 359–87.

6 Kathleen Mary Tillotson, Madeline House and Graham Storey, eds,
    The Pilgrim Edition of the Letters of Charles Dickens, vol. III: *1842–1843*
    (Oxford, 2016), p. 162.

7 London Metropolitan Archives (LMA), 726/14, 'William Whiteley
    Catalogue', 1885, pp. 1101–2.

8 *Cassell's Book of the Household: A Work of Reference on Domestic Economy*
    (London, 1893), p. 316.

9 See, for example, John G. Wood, *Petland Revisited* (London, 1884), p. 1.

10 Grace Foakes, *My Part of the River* (London, 1976), p. 49.

11 'Parrots Are Back. "Restrictions Off" Is Good News for the Trade', *Pet Store
    and Aquatic Trader*, January 1952, pp. 14–15.

12 Ingrid H. Tague, *Animal Companions: Pets and Social Change in Eighteenth
    Century Britain* (Philadelphia, PA, 2015), p. 23.

13 Joseph Smith, *Plain Instructions for Breeding and Rearing the Canary Finch
    in Its Most Admired Varieties of Feather and Song: With Practical Hints and
    Recipes for its Domestication* (London, 1830), p. 25.

14 Charles Dickens, *Martin Chuzzlewit* (London, 1842–4), pp. 415–16.

15 William Thomas Greene, *Canary Keeping for Amateurs* (London, 1902).

16 Science and Society Picture Library, 10597785, www.scienceandsociety.
    co.uk, accessed 9 February 2016.

17 *A Guide to Liverpool* [1902] (Liverpool, 2004).

18 Roger Scola, 'Food Markets and Shops in Manchester, 1770–1870',
    Journal of Historical Geography, 1/2 (1975), pp. 153–67.

19 James Greenwood, *In Strange Company: Being the Experiences of a Roving
    Correspondent* (London, 1874), pp. 225–6.

20 Beatrix Potter, 10 November 1884, in *The Journal of Beatrix Potter*,
    ed. Leslie Linder (London and New York, 1966), pp. 108–9.

21 *Grantham Journal*, 16 February 1878. He was fined £15 plus costs.

22 Census and probate returns for Caroline Towell, www.ancestry.co.uk,
    accessed 28 March 2019.

23 For London street sellers of animals and birds, see Mayhew, *London
    Labour*, vol. II, pp. 58–81.

24 Ibid., pp. 47–80.

25 Smith, *The Little World of London*, pp. 105–6.

26 Mayhew, *London Labour*, vol. II, pp. 47–80.

27 Elizabeth Roberts Working Class Oral History Archive (ERWCOHA),
    Lancaster University, Preston: Mrs B3P.

28 Bolton Archives and Local Studies (BALS), Bolton Oral History Project (BOHP), 105s and 47a.

29 'Leadenhall Market', *Leisure Hour*, 22 August 1861, pp. 539–41.

30 Simpson, 'Cat and Dog London', pp. 254–60.

31 Henry Scherren, 'Bird-Land and Pet-Land in London', in *Living London*, ed. Sims, pp. 324–9.

32 Manchester's Shude Hill boasted a dedicated bird market. See *Slater's Directory of Manchester and Salford* (Manchester, 1876). See also ERWCOHA, Miss B3P, who claimed any pet could be had for a shilling at Preston market.

33 *The Star*, 9 May 1873.

34 George R. Sims, *Off the Track in London* (London, 1911).

35 Edward Fairholme and Wellesley Pai, *A Century of Work for Animals: The History of the RSPCA* (London, 1924), p. 41.

36 *Cassell's Household Guide*, p. 118.

37 John G. Wood, *Every Little Boy's Book* [1856] (London, 1860), pp. 247–8, and John G. Wood, *Our Domestic Pets* (London, 1863), pp. 166–7.

38 *Book of Home Pets* (London, 1861), p. 258.

39 Mayhew, *London Labour*, vol. II, pp. 47–80.

40 Booth Archive, Special Collections, London School of Economics (LSE), Booth/B/351, George H. Duckworth's Notebook: Police and Publican District 7 and District 8, p. 159; Booth/A/23 Dealers, Clerks and Locomotion: Interviews, Questionnaires, Reports and Correspondence, 1891–1895, Report of London costermongers and their markets by Harold Hardy, 189, pp. 72–115.

41 J. Ewing Ritchie, *Days and Nights in London; or, Studies in Black and Gray* (London, 1880), pp. 99–102.

42 '"That Monkey!"', *Illustrated London News*, 4 July 1885, p. 20.

43 Miss Dyson, 'Home Amusements', in *The Home Book of Pleasure and Instruction*, ed. Mrs R. Valentine (London, 1867), p. 501.

44 Mrs R. Valentine, ed., *The Girl's Home Companion* (London, 1894), pp. 560–61.

45 Mayhew, *London Labour*, vol. II, pp. 48–52; Philip Howell, *At Home and Astray: The Domestic Dog in Victorian London* (Charlottesville, VA, 2015), pp. 50–72.

46 Mayhew, *London Labour*, vol. II, pp. 48–52.

47 For a fictionalized version of this, see Virginia Woolf, *Flush: A Biography* [1933] (London, 2015).

48 Jane Welsh Carlyle, 27 February 1850 in *Letters and Memorials of Jane Welsh Carlyle*, vol. II, ed. Thomas Carlyle and James Anthony Froude (Cambridge, 1883), pp. 102–3.

49 *Cassell's Book of the Household*, p. 307.

50 *Bell's Life in London and Sporting Chronicle*, 22 April 1885, p. 4.

51 Old Bailey, William Harley Clements, 19 May 1890, Animal Theft. Reference: 441.

52 Joseph Stamper, *So Long Ago* (London, 1960), pp. 133–4.

53 Charles Manby Smith, *Curiosities of London Life* (London, 1857), p. 160.

54 *Bell's Life in London and Sporting Chronicle*, 4 June 1870, p. 6.

55 Ibid., 8 June 1870, p. 4.

56 Valentine, *The Girl's Home Companion*, p. 225.

57 Devon Archives and Local Studies, 3177B/1/B/6, James Hutchings Letter Books, 1880–1895, p. 51.

58 Special Collections, University of Liverpool, Rathbone Papers: Emily Rathbone, 11 September 1907, RP X.3.15.

59 Valentine, *The Girl's Home Companion*, p. 226.

60 Old Bailey, Sarah Morris, John Davis and Joseph Onley, 21 November 1881, Fraud. Reference: 58.

61 Old Bailey, George Robert Short, George Sumby, George Edmundson and Henry Kerr, 25 February 1884, Fraud. Reference: 348.

62 24 April 1867, 23 September 1865, 23 October 1865, *The Pilgrim Edition of the Letters of Charles Dickens*, vol. VIII: *1856–1858*, ed. Kathleen Mary Tillotson, Madeline House and Graham Storey (Oxford, 2016), pp. 95–6, 101, 357–8.

63 Entry for 30 June 1935, *The Diary of Virginia Woolf*, vol. IV: *1931–1935*, ed. Anne Oliver (Harmondsworth, 1982), p. 328.

64 Highgate Literary and Scientific Institution, Highgate, United Kingdom, Alan Withington Diary, 27 July 1933.

65 May Eustace, *A Hundred Years of Siamese Cats* (London, 1978), pp. 24–5.

66 *Catalogue of the Siamese Cat Club's 1st Championship Show* [1924] (Oxford, facsimile edn, 2003), appended Historical Notes, n.p.

67 Rose Tenent, *The Book of the Siamese Cat* (London, 1950), p. 10.

68 Kit Wilson, 'Introduction', in Kathleen R. Williams, *The Breeding and Management of the Siamese Cat* (Feltham, 1950), p. 7.

69 Doreen Tovey, *Cats in the Belfry* [1957] (London, 2005), pp. 11–12.

70 Ibid., p. 15.

71 The introduction of the flat-rate dog licence in 1867 brought the cost of the former 'dog tax' down from twelve shillings, ostensibly making it more affordable for working-class people. In practice, the complicated administration of the dog tax meant that working-class people were largely able to ignore it. The streamlined dog licence was cheaper but easier to monitor, meaning working-class people without licences were far more likely to be prosecuted. Neil Pemberton and Michael Worboys, *Mad Dogs and Englishmen: Rabies in Britain, 1830–2000* (Basingstoke, 2007), p. 79.

72 'At Jamrach's', *Illustrated London News*, 19 February 1888, p. 215; 'Mr Jamrach's Wild Beast Depot, Ratcliff Highway', *The Graphic*, 24 July 1875.

73 *A Guide to Liverpool*.

74 Scherren, 'Bird-Land and Pet-Land', pp. 324–9.

75 Advertisement, *Avicultural Magazine*, November 1903, n.p. See also 'Augustus Zache's Pet Stores [196 Great Portland Street]', *The Referee*, 6 July 1902, p. 12.

76 Albert MacSelf, *Pets for Boys and Girls* (London, 1923), pp. 65–6.

77 Ella Alexander, 'Harrods Closes Its Animal Kingdom', *Vogue*, www.vogue.co.uk, 13 January 2014.

78 'Dave Meets Dusty', British Pathé, 16 December 1946.

79 Gerald Durrell, *Fillets of Plaice* (London, 1971), pp. 65, 71–2.

80 F. W. Jefkins, 'Display Your Salesman', *Pet Trade Journal* (November 1954), pp. 17–19.

81 Advertisement, *Avicultural Magazine*, November 1903, n.p., and 'Augustus Zache's Pet Stores', *The Referee*, 6 July 1902, p. 12.

82 'New Pet Shop, Babington Lane, Derby', *Derbyshire Advertiser and Journal*, 11 April 1924, p. 2.

83 MacSelf, *Pets for Boys and Girls*, p. 26.

84 'Dogs and the Home', *Ideal Home*, April 1925, p. 345.

85 Joseph Ackerley, *My Dog Tulip* [1956] (New York, 2011), p. 7.

86 *Hamlyn's Menagerie Magazine*, May 1916, backmatter.

87 Advertisement, *Ideal Home*, January 1922, p. 50.

88 James Herriot, *Vet in Harness* (London, 2012), pp. 24–5.

89 V. H. Drummond, *Mr Finch's Pet Shop* (London, 1953).

90 Mayhew, *London Labour*, pp. 47–80.

91 Dog collar worn by Keeper, 2000/2.1, and brass collar, HIII, Brontë Parsonage Museum Collections.

92 Tower Hamlets Archives, L/BGM/A/16/2/1, Report of the Special Meeting re: Street Trading, 31 October 1927.

93 Tower Hamlets Archives, L/BGM/A/16/1/1, Minutes of the Bethnal Green Street Trading Committee, 31 January 1928.

94 Kennel Club Library, catalogue of Crufts Dog Show (1960), pp. 12–13.

95 Spillers advertisement, *Daily Mail*, 10 October 1919, n.p.

96 Spillers advertisement, *Daily Mail*, 16 October 1931, n.p.

97 Kennel Club Library, catalogue of Crufts Dog Show, 1960, p. 16.

98 Spratts, *The Care of Cats and Kittens* (London, 1939).

99 Kit-E-Kat advertisement, *Cats and Kittens Magazine*, November 1950.

100 'Qualitative Research on Soft Moist Cat Food', CRAM (Cooper Research and Marketing Ltd) Peter Cooper Collection, Project A13 (July 1973). www.amsr.org.uk.

101 London Metropolitan Archives, National Canine Defence League Information Leaflet, *c.* 1930, A/FWA/C/D/268/001.

102 S. W. Slocombe, *Introduction to Police Duty* (Newport, 1946).

103 House of Commons Papers, 'Minutes of the Proceedings on the Pet Animals Bill', vol II.141, Paper 173 (London, 1951).

104 Michael Horsnell, 'Police Found Pub Bars Crowded with Caged Birds', *The Times*, 4 November 1977, p. 7.

105 'What Is Lucy's Law?', *The Week*, www.theweek.co.uk, 23 August 2018.

3 Rules Made and Broken: Pets at Home

1 'Christmas Now and Then!', *The Idler*, VII/5 (December 1897), pp. 683–96 (p. 686).

2 See, for instance, 'Mr G. R. Sims at Home', *Bookseller's Supplement* (7 September 1895), pp. 38–40; '"Dagonet" at Home', *The Princess* (9 November 1895), pp. 2–5; 'Quaint George Sims', *Sunday Advertiser* (29 April 1894); 'Journalists of Today', *The Sketch* (24 July 1895), p. 703.

3 *Bennett's Everyday Book* (London, 1880), pp. 1–3; William Smith, *The Uses and Abuses of Domestic Animals* (London, 1887), p. 183; Sidney Day, *London*

Born: A Memoir of a Forgotten City (London, New York, Toronto and
Sydney, 2013), p. 5.

4 Beatrix Potter, 10 August 1892, in *The Journal of Beatrix Potter*, ed. Leslie
Linder (London and New York, 1966), pp. 246–7.

5 Ibid., 28 March 1885, p. 138.

6 Frances Simpson, 'Cat and Dog London', in *Living London*, ed. George R.
Sims (London, 1901), vol. I, section 1, pp. 254–60 (p. 254).

7 Charles Dickens, 4 November 1858, in *The Pilgrim Edition of the Letters
of Charles Dickens*, vol. VIII: *1856–1858*, ed. Kathleen Mary Tillotson,
Madeline House and Graham Storey (Oxford, 2016).

8 Emma Davenport, *Little Toys; or, Anecdotes of Our Four Legged And Other
Pets* (London, 1862), pp. 69–71.

9 Mabel May, *The Picture Book of Mabel May, Her Friends, Her Pets, etc.*
(London, 1868).

10 Caroline Pridham, *Domestic Pets: Their Habits and Treatment* (London,
1895), p. 10. See also *The Book of Home Pets* (London, 1861), pp. 595–614;
Cassell's Book of the Household (London, 1893), p. 311; Gordon Stables,
The Dog: From Puppyhood to Age (London, 1893), p. 20.

11 John Maxtee, *Popular Dog-Keeping* (London, 1898), pp. 3–8.

12 Ibid., p. 6.

13 *The Book of Home Pets*, p. 500.

14 John George Wood, *Petland Revisited* (London, 1884), pp. 58–9.

15 William Plomer, ed., *Kilvert's Diary* (London, 2012), p. 54.

16 Simpson, 'Cat and Dog London', p. 254.

17 Egerton Leigh, *Pets: A Paper Dedicated to All Who Do Not Spell Pets Pests*
(Manchester, 1859), p. 17.

18 Jane Loudon, *Domestic Pets: Their Habits and Management* (London, 1851),
p. iii.

19 Plomer, ed., *Kilvert's Diary*, p. 58.

20 Ibid., pp. 83–4 and p. 89.

21 Grace Foakes, *My Part of the River* (London, 1976), p. 39, p. 113.

22 Hilda Kean, *Animal Rights: Political and Social Change in Britain since 1800*
(London, 1998), p. 97.

23 Diana Donald, *Women Against Cruelty: Protection of Animals in Nineteenth-
Century Britain* (Manchester, 2020), p. 75.

24 Arthur W. Moss, *Valiant Crusade: The History of the RSPCA* (London, 1961),
p. 64.

25 Prosecution lists, *Animal World*, 1883.

26 Henry Scherren, 'Bird-Land and Pet-Land in London', in *Living London*,
ed. Sims, pp. 324–9.

27 Harry M. Burton, *There Was a Young Man* (London, 1958), pp. 45–8.

28 James Rogers, *A Complete Directory for the Proper Treatment, Breeding,
Feeding and Management of all Kinds of Domestic Poultry, Pigeons, Rabbits,
Dogs, Bees, etc.* (London, 1854), p. 29.

29 Maxtee, *Popular Dog-Keeping*, p. 63.

30 Ibid., p. 82.

31 Thomas Jackson, *Our Dumb Companions; or, Conversations about Dogs,
Horses, Donkeys and Cats* [1860] (London, 1895), p. 30.

32 Pridham, *Domestic Pets*, p. 37.
33 Scherren, 'Bird-Land and Pet-Land', pp. 324–9.
34 Bolton History Centre , Bolton Oral History Project (BOHT), Transcript 100.
35 Scherren, 'Bird-Land and Pet-Land', pp. 324–9.
36 John Paton, *Proletarian Pilgrimage: The Autobiography of John Paton* (London, 1935), p. 3, and Robert Roberts, *The Classic Slum: Salford Life in the First Quarter of the Century* (London, 1973), p. 34.
37 Elizabeth Roberts Working Class Oral History Archive (ERWCOHA), Lancaster University, Lancaster: H4L.
38 Foakes, *My Side of the River*, p. 36.
39 See *The Book of Home Pets,* pp. 682–97; Pridham, *Domestic Pets*, pp. 83–92; Valerie Higgins, *Your Pets: Their Care and Welfare* (London, 1948), p. 88.
40 *The Book of Home Pets*, pp. 534–42.
41 Arthur Patterson, *Notes on Pet Monkeys and How to Manage Them* (London, 1888), p. 26.
42 Scherren, 'Bird-Land and Pet-Land', pp. 327–8.
43 John Timbs, ed., *Manual of Cage Birds, British and Foreign, with Directions for Breeding, Rearing and Keeping Them* (London, 1847), p. 78.
44 Davenport, *Little Toys*, pp. 10–11.
45 Maxtee, *Popular Dog-Keeping*, p. 63.
46 Jane Welsh Carlyle, 27 February 1850, in *Letters and Memorials of Jane Welsh Carlyle*, vol. II, ed. Thomas Carlyle and James Anthony Froude (Cambridge, 1883), p. 245.
47 Beatrix Potter, 9 September 1892, in *The Journal of Beatrix Potter*, ed. Linder, p. 256.
48 BOHT, Transcript 28b; BOHT, Transcript 18 (here, the dog ate pies destined for human dinner).
49 Elizabeth Roberts Working-Class Oral History Archive, Lancaster University (ERWCOHA). Preston: FIP.
50 Paton, *Proletarian Pilgrimage*, p. 3.
51 ERWCOHA, Lancaster: H2L.
52 BOHT, Transcript 55c.
53 ERWCOHA, Lancaster: DIP.
54 Wood, *Petland Revisited*, p. 127.
55 *The Book of Home Pets*, pp. 543–4.
56 Ibid., p. 104.
57 Beatrix Potter, May 1890, in *The Journal of Beatrix Potter*, ed. Linder, p. 204.
58 30 October 1892, ibid., p. 300.
59 27 January 1884, ibid., p. 62.
60 'Mr G. R. Sims Interviewed', *Illustrated Sporting and Dramatic News*, 6 February 1897, pp. 896–8.
61 'Quaint George Sims', *Sunday Advertiser,* 29 April 1894, in John Rylands University Library Manchester (JRULM), GRA/10/3/1.
62 Claire Tomalin, *Thomas Hardy: The Time-Torn Man* (London, 2007), p. 317.
63 Michael Millgate, *Thomas Hardy: A Biography Revisited* (Oxford, 2006), p. 489.

64 Foakes, *Four Meals and Fourpence: A Heartwarming Tale of Family Life in London's Old East End* (London, 2011), p. 224.

65 T. Sparrow, 'Poverty's Pets', *Quiver*, I/759 (1900), pp. 278–82.

66 Wood, *Petland Revisited*, p. 125.

67 Chris Pearson, *Dogopolis: How Dogs and Humans Made Modern New York, London and Paris* (Chicago, IL, and London, 2021), pp. 58–60, and Neil Pemberton and Michael Worboys, *Mad Dogs and Englishmen: Rabies in Britain, 1830–2000* (Basingstoke, 2007), p. 79.

68 Elizabeth Von Arnim, *All The Dogs of My Life* [1936] (London, 2006), pp. 70–73.

69 John Maxtee revd Capt. H. E. Hobbs, *Popular Dog-Keeping* (10th edn, London, 1947), p. 28.

70 A fictionalized name has been used. Day Survey, N DS 99, Mass-Observation.

71 London Metropolitan Archives (LMA), Canine Defence League, A/FWA/C/D/268/001, Information Leaflet 407, c. 1920s, and Edward George Fairholme, *A Century of Work for Animals: The History of the RSPCA, 1824–1924* (London, 1924), pp. 125–6.

72 'A Chained Up Dog', *Animal World*, August 1922, p. iii.

73 'A Starved and Neglected Dog', *Animal World*, September 1922, p. iii.

74 LMA, Canine Defence League, A/FWA/C/D/268/001, c. 1920s.

75 Hilda Kean, *The Great Cat and Dog Massacre: The Real Story of World War II's Unknown Tragedy* (Chicago, IL, and London, 2017), pp. 27–9.

76 'Cruelty to Twenty Three Dogs', *Animal World*, February 1935, p. iv.

77 Day, *London Born*, p. 9.

78 Kean, *The Great Cat and Dog Massacre*, pp. 70–76.

79 J. Bentley Aistrop, *Every Child's Book of Pets* (London, 1949), p. 40; Ian Harman, *Cats for Pets and Show* (London, 1948), p. 57; James Norbury, *Your Pets and Mine* (London, 1955), p. 84; Harper Cory, *You and Your Pets*, 5th edn (London, 1952), p. 9.

80 Sir John Smyth, *Beloved Cats* (London, 1963), p. 36.

81 Ibid., pp. 78–9

82 Ibid., p. 62.

83 Ibid., p. 84.

84 Simpson, 'Cat and Dog London', p. 254.

85 Robert Tressell, *The Ragged Trousered Philanthropists* (London, 1914), p. 91.

86 *An Enquiry into People's Homes: A Report Prepared by Mass Observation for the Advertising Service Guild* (London, 1943), p. xxiii.

87 On the middle-class belief that they had been pauperized by the First World War, see Ross McKibbin, *Classes and Cultures: England, 1918–1951* (Oxford, 1998), p. 52.

88 P. M. Soderberg, 'This Breed Makes an Excellent Pet: Cocker Spaniel', *Pets and Aquaria*, I/1 (October 1953), p. 9.

89 Robert Leighton, *Your Dog* (London, 1924), p. 38.

90 Higgins, *Your Pets*, p. 20.

91 Smyth, *Beloved Cats*, p. 7.

92 A fictionalized name has been used. Day Survey, Mass-Observation, DS 378.

93 J. R. Ackerley, *My Dog Tulip* [1956] (London and New York, 1999), p. 47.

94 Ibid., pp. 125–42.
95 *Moving from the Slums: Seventh Report of the Housing Management Sub-Committee of the Central Housing Advisory Committee* (London, 1956), p. 7.
96 'Flats and Pets', *Pets and Aquaria*, I/I (October 1953), p. 16.
97 LMA, Canine Defence League, A/FWA/C/D/268/001, Annual Report 1929.
98 *Daily Mail* (27 March 1947), p. 3.
99 *Daily Mail* (20 June 1950), p. 5.
100 Liverpool Record Office, 179 ANI 9, Liverpool RSPCA, Annual Report 1922.
101 RSPCA, *Cats on the Hearth* (1957), 9 minutes, available to watch for free at https://player.bfi.org.uk.
102 Ackerley, *My Dog Tulip*, p. 146.
103 Jeanette and Maureen Jonas, 5 November 1985, Oral History Transcript, Jewish Museum London, 22.
104 Millennium Memory Bank, Chana Joginder interviewed by Esella Hawkey, 25 November 1998. British Library.
105 LMA, Canine Defence League, A/FWA/C/D/268/001, *Dogs Bulletin*, October–November 1934.
106 Paul Gilroy, *Black Britain: A Photographic History* (London, 2007), p. 144.
107 Ackerley, *My Dog Tulip*, pp. 50–58.
108 Charlotte Mosley, ed, *The Mitfords: Letters Between Six Sisters* (London, 2007), p. 344.
109 Justyna Wlodarczyk, *Genealogy of Obedience: Reading North American Dog Training Literature, 1850s–2000s* (Leiden and Boston, MA, 2018), pp. 108–10.
110 Barbara Woodhouse, *Dog Training My Way* (London, 1954).
111 Percy Measdy Soderberg, *Your Cat: A Useful Handbook for All Cat Lovers* (London, 1951), p. 40.
112 Linda Cottrel, 'The Rochester Measdays' (2009), at www.geonius.com/family/rochester.html#PercyMeasdaySoderberg.
113 Wellcome Collection, Tavistock Institute for Human Relations, SA/TIH/T501, 'Notes for Discussion on the Nature of Pet Ownership (A Model Based on "Forces Underlying the Keeping of Pets", by H. Bridger and Stephanie F. T. White'), 24 February 1965.
114 Woodhouse, *Dog Training My Way*, p. 49.
115 Hansard Debate, 25 November 1959, vol. CCXIX, cc923–70, available at www.parliament.uk.
116 Doreen Tovey, *Cats in the Belfry* [1957] (London, 2005), p. 75.
117 Jewish Museum London, Oral History Collection Transcript, 194, interview with Mrs Nenk, 28 February 1989.
118 At www.dogsonthestreets.org, accessed 5 May 2022.
119 Matthew Lane, 'A Decade of Growth and Profit: Private Rented Sector Booms Over Last 10 Years', *Property Investor Today*, 9 December 2019, www.propertyinvestortoday.co.uk; Office of National Statistics, 'Private Rental Market Summary Statistics in England, April 2020 to March 2021', 16 June 2021, www.ons.gov.uk.
120 Dogs Trust, 'Lets with Pets Research', October 2011, at www.letswithpets.org.uk.
121 Dogs Trust, 'Lets with Pets: New Government Announcement to Make it Easier to Rent with Pets', www.dogstrust.org.uk, 14 January 2020.

4 We've Taken to You: Pets in the Family

1 Gwen Raverat, *Period Piece, A Cambridge Childhood* (London, 1952), p. 246.
2 Elizabeth Roberts Working-Class Oral History Archive (ERWCOHA), Lancaster University. Lancaster: DIP.
3 Leonore Davidoff, *Thicker Than Water: Siblings and Their Relations, 1780–1920* (Oxford, 2012).
4 Leonard Woolf, *Sowing: An Autobiography of the Years 1880–1904* (London, 1962), p. 27.
5 Nickie Charles, '"Animals Just Love You As You Are": Experiencing Kinship Across the Species Barrier', *Sociology*, XLVIII/4 (2014), p. 721, p. 726.
6 ERWCOHA, Barrow: A3B.
7 Sidney Day, *London Born: A Memoir of a Forgotten City* (London, New York, Toronto and Sydney, 2013), p. 5.
8 The postcard was posted to London in September 1907. Libby Hall, *These Were Our Dogs* (London, 2007), p. 14.
9 At www.thearchivegroup.org/national-trust, 9 June 2022.
10 *Cassell's Household Guide: To Every Department of Practical Life: Being a Complete Encyclopædia of Domestic and Social Economy* (London, 1897), p. 204.
11 *Bennett's Everyday Book* (London, 1880), p. 11.
12 Paul Thompson and Trevor Lummis, 'Family Life and Work Experience Before 1918: The Edwardians' (Oral History Collection), 7th edn, UK Data Service (SN, 2000) (hereafter, 'The Edwardians'). Mrs Skinner, b. 1897, and Mrs Morgan, b. 1880.
13 Ibid., Mrs Thomas, b. 1895.
14 Caroline Pridham, *Domestic Pets: Their Habits and Treatment* (London, 1895), p. 11.
15 Horace Collins, *My Best Riches: Story of a Stone Rolling Round the World and the Stage* (London, 1941), p. 11.
16 Ibid., p. 27.
17 Grace Foakes, *My Part of the River* (London, 1976), p. 102.
18 H. I. Port, 'Pets Reflections', 1986, West Sussex Record Office, Add. Mss 41506.
19 Theresa M. McBride, *The Domestic Revolution: The Modernisation of Household Service in England and France, 1820–1920* (London, 1976), p. 120.
20 Ibid., p. 25.
21 Thompson and Lummis, 'The Edwardians', Mrs Shearer, b. 1894.
22 Mrs. Jane Loudon, *Domestic Pets: Their Habits and Management* (London, 1851), p. 51.
23 Beryl Lee Booker, *Yesterday's Child, 1890–1909* (London, 1937), p. 80.
24 Diary of Stephen Bowditch, 26 June 1857, Lewisham Local Archives and History Centre, LSC PT78/200/1.
25 Olive Patch, *Familiar Friends* (London, 1880), p. 67.
26 Juliana Horatia Ewing, *Papa Poodle and Other Pets* (London, 1884).
27 *Book of Home Pets* (1861), p. 802.

28 John Wood, *Every Little Boy's Book* (London, 1864), pp. 263–6.
29 Port, 'Pets Reflections'.
30 Dorothy Scannell, *Mother Knew Best: An East End Childhood* (London, 1974), p. 108.
31 Foakes, *My Side of the River*, p. 50.
32 Thompson and Lummis, 'The Edwardians', Mrs Skinner, b. 1897.
33 Percy M. Clark, *The Autobiography of An Old Drifter: The Life-Story of Percy M. Clark of Victoria Falls* (London, 1936), p. 16.
34 Ibid, p. 18.
35 Bolton Archives and Local Studies, Bolton Oral History Project (BOHP), Transcript 114.
36 BOHP, Transcript 104.
37 Sir Oliver Lodge, *Past Years: An Autobiography* (London, 1931), p. 32.
38 Stanley Lupino, *From the Stocks to the Stars: An Unconventional Autobiography* (London, 1934), p. 20.
39 Foakes, *My Part of the River*, p. 112.
40 ERWCOHA, Barrow: A3B.
41 BBOHP, Transcript 114.
42 Thompson and Lummis, 'The Edwardians', Mrs Williams, b. *c.* 1898.
43 Grace Foakes, *My Life With Reuben* (London, 1975), pp. 3–4.
44 T. Sparrow, 'Poverty's Pets', *Quiver*, January 1900, p. 759.
45 ERWCOHA, Barrow: M2B.
46 Sparrow, 'Poverty's Pets', p. 759.
47 Ibid.
48 Manchester Archives and Local Collections. M38/4/2/11, Joe Lockhart, 'My Canine Friends and Acquaintances', *Odds and Ends: A Manuscript Magazine*, Easter 1865 (St Paul's Mutual Improvement Society), pp. 54–69.
49 Virginia Woolf, 30 June 1935, in *The Diary of Virginia Woolf*, vol. IV: *1931–1935*, ed. Anne Olivier Bell (London, 1982), p. 328.
50 Ibid., 21 April 1937, pp. 80–81.
51 Ibid., Sunday, 20 June 1937; Wednesday, 16 June 1937, pp. 94–5.
52 Virginia Woolf, letter to Ethel Smythe, Thursday, 27 June 1938, in *Leave the Letters till We're Dead: The Letters of Virginia Woolf*, vol. VI: *1936–1941*, ed. Nigel Nicolson (London, 1980), p. 209.
53 Patrick Brontë, before 19 January 1853, in *The Letters of Charlotte Brontë: With a Selection of Letters by Family and Friends*, vol. III: *1852–1855*, ed. Margaret Smith (Oxford, 2004).
54 Jane Welsh Carlyle, 29 January 1850, in *Letters and Memorials of Jane Welsh Carlyle*, vol. II, ed. Thomas Carlyle and James Anthony Froude (Cambridge, 1883), p. 100.
55 Michael Millgate, ed., *Letters of Emma and Florence Hardy* (Oxford, 1996), p. xii.
56 Claire Tomalin, *Thomas Hardy: The Time-Torn Man* (London, 2007).
57 Emma Hardy to Rebekah Owen, 4 April 1901, in *Letters of Emma and Florence Hardy*, ed. Millgate, p. 22.
58 Emma Hardy to Mr Shorter, 3 October 1904, in *Letters of Emma and Florence Hardy*, ed. Millgate, pp. 29–30.

59 Thomas Hardy to Hamo Thornycroft, 4 October 1904, in *The Collected Letters of Thomas Hardy, 1840–1928*, ed. Richard Little Purdy and Michael Millgate (Oxford, 2012), vol. III, p. 137.

60 Thomas Hardy, 'Last Words to a Dumb Friend', in *Thomas Hardy: Selected Poetry*, ed. Samuel Hynes (Oxford, 2009), pp. 162–4.

61 Thomas Hardy, 'The Roman Grave Mounds', in *Satires of Circumstance* (London, 1914). See also Anna West, *Thomas Hardy and Animals* (New York, 2017), pp. 179–86.

62 Florence Dugdale to Edward Clodd, 18 November 1910, in *Letters of Emma and Florence Hardy*, ed. Millgate, p. 68.

63 Thomas Hardy to Florence Dugdale, 29 January 1914, in *The Collected Letters of Thomas Hardy*, ed. Purdy and Millgate, vol. VIII, p. 8.

64 Florence Hardy to Rebekah Owen, 13 December 1917, in *Letters of Emma and Florence Hardy*, ed. Millgate, p. 136.

65 Florence Hardy to Rebekah Owen, 18 January 1916, ibid., p. 114.

66 Florence Hardy to Sydney Cockerell, 27 December 1919, ibid., pp. 164–5.

67 Thomas Hardy to Florence Hardy, 1 March 1922, in *The Collected Letters of Thomas Hardy*, ed. Purdy and Millgate, vol. VIII, p. 120.

68 Florence Hardy to Sydney Cockerell, 29 December 1926, in *Letters of Emma and Florence Hardy*, ed. Millgate, p. 247.

69 Simon Szreter and Kate Fisher, *Sex Before the Sexual Revolution: Intimate Life in England, 1918–1963* (Cambridge, 2010).

70 Michael Joseph, *Cats Company* [1930] (London, 1946), p. 39.

71 Ibid., p. 40.

72 Ibid., p. 43.

73 Michael Joseph, *Charles: The Story of a Friendship* (London, 1943), p. 45.

74 Joseph, *Cats Company*, p. 6.

75 Joseph, *Charles*, p. 10, p. 26.

76 Richard Joseph, *Michael Joseph: Master of Words* (Southampton, 1986), pp. 7–10.

77 A. Withington (1932–1992). Diaries. Highgate Literary and Scientific Institution, Highgate, United Kingdom.

78 Alan Withington, Diary, 28 July 1933.

79 Alan Withington, Diary, 12 November 1933.

80 Thompson and Lummis, 'The Edwardians', Mrs Embleton, b. 1899.

81 BOHP, Transcript 104, b. 1920.

82 A fictionalized name has been used, Mass-Observation, November 1944.

83 Ibid.

84 Ibid., 10 December 1944.

85 Ibid., 21 December 1944.

86 John Bowlby, *Attachment and Loss* (Harmondsworth, 1972).

87 Wellcome Collection, Tavistock Institute for Human Relations, SA/TIH/T501, 'Notes for Discussion on the Nature of Pet Ownership (A Model Based on "Forces Underlying the Keeping of Pets", by H. Bridger and Stephanie F. T. White)', 24 February 1965.

88 A *Reader's Digest* Survey in 1963 found that the most common household type to keep pets was families with children. The Archive of Market and Social Research (AMSR), R362, *Reader's Digest*, 'Products and People:

A Digest of the Marketing Survey of the European Common Market in 1963', Table 28: 'Domestic Animals'. In the 1970s market research on cat food also suggested that cats were often acquired to please children. AMSR, CRAMAI81, Qualitative Research on Soft Moist Cat Food and Packaging 1973.

89 'Our Ladies' Pets and What They Cost', *Tait's Edinburgh Magazine*, May 1856, pp. 270–75.

90 Florence Turtle Diaries (1917–1980), 7 May 1936. Wandsworth Heritage Service, D103/1.

91 Ibid., 18 February 1929.

92 Ibid., 30 July 1929.

93 Ibid., 14 July 1933.

94 Ibid., 18 September 1936.

95 Daniel José Gaztambide, *A People's History of Psychoanalysis: From Freud to Liberation Psychology* (Lanham, MD, 2019).

96 Jean Pratt Diary, 7 October 1946, Diarist 5401, Mass-Observation Archives.

97 Ibid., 29 September 1946.

98 Ibid., 24 February 1947.

99 Ibid., 27 April 1943.

100 Ibid., 19 November 1946.

101 A. L. Rowse, *Peter: The White Cat of Trenarren* (London, 1974), p. 5.

102 Richard Ollard, ed., *The Diaries of A. L. Rowse* (London, 2003), pp. 153, 160, 233–4.

103 Rowse, *Peter*, p. 24.

104 Ibid., p. 29.

105 Ibid., p. 48.

106 Ibid., p. 68.

107 Wellcome Collection, Tavistock Institute for Human Relations, SA/TIH/ T501, 'Notes for Discussion on the Nature of Pet Ownership (A Model Based on "Forces Underlying the Keeping of Pets", by H. Bridger and Stephanie F. T. White)', 24 February 1965.

108 Ibid.

109 Barry Hines, *Kes* (London, 1968).

110 'UK Pet Care Buyers Would Rather Cut Back Spending on Themselves than on Their Pet', Mintel press release, 16 October 2018, www.mintel.com.

111 Statista, 5 May 2021, www.statista.com.

5 In Sickness and in Health: Caring for Pets

1 Emma Davenport, *Little Toys; or, Anecdotes of Our Four Legged and Other Pets* (London, 1862), pp. 69–80.

2 Margaret Penn, *Manchester Fourteen Miles* (London, 1947), pp. 114–15.

3 *Veterinary Record*, 3 December 1898, p. 1.

4 Diary of Arthur Jones, 19 September 1893, p. 463. Lambeth Archives, IV/138/5.

5 Abigail Woods and Stephen Matthews, '"Little, If at All, Removed from the Illiterate Farrier or Cow-Leech": The English Veterinary Surgeon, *c.* 1860–1885, and the Campaign for Veterinary Reform', *Medical History*, LIV (2010), pp. 29–54.

6 Michael Worboys, Julie-Marie Strange and Neil Pemberton, *The Invention of the Modern Dog: Breed and Blood in Victorian Britain* (Baltimore, MD, 2018), pp. 173–5.

7 *The Household Encyclopedia; or, Family Dictionary of Everything Connected with Housekeeping* (London, 1858), p. 423. In 1880 *Bennett's Everyday Book* made no mention of vets but recommended that distemper in small dogs could be treated with Dr James's powders; for fleas, wash with tobacco water occasionally or use prepared dog soap. *Bennett's Everyday Book* (London, 1880), p. 16.

8 *Sylvia's Family Management* (London, 1886), p. 448.

9 *The Book of Home Pets* (London, 1861), pp. 624–31.

10 Jane Welsh Carlyle, 30 October 1859, in *Letters and Memorials of Jane Welsh Carlyle*, vol. III, ed. Thomas Carlyle and James Anthony Froude (Cambridge, 1883), p. 12.

11 Charles Dickens, 21 July 1865, in *The Pilgrim Edition of the Letters of Charles Dickens*, vol. XI: *1865–1867*, ed. Kathleen Mary Tillotson, Madeline House and Graham Storey (Oxford, 2016), pp. 74–5.

12 Jane Loudon, *Domestic Pets: Their Habits and Management* (London, 1851), pp. 75–9.

13 *Book of Home Pets*, pp. 29–32.

14 William Henry Betts, *The Pleasurable Art of Breeding Pet Canaries* (London, 1897).

15 *Cassell's Book of the Household* (London, 1893), p. 348.

16 For early cat enthusiasm see Loudon, *Domestic Pets*, pp. 41–54.

17 Beeton's *Book of Home Pets* drew mainly on Cust and was subsequently the source book for other advice texts: for example *Dogs and Cats: How to Manage and Keep Them* (London, 1882), p. 100 includes a section on scraps for dogs which directly replicates Beeton's paraphrasing of Cust.

18 Lady Cust, *The Cat, Its History and Diseases* (London, 1856).

19 Gordon Stables, *Cats: Their Points and Characteristics, with Curiosities of Cat Life and a Chapter on Feline Ailments* (London, 1876); Gordon Stables, *The Domestic Cat* (London, 1876).

20 Stables, *The Domestic Cat*, p. 381.

21 Ibid., pp. 385–6.

22 Ibid., p. 77.

23 Gordon Stables, *Our Friend the Dog: A Complete Guide to the Points and Properties of All Known Breeds and their Successful Management in Health and Sickness* (London, 1884). By 1895 it had gone through seven editions and it continued to be reprinted in the early twentieth century.

24 Gordon Stables, *Our Friend the Dog: A Complete Practical Guide to All that is Known about Every Breed of Dog in the World* [1884] (London, revd edn 1895), pp. 89–99. Suggests that vets were needed in the case of ulcerations p. 100; severe skin complaints p. 114; and deadly ailments p. 119.

25 Ibid., p. 99.

26 Ibid., p. 120.

27 John Maxtee, *Popular Dog-Keeping* (London, 1898), p. 93.

28 Worboys, Strange and Pemberton, *The Invention of the Modern Dog*, p. 129.

29 Stables, *Cats*, p. v.

30 *Cassell's Book of the Household*, pp. 313–17.
31 Gordon Stables, *The Dog: From Puppyhood to Age* (London, 1893).
32 Henry Mayhew, *London Labour and the London Poor* (London, 1862), vol. 1, pp. 181–3.
33 Worboys, Strange and Pemberton, *The Invention of the Modern Dog*, pp. 176–82.
34 Vero Kemball Shaw, *How to Choose a Dog and How to Select a Puppy* (London, 1897), ad inside front cover.
35 Stables, *Cats*, p. vii.
36 For example, the Army & Navy Stores have just one or two references to Spratt's cat food on their order list.
37 Dick Whittington, *The Cat Manual* (London, 1902), pp. 62–3.
38 Simpson, *Cats for Pleasure and Profit* (London, 1905), p. 43. This book was a revised and reprinted version of Simpson's earlier *Cats and All About Them* (London, 1902).
39 A. S. Jasper, *A Hoxton Childhood* (London, 1971), p. 86.
40 Ibid.
41 *Veterinary Record*, 31 March 1894.
42 James Herriot, *If Only They Could Talk* [1970] (London, 1973), pp. 194–8.
43 *Cassell's Household Guide to Every Department of Practical Life* (London, 1869), p. 266.
44 Walter Burt, 'Manuscript Day Book: 1807–1809', Royal College of Veterinary Surgeons, AHB.
45 H. J. Raynham, 'Manuscript Day Book and Accounts Records Commencing in 1849–1850,' Royal College of Veterinary Surgeons, AHB.
46 Harrison Weir, *Our Cats and All About Them* (Tunbridge Wells, 1889), p. 147.
47 *Kennel Club Show Catalogue* (1884), p. 6.
48 Simpson, *Cats for Pleasure and Profit*, p. 77.
49 *Veterinary Record*, 24 June 1899, p. 763; 18 March 1899, p. 539.
50 *Veterinary Record*, 23 December 1897, p. 358.
51 *Veterinary Record*, 7 September 1895.
52 Matthews and Woods point out that in some rural areas such as Cheshire there was a widespread belief that qualified vets lacked the knowledge to treat cattle. Matthews and Woods, '"Little, If at All"', p. 43.
53 Jane Carlyle, 1 February 1860, *Letters and Memorials*, ed. Carlyle and Froude, pp. 23–4.
54 Diary of Arthur Jones, 22 August 1894, p. 49.
55 T. Sparrow, 'Poverty's Pets', *Quiver*, January 1900, pp. 278–82.
56 *Veterinary Record*, 10 September 1892, pp. 135–8 and 10 March 1894, p. 509.
57 Manchester Archives and Local Collections M38/4/2/11. Joe Lockhart, 'My Canine Friends and Acquaintances', *Odds and Ends: A Manuscript Magazine*, Easter 1865 (St Paul's Mutual Improvement Society), pp. 54–69.
58 *Veterinary Record*, 18 March 1893.
59 *Veterinary Record*, 11 and 18 August 1894, p. 116.
60 Betts, *The Pleasurable Art of Breeding Pet Canaries*, p. 119.
61 H. I. Port, 'Pets Reflections', 1986, West Sussex Record Office, Add Mss 41506.

62 Jean Pratt Diary, 24 February 1947, Diarist 5401, Mass-Observation Archives.

63 Ibid., 1 March 1947.

64 Ibid., 2 March 1947.

65 Ibid., 10 March 1947.

66 Ibid., 13 March 1947.

67 Andrew Gardiner, 'Small Animal Practice in British Veterinary Medicine, 1920–1956', PhD thesis, University of Manchester, 2010, p. 95.

68 Ibid., p. 79; Frederick T. G. Hobday, *Canine and Feline Surgery* (Edinburgh and London, 1900); *Veterinary Record*, 31 December 1898, p. 387.

69 Gardiner, 'Small Animal Practice', p. 81. William Kirk, *The Diseases of the Cat and Its General Management* (London, 1925).

70 Gardiner, 'Small Animal Practice', p. 120.

71 Herriot, *If Only They Could Talk*, pp. 28–9.

72 Michael Bresalier and Michael Worboys, '"Saving the Lives of Our Dogs": The Development of the Canine Distemper Vaccine in Interwar Britain', *British Journal for the History of Science*, XLVII/2 (2014), pp. 327–31.

73 'Willett Practice Ledger: 1929–1962', Royal College of Veterinary Surgeons, ACC 2016/02.

74 Ibid.

75 Ibid.

76 Alison Uttley, 6 May 1934 and 9 July 1942, in *The Private Diaries of Alison Uttley, 1932–1971*, ed. Denis Judd (Barnsley, 2009), p. 40 and p. 102.

77 Alan Withington Diary, 14 November 1934. Highgate Literary and Scientific Institution, Highgate, United Kingdom.

78 Ibid., 28 August 1933.

79 Ibid., 23 December 1934, 17 May 1940.

80 Ibid., 17 November 1938.

81 Herriot, *If Only They Could Talk*, p. 19, p. 71; James Herriot, *It Shouldn't Happen to a Vet* [1972] (London, 2006), p. 23.

82 Herriot, *It Shouldn't Happen to a Vet*, p. 83.

83 '151 Years On: The Story of Maria Dickin and the PDSA', www.pdsa.org.uk.

84 Gardiner, 'Small Animal Practice'.

85 *Veterinary Record*, 20 January 1894, p. 399.

86 London Metropolitan Archives (LMA), A/FWA/C/D/256/001 and 002, Our Dumb Friends' League, Annual Reports, 1900 to 1908.

87 LMA, A/FWA/C/D/256/002, Our Dumb Friends' League, Annual Report 1921.

88 LMA, A/FWA/C/D/268/001, National Canine Defence League, Annual Reports, 1928, 1929 and 1933.

89 Liverpool Record Office (LRO), 179 ANI/9, Liverpool Royal Society for the Prevention of Cruelty to Animals (RSPCA), Annual Reports, 1901–1930.

90 LRO, 179 ANI/9 Liverpool RSPCA, Annual Report, 1935.

91 LRO, 179 ANI/9 Liverpool RSPCA, Annual Report, 1930.

92 LRO, 179 ANI/9, Alan Mikhail, 'Animal Hospital for Merseyside', unpublished doctoral thesis, University of Liverpool, 1949.

93 Antonia White, *Living with Minka and Curdy, a Marmalade Cat and His Siamese Wife* (London, 1970), pp. 52–3.

94 J. R. Ackerley, *My Dog Tulip* [1956] (London and New York, 1999), p. 10.

95 Ibid., pp. 14–15.
96 White, *Living with Minka and Curdy*, pp. 54–9.
97 Ackerley, *My Dog Tulip*, pp. 17–21.
98 *Veterinary Record*, 25 September 1897, p. 171.
99 *Veterinary Record*, 23 December 1897, p. 359.
100 Julie Hipperson, 'Roy Porter Student Prize Essay, Professional Entrepreneurs: Women Veterinary Surgeons as Small Business Owners in Interwar Britain', *Social History of Medicine,* xxxi/1 (2018), pp. 121–39 (pp. 135–7).
101 Florence Turtle Diary, 1 January 1955, Wandsworth Heritage Service, D103/1.
102 After the deaths of her mother's dogs, Florence yearned for a dog but did not allow herself one until Dinah arrived in the 1940s. The precise date of the arrival is not clear as there is a gap in the diaries.
103 Florence Turtle Diary, 15 August 1955.
104 Ibid., 2–4 July 1957.
105 Ibid., 13 July 1957.
106 Ibid., 19 July 1957.
107 Ibid.
108 'Willett Practice Ledger: 1929–1962', Royal College of Veterinary Surgeons, ACC 2016/02.
109 *Veterinary Record,* 30 July 1898, p. 67.
110 Herriot, *If Only They Could Talk*, pp. 94–100.
111 Ronald Blythe, *Akenfield: Portrait of an English Village* [1969] (Harmondsworth, 2005), p. 265.
112 Alan Withington Diary, 17 November 1938.
113 Budd of Ropley collection, Hampshire Record Office (HRO), 51M98.
114 Doreen Budd Diary, 25 February 1939, HRO, 51M98/2.
115 Doreen Budd Diary, 1 March, 5 April, 10 May 1939. 1939, HRO, 51M98/2.
116 Injured foot but no trip to the vets. Doreen Budd Diary, 26 January 1941, HRO, 51M98/4; unable to eat for three days, 24 January 1944, Doreen Budd Diary, HRO, 51M98/7.
117 Doreen Budd Diary, 8 February 1948, HRO, 51M98/11.
118 Doreen Budd Diary, 21 July 1948, HRO, 51M98/11.
119 Jennie Gauntlett Hill Diary, 1959, HRO, 130M82/27.
120 Ibid., 2 January 1959, HRO, 130M82/27 and 8 March and 9 June 1960, HRO, 130M82/28.
121 Ibid., 20 December 1959, HRO, 130M82/27.
122 Ibid., 8 January 1960, HRO, 130M82/28.
123 Ibid., 21 January 1961, HRO, 130M82/29.
124 LMA, A/FWA/C/D/256/002, Our Dumb Friends' League, Annual Report, 1921.
125 LMA, A/FWA/C/D Charity Organisation Society report (1905), refusing to recommend the Mayhew Home for Stray Cats because it did not destroy stray animals unless they were too sick to treat.
126 LRO, 179 ANI/9, Liverpool RSPCA, Annual Reports, 1901–50.
127 LMA, A/FWA/C/D/268/001, National Canine Defence League, Annual Report, 1925; LRO, 179 ANI/9 Annual Reports for Liverpool Temporary Home for Stray Dogs (RSPCA).

128 LMA, A/FWA/C/D/268/001, National Canine Defence League, Leaflet on 'Mongrel Pups', *c.* 1920s and '30s.

129 LRO, 179 ANI/9, Mikhail, 'Animal Hospital for Merseyside'.

130 LRO, 179 ANI/9, Liverpool RSPCA, Annual Reports, 1901–35.

131 A change in the law in 1919 demanded that neutering for animals over six months had to be done under general anaesthetic.

132 Kirk, *Diseases of the Cat*, pp. 284–94.

133 A vet recommended that Jennie Gauntlett Hill get her male cat Trixie 'doctored on' in 1936. Jennie Gauntlett Hill Diary, 30 April 1936, HRO, 130M82/17.

134 'Willett Practice Ledger: 1929–1962', Royal College of Veterinary Surgeons, ACC 2016/02.

135 White, *Living with Minka and Curdy*; Sir John Smyth, *Beloved Cats* (London, 1963); Doreen Tovey, *Cats in the Belfry* [1957] (London, 2005).

136 Wellcome Collections, Tavistock Institute for Human Relations, T159: F. E. Emery, 'Some Matters Affecting the Feeding of Cats'.

137 Smyth, *Beloved Cats*, p. 19.

138 White, *Living with Minka and Curdy*, p. 9.

139 Tovey, *Cats in the Belfry*, pp. 119–20.

140 Ibid., p. 90.

141 White, *Living with Minka and Curdy*, p. 9.

142 Smyth, *Beloved Cats*, p. 19.

143 Ibid., p. 56.

144 White, *Living with Minka and Curdy*, p. 16.

145 Tovey, *Cats in the Belfry*, p. 119.

146 Alan Withington Diary, 6 June 1961.

147 Ibid., 9 June 1961.

148 Ibid., 7 November 1961.

149 Monty Don, *Nigel: My Family and Other Dogs* (London, 2016), pp. 173–9.

150 The earliest evidence we have found for insurance was in advertisements placed in the catalogue for the Crystal Palace Kennel Club 59th show, held in 1910 (p. 20). Kennel Club Archives. These early insurance policies were aimed at breeders selling dogs and so slightly different to 'pet insurance' as we now know it.

151 'Pet Insurance in the UK', Statista, February 2020, at www.statista.com.

6 In Loving Memory: Mourning for Pets

1 Beatrix Potter, December 1886, in *The Journal of Beatrix Potter*, ed. Leslie Linder (London and New York, 1966), pp. 192–3.

2 Ibid., 2 July 1882, p. 19.

3 'A Break in the Family', *Illustrated London News*, 8 September 1906, pp. 338–9.

4 Emma Davenport, *Little Toys; or, Anecdotes of Our Four Legged and Other Pets* (London, 1862), pp. 56–7.

5 Ibid., pp. 79–80.

6 Ingrid H. Tague, *Animal Companions: Pets and Social Change in Eighteenth-Century Britain* (Philadelphia, PA, 2015), p. 12.

7 John Rylands University Library Special Collections (JRULSC), Alison Uttley Papers, GB 133 AJU/2/4/1, Letters from Children at Colwall Hill Infants School (1959–76).

8 Kent History and Library Centre, EK/1249, Diary of Oliver Henry Lloyd, 13 June 1870.

9 Ibid., 25 June 1872.

10 Beatrix Potter, 8 December 1883, in *The Journal of Beatrix Potter*, ed. Linder, p. 76.

11 Lewisham Local Archives and History Centre, LSC PT78/200/1, Diary of Stephen Bowditch, 26 June 1857.

12 Paul Thompson and Trevor Lummis, 'Family Life and Work Experience before 1918: The Edwardians' (Oral History Collection), 7th edn, UK Data Service (SN, 2000) (hereafter, 'The Edwardians'). Mr Morris, b. 1896.

13 Ibid., Mr Rush, b. 1894.

14 There are multiple versions but see *The Death of Cock Robin* (London, 1840) for an early edition.

15 Juliana Horatia Ewing, *Papa Poodle and Other Pets* (London, 1884).

16 Thompson and Lummis, 'The Edwardians', Mrs Pemberthy, b. 1899.

17 Ibid., Mrs Freeman, b. 1891.

18 Diary of Oliver Henry Lloyd, 23 June 1872.

19 Thompson and Lummis, 'The Edwardians', Miss Slamon, b. 1905.

20 Margaret Penn, *Manchester Fourteen Miles* (London, 1947), pp. 114–16.

21 Joseph Armitage, 'The Twenty-Three Years, or the Late Way of Life – and of Living. By the Exile' (Unpublished MS. Burnett Collection. Brunel University Library), p. 106.

22 Liverpool Record Office, 179 ANI/6/4, Liverpool RSPCA Ladies Committee, 24 June 1931 and 15 November 1934.

23 JRULSC, GB 133 PIL/3/1/1/12, Pilkington Papers, 27 April 1890.

24 'The Dogs' Cemetery', *Daily Mail* (24 September 1897), p. 7.

25 Nora Schuurman and David Redmalm, 'Transgressing Boundaries of Grievability: Ambiguous Emotions at Pet Cemeteries', *Emotion, Space and Society*, 31 (2019), pp. 32–40.

26 'A Cemetery for Pets', *Daily Mail* (18 April 1899), p. 5.

27 'Burial of a Dog in the Pets' Cemetery in Huntingdonshire', *Daily Mirror* (27 August 1912), p. 11.

28 'The Dogs' Cemetery', *Daily Mail* (24 September 1897), p. 7.

29 'Mourning for Dogs', *Daily Mail* (18 October 1907), p. 9.

30 Brayley Hodgetts, 'A Cemetery for Dogs', *Strand Magazine*, 6 (July–December 1893), pp. 625–33.

31 'Burial of a Dog in the Pets' Cemetery in Huntingdonshire', *Daily Mirror* (27 August 1912), p. 11.

32 'Crematorium for Dogs', *Daily Express* (28 December 1928), p. 11.

33 No title, *Daily Mirror* (17 January 1939), p. 25.

34 Jane Welsh Carlyle, 27 February 1850, in *Letters and Memorials of Jane Welsh Carlyle*, vol. III, ed. Thomas Carlyle and James Anthony Froude (Cambridge, 1883), pp. 102–3.

35 Glamorgan Archives, Dyffryn Estate Records, DBR/153/21, Edward Lear, Letter to Lord Aberdare, 29 November 1887.

36 Lambeth Archives, IV/138, Diary of Arthur Jones, 4 April 1895.

37 Ibid., 14 September 1909.

38 *The Diary of Virginia Woolf*, vol. IV: *1931–1935* ed. Anne Olivier Bell (London, 1984), 1 June 1935, p. 318.

39 JRULSC, GB 133 PIL/3/1/1/12, Pilkington Papers, 27 April 1890.

40 Wandsworth Heritage Service, D103/1, Diary of Florence Turtle, 17 September 1936.

41 JRULSC, George R. Sims Papers, GB 133 GRS 10–2–1, 'Our Character Sketch'.

42 'Journalists of Today', *The Sketch* (24 July 1895), p. 303.

43 'Where Women Weep for Lost Loved Ones', *Northampton Mercury* (14 April 1939), p. 1.

44 Philip Howell, *At Home and Astray: The Domestic Dog in Victorian London* (Charlottesville, VA, 2015), pp. 125–49. See also Diana Donald, *Women Against Cruelty: Protection of Animals Against Cruelty in Nineteenth Century Britain* (Manchester, 2020).

45 Charlotte Brontë, 7 December 1854, in *The Letters of Charlotte Brontë: With a Selection of Letters by Family and Friends*, vol. III: *1852–1855* ed. Margaret Smith (Oxford, 2004), p. 306.

46 Jane Welsh Carlyle, [n.d.] April 1850, in *Letters and Memorials*, ed. Carlyle and Froude, vol II, p. 105.

47 Ibid., 1 February 1860, vol. III, pp. 23–4.

48 Glamorgan Archives, Dyffryn Estate Records, DBR/179/1. Letter to Lady Aberdare, 25 March 1908.

49 HRO, 130M82/27, Jennie Gauntlett Hill Diary, 29 January 1936 and 14 December to 31 December 1938.

50 Diary of Florence Turtle, 16 September 1936 to 25 September 1936.

51 Jean Lucey Pratt, 15 August 1941, in *A Notable Woman: The Romantic Journals of Jean Lucey Pratt*, ed. Simon Garfield (London and Edinburgh, 2015), p. 246.

52 Ibid., 19 October 1943, pp. 295–6.

53 Ibid., 13–14 March 1947, pp. 417–18.

54 JRULSC, 9 April to 17 April 1944, Alison Uttley Papers, GB 133 AJU/2/3/18. See also *The Private Diaries of Alison Uttley: Author of Little Grey Rabbit and Sam Pig*, ed. Denis Judd (Barnsley, 2009), 10 April 1944, pp. 118–19.

55 JRULSC, 9 April to 17 April 1944, Alison Uttley Papers, GB 133 AJU/2/3/18.

56 Thomas Carlyle in *Letters and Memorials*, ed. Carlyle and Froude, vol. II, pp. 91–2.

57 31 May and 1 June 1935, in *The Diary of Virginia Woolf*, vol. IV: *1931–1935*, ed. Bell, pp. 317–18.

58 University of Liverpool Special Collections and Archives, Dr. Thomas Inman papers, D398/2/2, 9 September 1864.

59 Diary of Stephen Bowditch, 26 June 1857.

60 Lady Cust, *The Cat, Its History and Diseases* (London, 1856).

61 Jenny Uglow, *Edward Lear: A Life of Art and Nonsense* (London, 2017).

62 Glamorgan Archives, DBR/153/21, Dyffryn Estate Records, Letter to Lord Aberdare, 29 November 1887.

63 *Horses Illustrated*, 26 October 1907, p. 180.

64 J. R. Ackerley, *My Father and Myself* (London, 1968), p. 281.

65 J. R. Ackerley, *My Dog Tulip* (New York, 1999), p. 173.
66 Ibid., p. 190.
67 James Herriot, *If Only They Could Talk* [1970] (London, 1978), pp. 84–8.
68 Highgate Literary and Scientific Institution, Highgate, United Kingdom, Alan Withington Diary, 6 July 1940–18 July 1940.
69 William Beach Thomas, *The Way of a Dog* (London, 1948), pp. 7–72.
70 Ibid., pp. 68–72.
71 Thompson and Lummis, 'The Edwardians', Mrs Speight, b. 1890.
72 Ibid., Mrs Pike, b. *c.* 1900.
73 Elizabeth Roberts Working-Class Oral History Archive (ERWCOHA), Lancaster University. Lancaster: w6L, b. 1931.
74 University of Sussex Special Collections, SXMS-13/2/G/1, Mary Caisley to Leonard Woolf, 1 September 1963.
75 Charlotte Brontë, 7 December 1854, in *The Letters of Charlotte Brontë*, ed. Smith, vol. III: *1852–1855*, p. 306.
76 Letter to Lord Aberdare, 29 November 1887.
77 Lambeth Archives, IV/138, Arthur Jones, 4 April 1895.
78 Jane Welsh Carlyle, 27 February 1850, in *Letters and Memorials of Jane Welsh Carlyle*, ed. Carlyle and Froude, vol. III, pp. 23–4.
79 *Veterinary Record*, 28 March 1896.
80 London Metropolitan Archives (LMA), A/FWA/C/D/256/002, Our Dumb Friends' League, Annual Report, 1916 and 1921.
81 LMA, A/FWA/C/D/268/001, National Canine Defence League, Leaflet 417, *c.* 1925.
82 LMA, A/FWA/C/D/268/001, National Canine Defence League, *Dogs Bulletin*, Oct/ Nov 1934.
83 LRO, 179 ANI/9, Alan Mikhail, 'Animal Hospital for Merseyside', doctoral thesis, University of Liverpool, 1949.
84 Diary of Florence Turtle, 24 March 1939.
85 Ibid., 24 June 1956.
86 Thompson and Lummis, 'The Edwardians', Mrs Walisher, b. 1896.
87 Julie-Marie Strange, 'When John Met Benny: Class, Pets and Family Life in Late Victorian and Edwardian Britain', *The History of the Family*, 26 (2021), pp. 214–35.
88 HRO, 130M82/27, Jennie Gauntlett Hill Diary, 6 November 1964 to 21 December 1964.
89 Jean Lucey Pratt, 4 November 1950, in *A Notable Woman*, ed. Garfield, pp. 503–4.
90 Ibid., 24 to 28 January 1951, pp. 515–16.
91 Ibid., 19 February to 2 March 1952, pp. 542–4.
92 Ibid., 2 March 1963, pp. 649–50.
93 Diary of Florence Turtle, 18 August 1955.
94 Ibid., 13 April to 3 June 1957 and 31 December 1957.
95 *Daily Mail* (9 July 1937), p. 12.
96 *Daily Mail* (14 July 1937), p. 10.
97 LRO, 179 ANI/6/4, Liverpool RSPCA Ladies Committee.

98 Ibid.

99 Mintel Petcare, June 2017, at www.mintel.com.

100 Chris Packham, *Fingers in the Sparkle Jar* (London, 2016), pp. 318–24.

Epilogue: Pets and the Way We Live Now

1 'Street Cat Named Bob: Pet Who Inspired Book and Film Dies', www.theguardian.com, 16 June 2020.

2 James Bowen, *A Street Cat Named Bob* (London, 2012), and *A Street Cat Named Bob*, dir. Roger Spottiswoode (2016).

3 Blue Cross, 'Link in the Chain: Tackling Mental Health, Poverty and Loneliness through Pet Ownership', www.bluecross.org.uk, 2019.

4 'Households Buy 3.2 Million Pets in Lockdown', www.bbc.co.uk, 12 March 2021.

5 Michael Worboys, Julie-Marie Strange and Neil Pemberton, *The Invention of the Modern Dog: Breed and Blood in Victorian Britain* (Baltimore, MD, 2018), pp. 221–7.

6 The Archive of Market and Social Research (AMSR), The Harris Poll – The British People and Their Pets. February 1970.

7 'Nation of dog/pet/animal lovers' – frequently appears: for example Geoffrey Dennis, 'Britain – A Nation of Pet Lovers – Must Stand Up for Animals Overseas', www.huffingtonpost.co.uk, 6 July 2017.

8 'Pet Ownership GfK Survey', 2015, at www.cdn2.hubspot.net.

9 AMSR, The Harris Poll.

10 Kathleen Kete, *The Beast in the Boudoir: Pet Keeping in Nineteenth-Century Paris* (Berkeley, CA, 1994), p. 3.

11 Cihangir Gündoğdu, 'The Animal Rights Movement in the Late Ottoman Empire and the Early Republic: The Society for Protection of Animals (Istanbul, 1912)', in *Animals and People in the Ottoman Empire*, ed. Suraiya Faroqui (Istanbul, 2010), pp. 374–8.

12 Kete, *Beast in the Boudoir*, p. 4.

13 AMSR, R362, *Reader's Digest*, 'Products and People: A Digest of the Marketing Survey of the European Common Market in 1963', Table 28: 'Domestic Animals'.

14 Emma Bedford, 'Share of Households Owning At Least One Dog in the European Union in 2019, by Country', www.statista.com, 27 September 2021.

15 Lucy Jones, 'Claws Out! Why Pop Culture Clings to the Crazy Cat Lady', *The Guardian*, ww.theguardian.com, 16 April 2018. On the possibilities of post-human love see Joanna Bourke, *Loving Animals: On Bestiality, Zoophilia and Post-Human Love* (London, 2020).

16 Kete, *Beast in the Boudoir*, p. 4. Cihangir Gündoğdu, 'Dogs Feared and Dogs Loved: Human–Dog Relations in the Late Ottoman Empire', *Society and Animals*, 14 May 2020, at https://doi.org/10.1163/15685306–BJA10008.

17 A *Reader's Digest* survey in 1963 found that working-class families across Europe were more likely to keep birds as pets. AMSR, R362, *Reader's Digest*, 'Products and People: A Digest of the Marketing Survey of the European Common Market in 1963', Table 28: 'Domestic Animals'.

18 Quais Hussein, 'How Islam Conquered My Mother's Fear of Cats', *The Guardian*, www.guardian.com, 25 July 2021.

19 Damian Le Bas, *The Stopping Places: A Journey through Gypsy Britain* (London, 2018), pp. 8–9.

20 'Pet Ownership GfK survey', 2015, at www.cdn2.hubspot.net.

21 Emma Bedford, 'Value of the Pet Care Market in the United Kingdom in 2020, by Category', 16 June 2021, www.statista.com.

22 'Pets at Home Smash £1bn For First Time in Extraordinary Year', www.retailgazette.co.uk, 27 May 2021.

23 'What Feelings Do Owners Experience as a Result of Owning a Pet?', www.statista.com, 24 November 2020.

SELECT BIBLIOGRAPHY

Amato, Sarah, *Beastly Possessions: Animals in Victorian Consumer Culture*
  (Toronto, 2015)
Bourke, Joanna, *Loving Animals: On Bestiality, Zoophilia and
  Post-Human Love* (London, 2020)
Cockram, Sarah, and Andrew Wells, eds, *Interspecies Interactions:
  Animals and Humans Between the Middle Ages and Modernity*
  (London, 2017)
Cowie, Helen, *Exhibiting Animals in Nineteenth-Century Britain: Empathy,
  Education and Entertainment* (Basingstoke, 2014)
Cowie, Helen Louise, *Victims of Fashion: Animal Commodities in Victorian
  Britain* (Cambridge, 2021)
Donald, Diana, *Picturing Animals in Britain* (London, 2008)
—, *Women Against Cruelty: Protection of Animals Against Cruelty in
  Nineteenth-Century Britain* (Manchester, 2020)
Fudge, Erica, *Pets* (London, 2008)
—, *Quick Cattle and Dying Wishes: People and Their Animals in Early
  Modern England* (Ithaca, NY, 2018)
Grier, Katherine, *Pets in America: A History* (Durham, NC, 2006)
Grigson, Caroline, *Menagerie: The History of Exotic Animals in England*
  (Oxford, 2016)
Howell, Philip, *At Home and Astray: The Domestic Dog in Victorian
  London* (Charlottesville, VA, 2015)
Kean, Hilda, *Animal Rights: Political and Social Change in Britain
  since 1800* (London, 1998)
—, *The Great Cat and Dog Massacre: The Real Story of World War Two's
  Unknown Tragedy* (Chicago, IL, 2017)
Kete, Katherine, *The Beast in the Boudoir: Pet Keeping in Nineteenth-Century
  Paris* (Los Angeles, CA, 1994)
Pearson, Chris, *Dogopolis: How Dogs and Humans Made Modern New York,
  London and Paris* (Chicago, IL, 2021)
Pemberton, Neil, and Michael Worboys, *Mad Dogs and Englishmen:
  Rabies in Britain, 1830–2000* (Basingstoke, 2007)

Ritvo, Harriet, *The Animal Estate: The English and Other Creatures in the Victorian Age* (Cambridge, MA, 1987)

Simons, John, *Rossetti's Wombat: Pre-Raphaelites and Australian Animals in Victorian Britain* (London, 2008)

Tague, Ingrid H., *Animal Companions: Pets and Social Change in Eighteenth-Century Britain* (University Park, PA, 2015)

Thomas, Keith, *Man and the Natural World: Changing Attitudes in England, 1500–1800* (London, 1983)

Tuan, Yi-Fu, *Dominance and Affection: The Making of Pets* (New Haven, CT, 1984)

Walker-Meikle, Kathleen, *Medieval Pets* (Woodbridge, 2012)

Wlodarcyzk, Justyna, *Genealogy of Obedience: Reading North American Dog Training Literature, 1850s–2000s* (Leiden, 2018)

Worboys, Michael, Julie-Marie Strange and Neil Pemberton, *The Invention of the Modern Dog: Breed and Blood in Victorian Britain* (Baltimore, MD, 2018)

ACKNOWLEDGEMENTS

This book would not have been written without inspiration from our own companion animals. Jane has a long-term affinity with cats, first inspired by the activities of a friendly farm cat named (by Jane) 'Horror Teeth', who befriended the Hamletts in rural Hampshire in the early 1980s. A succession of other feline friends (as well as some rather short-lived guinea pigs) followed. For the past ten years, Jane's domestic life has been enlivened by two tortoiseshells – Kim and Kelley – whose chatty comments frequently helped with this book. Collie dogs were formative influences on Julie-Marie's childhood and have remained pivotal figures in her adult life. Pepper (Best Beloved) moved in from the incredible Barbara Sykes's collie dog rescue centre in Yorkshire just as this project began to gestate. More recently, we made space for much-loved cat companions too: first Maude and Percy (visiting guest), then Ronz and Bernard.

The research for this book was a collaborative effort and was supported by an Arts and Humanities Research Council Research Grant for the Pets and Family Life Project (AH/N003721/1). During 2016–19 we were helped by a research team – Dr Lesley Hoskins, Dr Luke Kelly and Dr Rebecca Preston. Enormous thanks are due to our team whose efforts bringing together a huge range of archival material were crucial to the project. Special thanks are due to Lesley and Rebecca for their work on the Withington and Turtle diaries, research ingenuity and clear thinking, which helped shape the book. Lucy Cory Allen skilfully supported the development of materials relating to pet bereavement. Elle Larson provided much-valued administrative support for the social media and events associated with the project as well as a wealth of animal history knowledge. Most recently, Michael Leaman and Alex Ciobanu from Reaktion provided helpful feedback and support in developing the final manuscript.

As this book is based on a new survey of archival material, we owe an enormous debt of thanks to a wide range of libraries and archives who continue to provide researchers like us with access to historical material in increasingly difficult circumstances. Particular thanks are due to Emma Anthony at Wandsworth Libraries and Heritage Service, Lorna Cahill Bannister at the Royal College of Veterinary Surgeons, Ciara Farrell at the Kennel Club Library, Katie Flannagan at the Burnett collection of Working-Class Autobiographies (Brunel University),

Phyllis MacFarlane at the Archive of Market and Social Research, Julian Pooley at Surrey History Centre and David Rymill at Hampshire Record Office. We would also like to thank the Rev. Michael Balchin for a very helpful discussion about the Jennie Gauntlett Hill diaries. We are grateful to the archivists and librarians at the following institutions: Bolton Archives and Local Studies, Brontë Parsonage Museum Collections (Haworth), Devon Archives and Local Studies (Exeter), the Elizabeth Roberts Oral History Archive Lancaster University, Glamorgan Record Office, the Highgate Literary and Scientific Institution, the John Rylands University of Manchester Special Collections, The Keep, the Kent History and Library Centre, Lambeth Archives, Lancashire Archives (Preston), Lewisham Local Archives and History Centre, Liverpool Record Office, Manchester Archives and Local History, the National Library of Wales, Tower Hamlets Archives, University of Liverpool Special Collections and the West Sussex Record Office. We are also grateful to Michelle Yunqué Alvarado, Katie Taylor and other colleagues at National Trust properties The Hardmans' House (Liverpool), where we hosted a Pet Portraits exhibition in 2019, and Speke Hall (Liverpool), who ran associated Pet Portrait events.

Support and feedback from other researchers has also been crucial. We would particularly like to thank Stephanie Howard-Smith, Ingrid Tague, Claudia Soares and Susan Nance. Harriet Ritvo, Phillip Howell, Seth Koven, Diana Donald and Hilda Kean read and commented on our research in its various forms. All research is collaborative but, here, we give a shout out to specific recent animal-studies collaborators: Michael Worboys, Neil Pemberton and Nora Schuurman. We thank the participants in the Animals and Emotions Workshop (Royal Holloway) and Pets and the Home Conference (Institute of Historical Research). Contributors brought our project blog (pethistories.wordpress.com) to life. We have presented research from this project at multiple conferences and seminar series over the past six years and are grateful for all the feedback. The project generated a partnership with the Blue Cross and the Museum of the Home, which we would like to thank for their interest in our research and support in bringing it to wider audiences. Julie-Marie would particularly like to thank Diane James, Blue Cross Pet Bereavement Support Services, for collaboration, friendship and enthusiasm. Long live the collective of practitioners, researchers and NGOs who have invested time and effort in 'The Pet Loss Network': thank you.

We both had the support of our institutions during this project. Jane would like to thank Royal Holloway and colleagues in the School of Humanities and History Departments for support and friendship, especially the staff and research students involved in the Centre for the Study of the Body and Material Culture. The bulk of research for this project was undertaken while Julie-Marie was at the University of Manchester. Thank you to colleagues for support and interest, especially the Modern British History and the Embodied Emotions research groups: JM misses you! Latterly, thanks to Durham University, especially for support in promoting awareness of pet bereavement.

Last but not least, we need to thank our human families . . . Jane wishes to thank David Wilson and Evie Wilson Hamlett for love, support and many cups of tea. Julie-Marie appreciates the humans in her life, especially George Dent, who tolerate her preference for time spent with animals: fanks.

PHOTO ACKNOWLEDGEMENTS

The authors and publishers wish to express their thanks to the below sources of illustrative material and/or permission to reproduce it. Some locations of artworks are also given below, in the interest of brevity:

From *Beeton's Book of Birds* (London, 1862): p. 26; Blue Cross Photo Library: pp. 164 (no. 7821), 165 (no. 7750); The British Museum, London: p. 23; from Juliana Horatia Ewing, *Papa Poodle and Other Pets* (London and New York, *c.* 1884): p. 184; courtesy of Gallery Oldham: p. 70; Hampshire Record Office, Winchester, reproduced with permission of Michael Balchin: pp. 191 (photograph album 1934–71, 130M82/52), 192 (photograph album 1922–39, 130M82/51); courtesy of Jewish Museum London: p. 109; from Michael Joseph, *Charles: The Story of a Friendship* (London, 1943): p. 135; courtesy of Libby Hall Dog Collection, Bishopsgate Institute, London: p. 119; Liverpool Record Office: p. 207; © Museum of London: p. 157; © Derek Parker, reproduced with permission, photo courtesy of Special Collections, University of Exeter: p. 142 (EUL MS 113/6/envelope 4); from Olive Patch, *Familiar Friends* (London, Paris and New York, 1880): p. 124; courtesy of Rebecca Preston: p. 120; from Caroline Pridham, *Domestic Pets: Their Habits and Treatment* (London, 1895): pp. 18, 29, 91, 126, 127; private collection: p. 89; from Frances Simpson, *Cats and All about Them* (New York, 1902): p. 156; from George R. Sims, ed., *Living London*, vol. II (London, Paris, New York and Melbourne, 1902): p. 92; from Gordon Stables, *Cats: Their Points and Characteristics . . .* (London, 1876): pp. 146, 155; from Gordon Stables, *Our Friend the Dog* (London, 1884): pp. 74, 83, 154; photo Julie-Marie Strange: p. 188; Tate Britain, London: p. 87; Touchstones Rochdale: p. 129; Walker Art Gallery, Liverpool: p. 117; Wandsworth Heritage Service, London, reproduced with permission: p. 170 (D102/3); courtesy of Withington Collection, Highgate Literary and Scientific Institution, London: p. 177.

INDEX

Page numbers in *italic* refer to illustrations.